the ARABIAN NIGHTS
cookbook

FROM LAMB KEBABS TO BABA GHANOUJ, DELICIOUS HOMESTYLE ARABIAN COOKING

Habeeb Salloum

Photography by **Suan I. Lim**
Styling by **Chow Chui Lin**

TUTTLE PUBLISHING
Tokyo • Rutland, Vermont • Singapore

Published by Tuttle Publishing, an imprint of
Periplus Editions (HK) Ltd.

www.tuttlepublishing.com

ISBN: 978-0-8048-4102-3

Distributed by

North America, Latin America & Europe
Tuttle Publishing
364 Innovation Drive
North Clarendon, VT 05759-9436 U.S.A.
Tel: 1 (802) 773-8930; Fax: 1 (802) 773-6993
info@tuttlepublishing.com
www.tuttlepublishing.com

Japan
Tuttle Publishing
Yaekari Building, 3rd Floor
5-4-12 Osaki; Shinagawa-ku; Tokyo 141 0032
Tel: (81) 3 5437-0171; Fax: (81) 3 5437-0755
tuttle-sales@gol.com
www.tuttlepublishing.com

Asia Pacific
Berkeley Books Pte. Ltd.
61 Tai Seng Avenue, #02-12, Singapore 534167
Tel: (65) 6280-1330; Fax: (65) 6280-6290
inquiries@periplus.com.sg
www.periplus.com

12 11 10
8 7 6 5 4 3 2 1

Printed in Singapore

CONTENTS

The diversity of modern Arab Gulf cooking

The first time I was introduced to the modern style of Arab Gulf cooking was in the early 1980s, during a trip to the United Arab Emirates. A gentleman in Dubai, whom I barely knew, invited me to a wedding. I had known this person for only a few days but in the true spirit of Arab hospitality, which is still widely practiced in the Arab Gulf countries, he invited me to his son's wedding. As is the case in all the Gulf countries, when it comes to festive occasions, the mainstay is traditional food.

Kharouf Mihshee (whole roast stuffed lamb), Makbous (fish with lentils and rice), Harees (lamb stew) and other traditional Arab Gulf dishes were all there. What surprised me at that time was that these old standards were enhanced by a good number of other dishes, mostly from the Greater Syria area—such as Baklava, Classic Hummus Chickpea Purée, Baba Ghanouj (Roasted Eggplant Purée), and Shawarma (Barbecued Chicken Slices). In the ensuing years, during more than a dozen trips to the region, I found that the number of foreign dishes appearing on Arab Gulf tables kept increasing year after year, but were almost always adapted to the tastes of the cook or region.

It was the same in Oman, Qatar, Bahrain and Kuwait. Roaming through these countries, I dined in the homes of a number of locals and expatriates, and in many restaurants and hotels, and it was always the same—traditional dishes were served alongside what once had been foreign dishes. An offering of both the old and new had become standard fare. The people of the Gulf countries had become cosmopolitan, especially in their cuisine.

Yet this was not always so.

Traditional Arab Gulf Cooking

Long before the modern boundaries were drawn in the sand to create the Arab Gulf nations, the people who inhabited this area were either nomadic (with a meat-based diet) or were clustered along the coastlines and followed a fishing and a merchant lifestyle (and seafood-based diet). For untold centuries, the simple Bedouin foods of the Arabian Peninsula, a largely desert landscape, and the pearl diver's foods along the coasts, dominated the cuisine of the region. The choice of ingredients was limited. It basically consisted of rice and seafood brought by Arab dhows—the Arab lateen-rigged boats that traded along the coasts of East Africa and the Indian subcontinent. As the centuries rolled by, these renowned ships of commerce returned with the spices of India and of the Indonesian archipelago. Soon, the simple yet delicious foods of Arab lands became infused with the aromatic fragrances of these exotic spices.

Despite the simplicity of their everyday foods, for honored guests the Bedouin would always serve roast lamb with rice in their desert tents (and continue to do so to this day!). Along the eastern coast of this ancient land, where merchant ships brought spices, the inhabitants created their own version of roast lamb by adding many more spices to the rice, and sometimes served fish instead of lamb. Roast lamb has come down to us today as the quintessential Arab Gulf dish—one that is reserved for special occasions.

The historical links between the Arab Gulf countries and the Indian sub-continent through shipping and trade led to

Arab Hospitality

Western visitors usually dine on tables set with plates, knives, forks and china while Arab guests are served in the traditional manner—dishes of food are set on a cloth spread over a carpet on the floor, a centuries-old tradition with its roots in Bedouin tent dining. Arab hospitality ensures that visitors, no matter from what part of the world, feast in comfort. It is common for guests to be given the best seats around the platter of food, with distinguished guests of honor typically being seated near the host, and to be served the choicest cuts of meat. The host might say: "You have honored our home!" or "We feel you are part of the family!" and "Do not stay away too long—our home is your home!" Guests are made to feel that they are part of the family and are never allowed to feel that they are strangers.

the development of home-grown dishes incorporating the spicy flavors of Indian and Pakistani foods. Exotic herbs such as fresh coriander leaf (cilantro) and mint, aromatics such as ginger, and spices such as cinnamon, coriander, cumin, nutmeg and cardamom have long been used by Arab Gulf cooks to create delicious, nuanced dishes. Through the years, the spices of the East became an integral part of their cooking. The restricted but wholesome and tasty cuisine of the traditional Arab kitchen—fish, meat and rice enhanced by the spices of the East—virtually did not change for centuries. But the discovery of petroleum would soon change all that.

With the discovery of oil and the wealth it brought, everything about the Arab Gulf countries changed dramatically, including their cuisine. There was a huge explosion of the culinary arts—a different world indeed! Added wealth meant that fruits and vegetables from less arid lands could be shipped in and costly irrigation was employed to grow crops in these lands that were unimaginable to the Bedouin of earlier centuries. The old meat- and fish-based diet became much more diverse.

Oil wealth attracted millions of workers from around the world whose own food traditions have had an enormous impact on the Arab Gulf table. While traditional roast lamb remains a universal favorite among locals as well as foreigners, it now vies for space with a multitude of new "foreign" dishes introduced to the Gulf countries by those who have come to work in the thriving petroleum industry. The culinary traditions of these foreigners have enriched and enlivened the once basic and frugal cuisine of the Arabian Peninsula, and dining has moved from the desert tent to elegant villas and plush urban restaurants.

What is Modern Arab Gulf Cooking?

The answer to this question is quite simple—it is multinational. In the main, the traditional cuisine of the Arab Gulf countries has adapted to the modern age, which in this part of world did not truly begin until the "Oil Age" was underway, around the middle of the 20th century. Since then the evolution has been swift. Foods like Tabbouleh (page 53), from Greater Syria, and Tandoori Chicken, Omani-Style (page 70) and Baqoura (Aromatic Chickpea Fritters, page 39), both originating in India, are now incorporated into the culinary arts of the Arab Gulf countries.

A dinner at a home or in a restaurant might include dishes from Iraq, Iran and the Indian sub-continent, and from the Greater Syria region—modern-day Syria, Lebanon, Jordan and

A Geography Lesson

The nations in the modern Arab Gulf region include Bahrain, Kuwait, Oman, Qatar, Saudi Arabia and the United Arab Emirates (UAE). Known collectively as the "Arab Gulf countries," these oil-rich nations are also referred to as the "Persian Gulf countries." Geographically, the Arab Gulf countries are all located on the Arabian Peninsula and are part of the eastern Arab World, which also includes Syria, Iraq, Lebanon, Jordan, the Palestinian territories and Yemen. The eastern Arab world is bordered on the east by the Arabian (aka Persian) Gulf and Iran; on the north by Turkey; on the west by the Mediterranean Sea and the Red Sea; and on the south by the Arabian Sea. Egypt is often included in the eastern Arab World. However, Egypt and the other North African countries of Sudan, Libya, Tunis, Algeria, Morocco and Mauritania, being part of a different continent, are more properly referred to as the North African Arab nations, or "Arab North Africa." Collectively, all of these countries from Syria in the north to Oman in the east, the Sudan in the south and Morocco and Mauritania in the west, are sometimes referred to generally and in a wider sense as the "Arab World" due to a shared language, religion and/or their geographic contiguity. The countries of the eastern Arab World, along with Egypt and the non-Arab countries of Turkey, Iran and Israel are considered to be part of the world that is often referred to, especially in the West, as the Middle East or Near East.

Palestine. On a smaller scale, the foods of the North African countries from Egypt to Morocco and those from the West and Far Eastern countries—such as steaks from the United States and Chebeh Rubyan (Shrimp Balls in a Tangy Sauce, page 102), a shrimp dish originating in Malaysia—have crept into the kitchens of the Arab lands. Many of the dishes, especially those of Syria, Lebanon, Jordan and Palestine, are now fully integrated into the cuisine of the Arab Gulf countries. The foreign dishes are sometimes incorporated as is; yet, more often, and better still, they have been enhanced with tidbits borrowed from other lands, making them even more appetizing than the original version, which I can vouch for personally. (I have never eaten such tasty Shawarma sandwiches as I had in a small Lebanese restaurant in Dubai. The addition of a few spices has created wonderful new taste sensations. That Shawarma [Barbecued Chicken Slices] was more succulent than any I have eaten in Lebanon!)

Oil wealth has made it possible to purchase the best ingredients from every country in the world. Moreover, the mil-lions of people who have come to work in this region, and the millions of tourists who now travel to the Arab Gulf nations, especially Dubai, have brought their own regional dishes and tastes—which have percolated into home and restaurant kitchens. Many younger people growing up in the Arab Gulf countries are likely unaware that when they enjoy their 'Aysh as-Saraaya (Sweet Bread Pudding, page 141) or Muhammara (Red Bell Pepper Dip with Pine Nuts, page 43) and Tabbou-leh (page 53)—a world-famous Lebanese salad—that these dishes did not exist here until the mid-20th century.

The Romance of the Arabian Nights—A Reminiscence

During one of my first trips to the Arab Gulf region we spent an evening at Al Safina, a restaurant in Abu Dhabi (the capital of the United Arab Emirates). This famous eating establish-ment was once the personal dhow of Sultan Zayed bin Sultan Al Nahyan, the late President of the United Arab Emirates. Like its sister dhows whose sails once traversed the Arabian Sea and the Indian Ocean, it had now become obsolete.

However, unlike the majority of these historic vessels, it had found a new purpose offering the best in Arab Gulf dining amid the ambience of the past.

We had chosen Al Safina to savor the pleasures of genuine United Arab Emirates cuisine in an authentic surrounding—an environment that Sinbad the Sailor would have quickly recognized. After we sat down, we were informed that the famous Roast Lamb cooked Arab style was on the menu this day. I was surprised.

Whole roasted lamb, which the Arabs call Kharouf Mihshee, Ouzi or Zarb, is usually prepared on feast days for a special occasion or to honor an important guest. Traditionally, the lamb is slowly cooked in an underground pit over red-hot coals. It is then served piping hot atop a mountain of rice—its enticing aroma making one anxious for the first bite. When the food came, it was tastier than any of the many roast lambs I have enjoyed both in the countries of the Arabian Peninsula and North America. To finish the meal, we lingered aboard the moored dhow, sipping aromatic cardamom-spiced coffee.

That night, as we dined in the converted dhow on the finest of Arab foods and enjoyed the stunning panoramic views of ultra-modern Abu Dhabi ablaze with lights, I took a nostalgic journey to the past. The heritage and atmosphere of the dhow, enhanced by the authentic spiced dishes of the Arabian Gulf, took me back to the era of the Arabian Nights and Sinbad the Sailor, in whose day these dhows would have brought riches, poetry, romance and spices from distant lands. On such a ship, Sinbad could very well have sailed to bring back cherished spices to the Arab lands to enrich their cuisine. I was no Sinbad, but the magic of the evening and our dinner at Al Safina will linger for a long time to come—always bringing to mind the joys of Arab Gulf cooking.

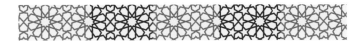

In this book I have not included a recipe for Kharouf Mihshee (a whole roasted lamb, which will feed at least 20 to 25 people) since this is a huge undertaking and is not considered practical for most home kitchens. However, I have included more manageable homestyle roast lamb dishes with similar spicing (see Aromatic Roast Leg of Lamb, page 84, and Stuffed Lamb or Veal, page 88) as well as plenty of other traditional Arab Gulf recipes. I hope these will transport you back to the romantic era of the Arabian Nights, even if you are not enjoying your meal on a historic dhow. You will also find numerous recipes for the very popular "new" Arab Gulf dishes. For those who have yet to savor the flavors of Arab Gulf cooking, this cookbook provides the adventurous cook and the would-be traveler a door to the traditional and contemporary cuisine of the region. In some ways, it is not surprising that Arab Gulf cooking is little understood or appreciated in many parts of the world—its evolution has been very swift during the past few decades. But I hope that after trying a few of the recipes in this book, you will gain a greater understanding and appreciation for Arab Gulf cooking and find it as delicious as I do (and all of the numerous friends and family I have served these dishes to!).

The recipes in this book are all authentic—I have gathered them from everyday cooks and chefs while traveling in the Arab Gulf countries. When I returned home to test and retest them, I made small changes in the ingredients and techniques to make the recipes easier to prepare in Western kitchens, and to give as many options for ingredients as possible. For example, when a traditional recipe calls for dried limes I have substituted, in some cases, lemon juice. However, for those who want to use dried limes, and do not live near an Arab or Middle Eastern food market, I have included a recipe for making dried limes at home. Lastly, dried limes, or any of the ingredients that are not available at a regular grocery store, can be ordered from an online supplier (see Resource Guide, page 154). And I sometimes tweaked the flavor of a recipe, but always to improve it! None of the slight changes made have taken anything away from the quality of the traditional dish. In the words of my daughter Muna, "You have enhanced the foods of the Arab Gulf countries."

My family, friends and colleagues relish these Gulf dishes. After compiling and testing a series of my dishes I would quite often make a dinner for a dozen or so friends and colleagues, anticipating their comments as they enjoyed their culinary journey. In the end, satisfaction on my part came with their usual request: "When are you going to invite us again?" Hopefully, you will soon be hearing that request from your own dinner guests.

Habeeb Salloum

useful tools and implements

All of the recipes in this book can be made with common everyday kitchen implements. Below are some of the items that I find most indispensable, many of which will be familiar to you. Occasionally I prefer to use a specialized tool because it is more authentic, and simply because it is what my mother used. However, none of the specialized tools are required: garlic can be crushed to a paste using a garlic press rather than a mortar and pestle; falafel can be formed by hand rather than with a specialized mold; and rather than being cored with a specialized corer, zucchini can be cut in half and cored with a spoon. And of course the Arab coffee service isn't necessary, but serving coffee with it does add flair to your dinner parties.

Blender I use this tool for puréeing food. A large food processor can be substituted. In many Arab Gulf foods, a blender has much simplified the time-consuming method of hand blending. Date syrup is now processed in a blender as are the well-known yogurt drinks of the region. Soups such as Spicy Broad Bean Soup

(page 57) and Mixed Vegetable Puréed Soup (page 60) come out a lot smoother with a blender, as do salad dressings, especially those made with tahini. The blender can even be used when making traditional beverages, such as Iced Yogurt Drink with Fresh Mint (page 146), a refreshing yogurt beverage enjoyed throughout the Arab world. Traditional Arab Gulf cooks may feel that using a blender is "cheating," but I have found that using it cuts preparation time in half and the results are just as excellent.

China Cups (*demitasse*) In the Arab Gulf countries, coffee is served in small handle-less demitasse cups that are typically part of a coffee set. They are set in fitted brass cups or are used on their own and are placed on a brass serving tray around a steaming brass coffee pot. Some cups resemble European-

style demitasse cups, complete with saucers. Any type of demitasse or espresso-size cups can be used.

Coffee Thermos (*midlah*) In the Arab Gulf countries, thermos bottles, called *midlahs*, are made in the shape of Arab coffee pots (*dallahs*). They are usually large enough to hold a large ibrik-size amount of Arab coffee or more. The multi-purpose midlah is used to keep coffee hot and it's used as a serving pot; however, unlike the dallah, coffee is not prepared in the midlah. In the past, the traditional way of keeping coffee hot was over hot embers. Today the coffee thermos bottle serves the same purpose. Of course, you can use any type of thermos to keep coffee warm if you will not be drinking it right away.

Dallah A brass coffee pot for service with a hinged lid. It has a two-fold function: coffee can be made in it and also served from it. It often is part of a set that includes a brass tray and brass "cup" holders meant to hold small handle-less, ceramic, demitasse cups. A *dallah* is a symbol of true hospitality; guests are served coffee from it upon their arrival to welcome them. The dallah is also a symbol of tradition and formal ceremony. I know that when I prepare and serve coffee in my dallah, my guests feel particularly special.

Falafel Molds These molds are made especially for shaping falafel patties. They come in many sizes and shapes, such as those creating the standard round-shaped falafel or those with a punch in the middle producing round doughnut-like falafel. Some molds even come in heart or other whimsical shapes. There are advantages to using a falafel mold: it will enable you to form falafel much more quickly and with it you avoid falafel batter sticking to your hands and, of course, all of them will be the same shape. However, do not feel as if a mold is necessary; when it is prepared at home in Arab countries it is often shaped into patties or balls by hand. Falafel molds are available in Middle Eastern grocery stores and online. Tips for using a falafel mold or forming falafel by hand can be found on page 109.

Food Processor I use food processors for chopping vegetables and even grinding meat. Both a large food processor and "mini" food processor are handy to have in a kitchen. Large food processors, in most cases, have interchangeable blades and disk attachments that can be used for chopping, shredding, mixing, grinding, blending, puréeing and processing foods. Some come with an attachment that allows for kneading dough. **Meat grinders** were once very important in Arab kitchens. However, today they are rarely used since a food processor can serve the same function, and in some cases does a better job. Although a meat grinder is necessary when grinding meat to the texture of hamburger, a food processor is capable of grinding the meat to a smoother, paste-like consistency, which is sometimes preferable. For instance, for centuries women of the Arab World pounded their meat to make *Kibbe* (a meat and bulghur dish) or Savory Lamb Tartare (page 90), while today the food processor has virtually eliminated the pounding ritual. When processing smaller amounts of food, a mini food processor is useful (and it will give you more control). I always use my mini processor when chopping or grinding nuts for use as a garnish, when a more uniform appearance is desired.

Garlic Presses, Mincers or Crushers
Many versions of these handy garlic tools are sold worldwide. A garlic press makes fast work of chopping or mincing garlic, as opposed to doing this by hand with a knife. Mini food processors can be used to quickly chop or mince garlic. A garlic press can also be used in lieu of a mortar and pestle both to crush garlic and to create a garlic paste consistency. Though the texture of the paste will not be as fine as that created using a mortar and pestle, it will work nonetheless. (See page 30 for guidance on how to do this.)

Ibrik (also Ibreeq or Ibriq) This small, spouted pot with a long handle is used to brew Arab coffee. In Arab countries of the Middle or Near East it is known as a *rakwah*. Though a small saucepan can be substituted, the *ibrik*'s handy spout makes it easier to pour brewed coffee into the small coffee cups typically used when serving Arab coffee. If you find you enjoy serving authentic, Arab-style coffee to friends and family, an ibrik is worth the investment. Ibriks come in various sizes: a 3.3-oz (100-ml) ibrik will make enough coffee for one small (demitasse) cup serving, a 6-oz (185-ml) serves three demitasse cups; an 8-oz (250-ml) serves four demitasse cups, a 10-oz (300-ml) serves six demitasse cups, a 12-oz (355-ml) serves seven demitasse cups, a 14-oz (400-ml) ibrik serves eight demitasse cups; and an ibrik with a 2-cup (500-ml) capacity serves ten demitasse servings.

Knives Though I own several types of knives, the two that I most commonly use are a small paring knife with a 4-inch (10-cm)-long blade and a hard-steel Chef's knife with a 10-inch (25-cm) blade. I use a paring knife to peel fruits and vegetables such as apples, carrots, potatoes, and garlic and onion skins. I use the large one to cut meat and dice vegetables. I keep both knives razor-sharp, which helps greatly in the preparation of food.

Metal Skewers These are sharpened metal rods used in barbecuing all types of meat, chicken and fish such as Grilled Marinated Fish Kebabs (page 95). They are available with rounded or squared sides and with or without handles. The modern kitchen also includes the bamboo skewer (typically shorter). However, I do not recommend these because unless they are soaked in water for 30 minutes before cooking (adding an extra step), they tend to burn before what is being grilled is cooked. If you do not have metal skewers on hand, a thick wire can be used as a substitute.

Mortar and Pestle This consists of a wooden, metal, stone, or porcelain bowl (the mortar) and rounded bat-like tool (the pestle). The mortar and pestle have been used since ancient times to crush coffee, garlic cloves, nuts and spices, and to create spice pastes. A rolling pin (rolling over spices in a plastic bag) or an electric coffee grinder (one used only for spices so as not to inadvertently flavor your coffee) can be substituted for crushing and grinding spices, and a blender to create pastes. However, the mortar and pestle is inexpensive and a great kitchen tool to keep on hand. Once you are accustomed to using it, you will find there is really no good substitute. Although most Middle Eastern and Arab Gulf kitchens have blenders, according to traditional cooks, the mortar and pestle is the best tool for grinding and crushing spices, and bringing out the true flavor of spices, and the only true way of producing the fresh taste of garlic with a fine paste-like texture.

Pastry Bag A good pastry bag is usually made from nylon or polyester, but can be made from other tightly woven fabric. Normally, it comes with various interchangeable cone-shaped tips called nozzles. The bag is filled through the wider opening at one end and is employed to pipe semi-solid foods, such as soft doughs, by pressing them through the nozzle opening at the other end. The bag is rolled or twisted closed, then squeezed to push out its contents into the shapes needed. The zigzagged nozzle is used to shape numerous types of food, including Cardamom Fritters with Walnuts in Orange-Blossom Syrup (page 133).

Pastry Brush A small, soft-bristle brush used to brush butter or oil over foods before they are cooked, during cooking or after cooking. A pastry brush is very useful especially when making pastries such as Irresistable Baklava (page 134), which entails buttering several layers of paper-thin sheets of filo dough. I own a 1 1/2-inch (3.75-cm)-wide brush, which is a very versatile size.

Sieve or Colander A sieve, sometimes called a "strainer," is used to strain liquids or semi-liquids. It has a perforated or mesh bottom and/or sides. A colander lined with cheesecloth can serve as a sieve. I use a sieve to wash and drain the water from rice and to press the water out of soaked bulghur when preparing Tabbouleh (page 53). A colander is a bowl-shaped container with perforated holes, generally larger in size than those of a sieve. It is used to drain liquid from food, such as pasta, or from washed or cooked vegetables, such as the cooked spinach used in Deviled Eggs, Arabian-Style (page 41).

Zucchini Corer This tool is used for removing pulp from zucchini, small eggplants, etc. before stuffing them with a filling. It is about 10 inches (25 cm) long with a 5-to 6-inch (12.75 to15-cm)-long blade. It is used to prepare Delicious Stuffed Zucchini (page 128). It is an essential kitchen utensil in the Arab Gulf countries, and in the kitchens of Arab expatriates around the world, as it is considered the best tool for preparing stuffed vegetables— an all-time favorite dish among Arabs and nearly all peoples of the Middle East. A corer enables the cook to clear the pulp all the way to the uncut end of the vegetable. Corers are available in Middle Eastern grocery stores and online. If you do not own a corer, you may still make stuffed zucchini by following the instructions for the non-traditional method described in the recipe (page 128).

essential arabian ingredients

Allspice Called *baharat* in Arabic (not to be confused with the famous spice mixture of the Arab Gulf—see next listing), allspice is the berry of the small, evergreen pimento tree, originally found in the Caribbean.

The dried, dark brown berry, resembling a smooth round ball, is indispensable in Middle Eastern cooking. It is typically ground and then used to flavor a wide variety of stews and other meat dishes—in some parts, it is virtually the only spice added for flavoring. It is used in all of the Arab Gulf countries, although somewhat less than in the Greater Syria region.

One cannot honestly say which of the Gulf countries use it more than another because it really depends on the dish, the cook and the location. Also found under the name Jamaica Pepper, allspice can be bought in ground or seed form. The whole allspice berries can last up to four years and the ground version up to three months, as long as both types are stored in airtight containers. As a substitute for allspice, combine one part nutmeg with two parts each of cinnamon and cloves.

Baharat In Arabic, the word *baharat* simply means "spices." Here it refers to a mixture of spices much used in the Greater Syria region and the Arab Gulf countries. Along with Ibzar, a similar spice mixture, it is employed as an all-purpose food pep-up for appetizers, barbecues, pilaffs, sauces and all kinds of soups, stews and all types of meat dishes. A relative to the Indian *garam masala*, it can be used for most dishes that call for that Indian spice mixture. The most common spices used to create this spice mix are cardamom, cloves, coriander, cumin, nutmeg, paprika and pepper.

A Turkish type of Baharat, similar to the Arab version but often including mint, is also found in the Arab Gulf area. In North America, Baharat can be purchased at Middle Eastern markets and stores. However, my preference is to make the mixture fresh in small quantities and store any leftovers in a tightly sealed jar in the refrigerator. Baharat should keep for some period of time stored this way; yet, to make sure the spices are still potent, it's a good idea to smell the spice blend before using it. If the aroma is very faint or non-existent, it's time to discard the blend and make a fresh batch.

Bulghur Also known as *bulgar*, *bulgur* or *burghul*, it is made from wheat kernels that are boiled, then dried and crushed. A wheat product known in the Middle East since the ancient civilizations of Mesopotamia, it is today famous in the Greater Syria area and to a lesser extent in and around the surrounding lands for being the main ingredient in Kubba (also Kibbe), a meat and bulghur dish, and Tabbouleh (page 53)—known worldwide as a delicious healthy salad. Research and experience have proven to the health conscious diners that bulghur has very few equals in food value. The cooking of the wheat preserves most of the nutrients, even when some of the bran is removed after the grain is smashed. The calcium, carbohydrates, iron, phosphorous, potassium, vitamin B, and protein content are almost all retained. These are not lost even when bulghur is stored for a long period of time. The cereal can be kept for years without loss of food value and any other type of deterioration. Bulghur can be purchased in bulk or packaged. It comes in three sizes: coarse, medium and fine. The coarse is utilized in pottage dishes. The medium and fine as ingredients in salads, as a main component in vegetarian and other meat patties, as a breakfast cereal, and as a principal element in some desserts. In North America, cracked wheat causes some confusion when buying bulghur. **Cracked wheat**, crushed when raw, is a quite different product. Both bulghur and cracked wheat are different forms of processed wheat, and yet not alike in taste and aroma. Cooked bulghur has a pleasant chewy texture and a tasty-nutty flavor as well as a mouth-watering aroma when being cooked—putting cracked wheat to shame. Also, bulghur resists insects hence giving it a very long storage life. When our family made large amounts of bulghur on our farm in western Canada we often stored it for 3 years or more in a cool area in airtight tin containers and it did not spoil. If bulghur is left in a warm area, especially near the oven area in the kitchen, it will tend to go bad. It is available in Middle East grocery stores usually pre-packed in 1-lb (500-g) bags.

Cardamom (*haal*) This aromatic dried pod of the cardamom plant is used as a flavoring in Arab coffee, tea, pastries, and other food dishes and is one of the main spices in the Arabian Gulf spice mixture known as Baharat. It is one of the world's most ancient spices and is extensively used in Arab Gulf cooking. Green cardamom is found from India to Malaysia while black cardamom is found in parts of Asia and Australia. The seedpod has a thin papery outer shell and contains small black seeds that are often ground. The most used form of the spice in Arab cooking is ground cardamom—ground from the seeds of the green variety of cardamom. Cardamom is best stored in pod form because the seeds, once extracted (and exposed to air) or ground, will lose their flavor much more quickly. Pre-ground cardamom, however, is more readily available and less expensive, and can be used for all of the recipes in this book. The

pods will last about a year when kept in a sealed container in a cool place and up to 2 months when ground before they begin to lose their aroma. To make a ¹/₂ teaspoon of **freshly pulverized cardamom**, you will need 6 large pods containing approximately 20 seeds each totalling 120 seeds. To lessen your work, use the largest pods you can find. The pods I use are about ¹/₄ x ³/₄ inch (6 mm x 2 cm). Many stores that sell the pods will offer a mixture of large, medium and small pods. If you cannot find pods that large, count on needing additional pods. To extract the seeds from cardamom pods, lay a pod on a cutting board. Place the side of a chef's knife or other large knife on top of the pod. Press firmly on the side of the knife to smash the shell. Pick out the seeds with your fingers then pulverize the seeds with a mortar and pestle, in a coffee grinder, or by placing them in a plastic bag and rolling over them with a rolling pin. Try using freshly pulverized cardamom seeds in all types of Arab coffee, Aromatic Rice with Almonds (page 123) or Sweet Saffron Custard with Pistachios and Pine Nuts (page 132).

Chickpea Flour (*taheen al-hummus*) Much used in the Indian sub-continent, it is today found in all the Arab Gulf countries. There are two types available: roasted and un-roasted. In Indian cooking, throughout the Gulf countries, chickpea flour is used in fritters and pancakes. In North America the flour can be purchased in Asian/Indian and Chinese markets and some Italian stores. The shelf life of chickpea flour is approximately one year when stored in a dry and cool place and in an airtight container.

Chickpeas (*hummus*) Popular worldwide, this legume is known as chickpeas in North America, as *hummus* in Arabic, *garbanzo*

in Spanish, *chiches* in French and *cecci* in Italian. In North America, canned chickpeas can be purchased in any supermarket. Dried chickpeas are available in almost all supermarkets and grocery stores (especially health food stores). Both the canned and dried variety can be found in markets selling Arab, Armenian, Greek, Indian, Italian and Spanish products. Both can be stored indefinitely in a cool dry place. Chickpeas are filling and add a burst of flavor to plain-tasting foods. As well, they are a pleasant change from pasta, potatoes and rice. Chickpeas can be prepared and served in numerous ways. The mature pods, when still green, can be roasted, then peeled and served as appetizers or stripped and utilized raw in cooking in the same manner as green peas. However, it is more common for chickpeas to be harvested when fully matured and dried and sold in this way. Just like other dried beans and peas they make an excellent ingredient in all types of soups and stews. Either precooked canned chickpeas or dried chickpeas can be used interchangeably in almost all the recipes that call for chickpeas. I prefer to use dried chickpeas only because I find them tastier and, simply, because the dried variety is the type I grew up with and to which I am accustomed. **To use dried chickpeas for a recipe,** soak the chickpeas overnight by covering them with about 4 inches (10 cm) of water.

A half-teaspoon of baking soda can be added to the water when soaking the chickpeas as the baking soda will quicken the softening process of the chickpeas and cut the cooking time in half. Drain the chickpeas and then place them in a large saucepan. Cover with fresh cold water to about 4 inches (10 cm) above the chickpeas. Cover and bring to a boil. Cook over medium-low heat until tender, skimming off any foam. Drain before using. They will keep for few days in the refrigerator. Canned and dried chickpea equivalents: 1 cup (200 g) dried chickpeas yields 2 cups (400 g) cooked chickpeas. One 15.5-oz (439 g) can of precooked chickpeas, drained = 1¹/₂ cups (300 g); one 19-oz (583 g) can, drained = 2 cups (400 g); one 30-oz (850 g) canned chickpeas, drained = 3 cups (600 g).

Jalapeño Dried chili Green and red fresh chili

Bird's-eye chili pepper

Chili Peppers (*filfil harr, akhdar*) These are a fiery type of peppers (capsicum). They can be eaten interchangeably, fresh, canned or dried. They can be utilized whole in pickles or pickled themselves and served as a relish. When they fully ripen and turn red, they are dried whole or dried and then ground into a powder for use as a spice. The larger the chili the milder it will be and the smaller the fruit, the more volcanic it becomes. The seeds are the hottest part and if a fiery effect is wanted, they are left in. Without the seeds, the dish will still be hot but somewhat subdued. I like my food with the hot kick of chili peppers and so generally leave the seeds in. If you don't care for the heat of chili peppers, remove the seeds. In the Arab Gulf countries, all the chili peppers of the world are to be found in the markets such as Jalapeño, red or green and from 2- to 3-inches (5- to 7.5-cm) long; Serrano, about 2-inches (5-cm) long, green and hotter than the Jalapeño; and as well, numerous other types of chilies, mostly imported from India. I use the Jalapeño simply because it is easy to find in North America, and because it is used in the Arab Gulf countries. You can use another fresh green chili pepper of your choice, but do use less of it if it is an exceptionally hot chili pepper (such as the small bird's-eye chili pepper). All fresh peppers should be stored in the refrigerator; the dried stored in airtight containers.

Cloves (*kurunful*) The dried unopened bud of an evergreen tree has an infinite variety of uses as a spice. Cloves are best bought whole as, when ground, their aroma quickly subsides. A strong spice, cloves can easily overpower a dish, particularly when freshly ground, so only a very small amount needs to be used. Being extremely hard, it is difficult to grind by hand—a coffee grinder is recommended. Store in an airtight glass container out of direct light and in a dry place. Ground cloves will remain at full flavor for about six months while whole cloves, if stored properly, will keep for about a year, and if stored in the refrigerator, even longer. It is one of the main spices in the Arabian Gulf spice mix known as Baharat and in the Arab Gulf countries it is used in all types of dishes, including the drink Pomegranate Juice Spritzer (page 152) and the dessert Creamy Custard Perfumed with Rosewater (page 137). Cloves are available in all supermarkets and grocery stores.

Coffee (*qahwah*) This cherished beverage is associated with the exotic Middle East—a legacy of the people of the Arabian Desert and the romantic land from where its use as a beverage spread around the globe. For many centuries coffee and Arabia, where it is a symbol of welcome and friendship, have been inseparable. The Arabs use so much coffee that the English-speaking world once called it "the wine of Araby." In Arab lands, coffee is more than just a beverage, it is the social beverage of cultural identity. It is always offered in any home not only for its flavor and aroma but because of its time-honored tradition. Coffee in the Arab World offers a good stimulant to begin the morning but it is coffee that forms the social bonding of friend and friend, of guest and host and of family members. Over a hot cup of deep and rich coffee, family issues are discussed and world problems solved—it is the ideal tool for socializing. The roasting process of the raw, greyish-green beans is what gives coffee its aroma and flavor. Coffee beans are now grown in numerous parts of the world and roasted in even more. In the Arabian Gulf, coffee beans from Yemen, at an earlier time, would have been the primary beans used to make coffee. Today, beans from around the world (raw and pre-roasted) are imported by the Arab Gulf countries. However, the Mocha beans of Yemen are still used and produce a delicate flavor and rich aroma. The people of the Arab Gulf countries do still roast raw coffee beans at home for the freshest possible flavor. **To roast raw coffee beans at home,** place the beans in a shallow skillet over medium heat and evenly roast them, constantly turning and mixing them until they turn golden brown. If you roast them longer their delicate aroma will be lost and they will become too dark, which creates a bitter taste when the coffee is prepared. Allow the beans to slightly cool then grind finely to a very fine texture. Immediately store in an airtight glass container. In many cases, various types of beans are blended to produce the desired combination of aroma, flavor and richness. To keep these elements, after the coffee is ground it must be utilized as soon as possible.

Coriander Seeds (*kuzbara*) These are the seeds of the same plant that gives us fresh coriander leaves (or cilantro). Coriander seeds are utilized worldwide whole or ground as a spice. In the Arab Gulf countries the seeds have been used since ancient times, in the main, ground. It is one of the main spices in the Arabian Gulf spice mixture known as Baharat and is used in all types of meat dishes and soups, such as Thick and Rich Lamb Pottage (page 85) and Spicy Broad Bean Soup (page 57). Coriander seeds, whole or ground, although not as potent as the fresh coriander leaves are flavorful enough to use as a substitute. The seeds are available in most supermarkets and grocery stores. Like any other spice, over a long period, they lose their flavor.

Cumin (*kammun*) A small, dried, slightly bitter fruit of the parsley family, it is used as a spice in many dishes, adding a distinctive flavor to food. If kept too long cumin loses its flavor and agreeable scent. Hence, it should be bought in very small quantities. Cumin is used to flavor breads, cheeses; and all types of meats, grains and vegetables. Above all, this spice goes especially well with beans, cabbage, carrots, lentils, peas, peppers, potatoes, rice and tomatoes, giving them an appealing and appetizing flavor. In the Arab Gulf countries the seeds have been used since ancient times, and in the main, ground. It is one of the main spices in the spice mixture Baharat, and is used in all types of meat dishes and soups such as Lamb and Okra Stew (page 90) and Spiced Lentil Soup with Lemon (page 59).

Curry Powder (*karree*) is a blend of spices that varies from region to region in the Indian subcontinent. Hence, there are thousands of curry powders, known in India by other names, to be found in the Indian subcontinent alone. Today, several of these can be found in the Arab Gulf countries. "Curry" is an English word designating this mixture of spices. Most recipes and manufacturers of curry powder usually include coriander, cumin, fenugreek and turmeric as the base spices. Depending on the recipe, these are

Parsley

Mint

Coriander Leaves

Fresh Herbs (*a'shaab al-khadraa'*) Persia and India, historically, through trade and contact, have played a key role in introducing herbs to the Arab Gulf countries. The ancient Mesopotamian civilizations also had contact with the Gulf thereby introducing new dishes, techniques and ingredients to Gulf cooking. Fresh basil, coriander leaves, marjoram, mint leaves, parsley, tarragon and thyme were all known and used when available. The fresh herbs used in the recipes in this book can be found in all supermarkets and vegetable markets. The three that follow are the most commonly used fresh herbs in Arab Gulf cooking. Of these, my favorite is **coriander leaves** (also known as cilantro or Chinese parsley). The racy flavor of this herb adds a pronounced pungency and exotic touch to the taste of salads, soups and stews. **Fresh parsley** is another popular herb in Arab Gulf cooking. It is used in all kinds of salads and to some extent in other dishes. It is a shame that it is often relegated to mere decorative garnish in North America! Parsley reaches its shining glory in Tabbouleh (page 53)—a salad now sold in the health stores in North America. Flat-leaf parsley, sometimes referred to as Italian parsley, is preferred over the curly variety, but if all you can find is the curly type, you can use that. In the Middle East, including the Arab Gulf countries, **mint leaves** are utilized in every

course of the meal, from appetizers to desserts and drinks, especially in salads and in tea. In addition, mint is often utilized to give a tang to a wide variety of yogurt and stuffed vegetable dishes. For many Arabs, nothing is tastier than a few fresh mint leaves tossed over Creamy Yogurt Spread (page 29) scooped up with a piece of Arab pita bread. The leaves are at their epitome of flavor when picked fresh. Dried mint leaves can be used as well, though they lose some flavor and aroma when dried. If you do not have fresh mint, you may substitute 4 tablespoons of fresh chopped mint leaves with 1 teaspoon of dried, finely crushed mint leaves. Last, but not least, mint is one of the great decorating herbs. In the Middle East and North Africa, it is utilized daily to embellish all types of food. **To store fresh herbs,** place them in a jar or glass with a couple inches of water, cover loosely with a plastic bag (secure with a rubber band), and place in the refrigerator, changing the water every couple of days. Stored this way, herbs will keep well for about a week or more.

Dried Herbs (*a'shaab mujaffafa*) Today almost all the dried herbs in the world are to be found in the Arab Gulf countries and they are extensively used in the cuisines of these Arab nations. Dried basil, marjoram, mint, oregano, rosemary, sage, tarragon and thyme are used in countless dishes from appetizers and soups to stews and all types of meat dishes. As well, rosemary, and sage, more recent introductions to Gulf cooking, generally are used when cooking poultry dishes, such as Roast Chicken with Saffron Rice Stuffing (page 73). Though dried herbs can often be used as a substitute for fresh herbs, they are, as a rule, not used to replace fresh herbs in salads and in some appetizers. If you wish to substitute dried herbs for fresh, the rule of thumb is: one teaspoon dried herbs for every tablespoon of fresh. This is because dried herbs generally have a more concentrated flavor. Dried herbs can be stored in a cool dark place for up to six months. The whole herb will keep better than ground.

augmented with other spices and herbs to one's taste. In North America curry powders are found in many supermarkets and all the Asian/Indian markets. Store curry powder in an airtight container in a cool dry place and it can last up to two years, though it will begin to lose much of its potency after one year.

Filo Dough (*'ajeenat al-baklawa*) Also called "phyllo," "strudel," "baklawa" in the Arab East and known in the West as "baklava" dough, this famous paper-thin dough originated in the Middle East, where it is a popular base for pastries. This dough is used in many varieties of syrup-soaked-sweets such as Irresistible Baklava (page 134) and Filo Wrapped Nut Rolls (page 142).

At one time in the Arab East it was said that no young lady would make a good wife unless she knew how to make baklava dough. Fortunately today, not only in the Arab countries but also throughout the Western world, this dough is prepared commercially and sold frozen in most supermarkets, sparing the young ladies the ordeal of proving their suitability for marriage.

Filo dough is typically sold frozen in 1-lb (500-g) packages in the frozen food section of supermarkets and Mediterranean and Middle Eastern markets. Before being used, the box of filo dough should be defrosted in a refrigerator overnight for about 8 hours and then allowed to sit at room temperature for about one-half hour. With the commercially produced dough, anyone can easily make Baklava in its various forms whether baked in its tray form (cut into squares before baking), or in stuffed squares or in stuffed triangle shapes. Other types like Filo Wrapped Nut Rolls are rolled into cylinders.

When working with filo dough, work as quickly as you can to keep it from drying out. Also, always keep any portion of the dough you are not working with covered with a dampened tea towel to keep the sheets from drying out too quickly. When making any recipe that uses filo, I make sure to prepare and assemble all the ingredients so that one can work as quickly as possible with the dough without interruption. It's best to keep frozen filo on hand for only about two months.

Ground Red Pepper (Cayenne) *(filfil ahmar)* When dried, cayenne peppers are crushed into flakes or ground into powder, known as "cayenne pepper"—a spice highly favored in countries with hot climates. It gives an essential zest to food and is used to season curries and sauces as well as egg, fish, meat and vegetable dishes. It is quite hot, so just a small pinch will give a powerful stimulant that produces heat in the stomach and sends a glow throughout the body. When ground cayenne pepper is mixed with other spices, the product is called "chili powder"—a versatile spice utilized to flavor fish sauces, omelets, stews and other foods. In many dishes, it can be used as a replacement for cayenne. Store ground red pepper in the refrigerator or freezer to maintain its potency.

Lentils (*'adas*) In the lands where lentils have been consumed for centuries, the number of soups and stews made from this vegetable are legion. Flavorful and hearty with a meaty taste, these dishes and countless others, prepared with meat or without, are all enticing. A mouth-watering food, one can easily believe that a hungry person, like the Biblical Esau who sold his birthright for a bowl of lentils, would give almost anything for a dish of this healthy legume.

Called *dal* in the Indian sub-continent, a name understood in the Arab Gulf countries, lentils come in brown, green, grey, red, yellow, black and other colors in between. Some types of lentils can be purchased split—the split take half the time to cook. Middle Eastern cooks prefer to use green lentils—a large variety with a light greenish-tan color best described as a pale khaki. Do not confuse these with the much smaller French green lentil. A medium-size brown lentil, which

comes in various shades of light brown with khaki undertones, is also used. The third type of lentil used in this book is a split red lentil. When they are cooked they turn a brownish yellow color similar to the color of the cooked brown and green lentils. Both the green and brown hold their shape well if not overcooked. The split red lentils cook more quickly, and are more liable to become mushy if overcooked. In Middle Eastern, Mediterranean, Indian or natural foods stores, you may be able to purchase lentils in bulk, but usually they are packaged in plastic bags and sold under various trade names such as Cedar, Clic, and Nupak or simply as green lentils or brown lentils. If a bag of lentils just says "lentils," it most likely contains brown lentils, which are the most common and can be found in standard supermarkets and even in small corner grocery stores in some cities. In Indian markets, lentils are found in various types, including whole and split (and a small brown variety not to be confused with the larger brown variety that I use). Some Indian stores may carry other types used in Middle Eastern cooking. For the recipes in this cookbook, you need only ask for green, brown or split red lentils, or, if buying from an Indian shop, request *dal*—a name covering various varieties of beans and lentils. Almost any type of lentil can be used interchangeably in the recipes in the book—just keep in mind that some types take longer to cook. *Note:* When cooking with lentils (or any dry pulse), it's important to keep an eye on the water level. During slow cooking, a lot of water will be evaporated and absorbed by the lentils, so you may need to add water from time to time. Also, the amount of water dried lentils or any type of dried pulse absorbs will vary depending on the brand, age and so on.

Dried lentils have an indefinite shelf life as long as they are stored in a sealed package or airtight container in a cool and dry place. However, to ensure the best flavor, it's best to use dried lentils within one year. Cooked lentils, on the other hand, may be refrigerated in a sealed container for up to one week or frozen up to six months. It is best, however, to avoid freezing them as they may fall apart when re-heating.

Nuts (*al-mukassaraat*) Almonds, pine nuts, pistachios, walnuts and cashews are the most common nuts used in cooking in the Arabian (aka Persian) Gulf region. Nuts keep well for months if they are stored in the refrigerator in a tightly covered glass jar. If to be stored for a long period of time they should be frozen in vacuum packed bags. If stored in the pantry, they will, in most cases, eventually become rancid and develop a bitter offensive taste. In some recipes, nuts are toasted before they are added to the dish. Toasting nuts brings out their flavor and aroma and gives them a nice light brown color. **To toast nuts**, place a small skillet over medium heat. Add the nuts and, shaking the pan frequently, toast the nuts until they start to release an aroma and turn a light golden brown color, about 2 to 3 minutes. Immediately remove the nuts from the skillet. Be careful not to burn the nuts. Nuts can also be toasted in the oven. Pre-heat the oven to 350°F (175°C). Place the nuts evenly on a sheet pan and bake about 10 minutes until they begin to turn a light golden brown color, shaking the pan a couple of times so as to turn the nuts and have them uniform in golden color. Remove immediately.

Almonds (*lawz*) This versatile nut is one of the most popular in Arab Gulf cooking. They are employed extensively in the kitchens of the Middle East, including the Gulf region, North Africa, the Iberian Peninsula and Sicily. Delicious when served alone for snacks, they are also used for decorative purposes, but in the main they are used as ingredients in drinks, sauces, *tajines* (stews), soups, candies, chocolates and pastries. No one who has tried the almond-filled pastries of North Africa or the Arab introduced-candies of Spain can deny that almonds are a gourmet delight.

When used in cooking, almonds are very often blanched to remove their skins. You can buy pre-blanched almond slivers or slices, or you can blanch whole almonds at home. **To blanch almonds**, bring some water to a boil in a saucepan. Add the al-

monds and boil for two minutes. Drain and immediately place in ice cold water. Allow to stand for 3 minutes, and then drain. Take a nut between your thumb and the forefinger and squeeze—the blanched nut will pop out. Almonds keep well for months when stored in the refrigerator.

Cashews (*al-kaju*) Related to pistachios, they are at their best when bought plain roasted without added salt. They are often eaten raw for snacks and used in salads, desserts, vegetable and meat dishes. It is best to add cashews near the end of the cooking time since they will soften if cooked over a long period.

Pine Nuts (*sanawbar*) This white rice-shaped nut, also known as pignolia or pinon, is taken from the cones of certain pine trees which grow on the shores of the Mediterranean and the Far East. About 1/2-inch (1.25-cm) long, they have a soft-sweet texture and a buttery flavor, which is at its best when the nuts are lightly toasted.

Their flavor and texture go very well with salads, sweets as well as meats, cheese, vegetables and fruit. To help in keeping pine nuts from becoming rancid, refrigerate in an airtight jar. Two varieties are retailed in North America: the Chinese and Mediterranean types. In most recipes, slivered almonds, not quite as tasty, can be substituted for pine nuts. These are best stored in an airtight container in the refrigerator.

Pistachios (*fustaq Halabi*) Considered one of the best of the well-known nuts, in the majority of cases, pistachios are roasted and salted un-shelled. From 80 to 90 percent of pistachios are prepared in this way and consumed as snacks. Un-roasted and shelled pistachios have a sweet flavor and are used in cooking. In the Middle East they are mainly utilized in desserts both as ingredients and for decorative purposes. They keep well for months if stored in a refrigerator in an airtight jar.

Walnuts (*jawz*) Believed to be the oldest nut cultivated by man, walnuts are somewhat sweet to the taste and with a meaty flesh. As a food, walnuts are great for snacks and as ingredients in other foods, especially pastries.

Limes, Dried (*loomi*) These flavor enhancers are created by leaving whole limes in the sun to dry out for approximately two weeks. In Oman, they are known as *loomi*, in Iran as *limoo omani* and in Iraq, as *noumi basra*—all names known in the Arab Gulf countries. Their addition to a stew or fish dish creates a tangy flavor. If not used whole, dried limes are ground into a powder and sprinkled on soups and stews to add a tartness to vegetable and meat dishes. A type of tea can also be prepared by breaking open the dried limes and pouring boiling water over them. Dried lime is available either whole or ground in Middle Eastern or Indian specialty stores in North America's large urban centers. If you are patient and live in a sunny, hot area or have an oven with a low setting, you can make dried limes at home. **To dry limes,** set the fresh limes out in the hot sun for about fourteen days. Or, dry the limes in a very low oven (170°F/77°C) until they become hard, sound hollow when tapped, and are easily breakable. I buy my dried limes already dried—less headaches. Always store dried limes in an airtight container and avoid any humidity.

Nutmeg (*jawz al-teeb*) Called the "queen of tropical flora," the nutmeg-mace tree is the only tree that is the source of two spices. The nutmeg-mace fruit is soft and fleshy, similar in appearance to an apricot.

When ripe and the fruit is split in two, a seed with a scarlet-colored, pulpy and net-like covering is revealed. Inside the outer skin, the bright-red membrane is the mace. This mace membrane covers the nutmeg seed, one of the main spices in the spice mixture called Baharat. **Mace** is usually sold ground, but nutmeg is retailed in the shell or ground. It is better to buy the nutmeg seeds in their shells since it quickly loses its fragrance when ground. Purchased in the shell, nutmeg seeds can be stored without loss of potency for a long period of time. Only the necessary amount should be ground immediately before use. The nutmeg seed can be grated on the very fine teeth on a box grater, on a microplane, or a specially designed nutmeg grinder or grater.

Oil (*zayt*) Olive oil (*zayt zaytun*), a natural, healthy cold-pressed oil, is superior for use in salad dressings, drizzling over the top of foods as a finishing oil, for sautéing (frying) and even deep-frying. It can be used for most recipes in this book except the desserts, such as Crispy Doughnuts in Sweet Syrup (page 137) and Filo Wrapped Nut Rolls (page 142), that call for deep-frying, as olive oil will flavor the sweet with a slight olive taste. Deemed to be the soul and secret of Middle Eastern and Mediterranean cooking, olive oil, believed to have been first domesticated in Syria, and from where in my view, the best olive oil is still produced, is employed to make all types of foods and in countless sauces and salad dressings. Olive oil is recognized to be of superb quality and aromatic flavor, especially its top grade "extra-virgin" variety, the unadulterated first press oil of the olive and chemical-free. Vegetables are fried in olive oil, and no other kitchen aroma beats that of onions and garlic being fried in it. For salads and numerous types of cold dips, extra-virgin olive oil is the best choice. So ingrained is olive oil in Arab cooking that it is even used as one might use a garnish or a fresh herb, drizzled on a plate of Classic Hummus Chickpea Purée (page 35) or Roasted Eggplant Purée (page 34) or atop Creamy Yogurt Spread (page 29) just before serving

to give that slight olive taste and aroma, and to give that extra enticement. Olive oil is not indigenous to the Arab Gulf countries and cooks in that part of the world rely heavily on imported olive oil, in the main, from Tunisia, Syria, Lebanon, Jordan, Turkey, Greece, Italy and Spain, and less so from Palestine. The taste of the oil depends on the area in which the olives grow, their quality and the style of processing the oil. Most of these oils are available in the North American markets under countless brand names.

In most of the recipes in this book, I call for extra-virgin olive oil. In Arab Gulf cooking, and generally throughout the Arab World, extra-virgin olive is the preferred choice. However, generally, when foods are fried or deep-fried, I simply call for "oil." In either case you may use the oil of your choice, though if not using extra-virgin olive oil, I recommend using another high-quality oil obtained from cold pressing, such as peanut, safflower, untoasted sesame, and sunflower oil. These are the next best choices for sautéing and deep-frying, though they tend not to be used for salads or as a finishing oil. All of these high-quality oils retain most of their unique taste and aroma, and contain natural antioxidants that help to keep them from going rancid. Processed and refined vegetable oils are a less healthy choice for frying. However, all of these oils can be used for frying when a recipe calls for simply "oil." A good many diners will not know the difference but the pressed oils, especially olive oil, are the healthiest.

Note: There is a common misconception that one should not deep-fry in olive oil. In fact, olive oil lends itself well to deep-frying since it tolerates, without changing, a temperature of about 410°F (210°C), though each time the oil is reused, the smoke-point will lower slightly. Its high amount of mono-unsaturated fatty acids enables olive oil to stay stable at relatively high temperatures. Foods fried in olive oil retain more nutritional value than those fried in any other kind of oil or fat. Virgin or Extra-virgin olive oil is recommended for deep-frying. When deep-frying with olive oil, do your best to not allow the temperature of the oil to exceed 380°F (193°C), particularly if the oil has been previously used.

Orange Blossom Water (*mazahar*)

A distilled water that has been infused with essential oil extracted from the fragrant blossoms of the bitter Seville orange, which is noted for its fresh citrus scent more than its bitter fruit. Native to China, the bitter orange was introduced into the Iberian Peninsula by the Arabs in the eighth century and planted throughout southern Spain. Today, *mazahar* is a popular flavoring in Iranian and Arabic cooking, especially in sweets and syrups. It is available throughout the Arab Gulf, the Middle East, North Africa, Europe and North America. Orange blossom water, in Europe and North America, can be purchased in any of the Arab, Indian, Iranian and Turkish grocery stores or from international food specialty stores. Orange blossom water is used in all types of cooking, bringing the sweet perfume of the orange grove to the table. Just a few drops enhance cakes, candies, fruit salads, ice cream, puddings, pastries, stewed fruit and syrups. As well, mazahar gives an exotic touch to meat, fresh fruit, and rice dishes cooked Arab or Iranian style. In some areas of the Arab World, mazahar is used to rinse hair and hands. I remember as well when as a young boy and complaining to my mother about an upset tummy, relief would come by way of a teaspoon of mazahar. When I had my own children, my wife did the same and as customs pass down generation to generation, my daughter, when asking for advice to deal with an upset stomach for my grandchildren was advised by mom and dad to do the same—and for some reason it worked! Store in the refrigerator once the bottle is opened.

mildly hot. It can be used to both season and color foods. Paprika is one of the main spices in the Arabian Gulf spice mixture known as Baharat and in the Arab Gulf countries is used in all types of dishes such as Aromatic Baked Tomato Slices (page 127) and Cauliflower Sautéed with Chili Peppers and Fresh Coriander (page 126). Store paprika in the refrigerator or freezer to maintain its potency.

Pomegranate (*rumman*) This brightly colored fruit ranges in hue from pinkish to purple-red and is about the size of a large orange. The choicest are a bright reddish color with a thin leathery skin. Inside, they are filled with a myriad of large red seeds that appear like masses of scarlet berries embedded in a translucent slightly pinkish pulp. An excellent autumn fruit, pomegranates are picked before they are fully matured. However, they continue to ripen in cold storage where they will keep in excellent condition for long periods of time. The seeds are employed to garnish salads and a number of desserts. They are especially tantalizing when sprinkled on ice cream. Besides giving a bright adornment to these foods, they also add a pleasant savory flavor. In the lands of the Arabian Peninsula the fresh seeds are also utilized in stuffings for both vegetables and meats, while in India they are dried and employed in all types of cooking. **To remove seeds from pomegranates,** press and roll the pomegranate on a hard surface, then remove the stem. With a sharp knife, score the outer skin from top to bottom at 1-inch (2.5-cm) intervals. After this, the fruit can be easily broken into pieces with the fingers and the seeds removed. Or you may try this alternate method, which works just as well. After rolling the pomegranate on a hard surface, score

the skin around the widest part. Twist to open the fruit. Take one half, and holding it in the palm of your hand, face it cut-side down over an empty bowl. With your other hand tap the underside with a heavy wooden spoon. This will release the seeds and they will fall into the bowl. Repeat with the other half. Remember, pomegranate juice stains clothing quickly and, thus, an apron is suggested as protective kitchen wear. In North America, these are seasonal fruit, easily available in the autumn throughout early winter.

Pomegranate Syrup (*Dibs Rumman*)

Also called "pomegranate concentrate" and sometimes "pomegranate molasses," this product, prepared by boiling the juice of the pomegranate until it becomes thick and turns brownish, is employed in everyday cooking. This condensed and thick juice is used to make drinks or to give soups and sauces a pleasingly tart and somewhat sour and tangy taste. It is a great addition to any type of meat filling as it provides a piquant twist. In many cases, it is utilized as a replacement for lemon juice, such as in the meat topping for Mini Saudi Pizzas (page 82). Ground meat or fried eggs and salad dressings are always enhanced with a little of this concentrate. Pomegranate syrup can be found in Middle Eastern food stores all across western Europe and North America or it can be ordered on online (see Resource Guide, page 154). Other types of pomegranate syrups such as Grenadine sold in North America are not the true products. Most have sugar and other ingredients. However, they can be used as substitutes if you do not have Pomegranate Syrup on hand. If you do use grenadine, consider adding a squeeze of fresh lemon juice to maintain the correct sweet to tart balance. When a bottle is opened, I return it to the refrigerator until ready for the next use.

Rice (*ruzz*) Some food writers claim that there are some 40,000 different varieties of rice grown throughout the world. However, all of these varieties can be divided into long-, medium-, and short-grain rice. Today, people living in the Arab Gulf nations come from all over the world and thus prefer the type of rice to which they are accustomed. Thus, the three types of rice are used. Those from the Greater Syria area, for example, may opt to use short or medium-grain rice to stuff their vegetables. However, to simplify, when I cook Arab Gulf dishes I use Basmati for everything—from savory meals to sweet rice puddings. Basmati is always a sure bet—cooking-wise, flavor-wise, aroma-wise and taste-wise. Rice is bought, in the main, polished after the grain is hulled or husked then milled until the rice turns white. On the other hand rice can be purchased brown with only the hull removed. The bran layers, responsible for its color are rich in minerals and vitamins and give it a chewy texture and a nutlike flavor. My favorite, Basmati rice, is famous for its mouth-watering fragrance and delicate flavor—in fact, it gets its name from the Sanskrit (the fragrant one). One of the favored brands in the Arab Gulf countries it is a long-grained type of rice, grown mainly in the Punjab region of the Indian sub-continent. Other long-grain rice brands can be substituted but in my view Basmati is the long-grain rice par excellence. In Asian and the Middle Eastern countries rice is soaked and/or washed and then rinsed before use. This lessens the starch in the rice, which creates the ideal texture when cooked. Every country or region seems to have its own method of preparing rice before cooking it. From Japan, through China and the other countries of the Far East and westward to the Middle East and beyond, rinsing or washing rice is done in various ways. Some just place the rice in water for a few minutes and then drain; some run water over the rice until the water runs clear; others soak it for an hour or more and then drain; some even include a long draining period; and some, like myself, at times use rice, to the horror of Arab housewives, as is, without washing. The method I use most often, however, for convenience and to achieve fluffy, delicious rice is to do a five-minute soak and then thoroughly rinse.

How to Prepare Rice for Cooking: Cooking a great pot of rice is not only related to the quality of the rice and how the rice is cooked while it's on the stove, but also how the rice is prepped before it is cooked. To make the best rice, it is briefly soaked and then rinsed and drained. **To soak rice,** place the rice in a bowl and cover with cold water. Let soak for the time specified in the recipe. Generally, the soaking time is a brief 5 minutes. Occasionally I specify a longer soaking time. **To rinse rice,** place the rice in fine-mesh sieve and run cold water over it to rinse thoroughly (the water should run clear). *Note:* Do not use a colander as the rice grains will get stuck in the perforated holes, which is very frustrating and annoying! **To drain rice,** allow the rice to drain in the fine-mesh sieve over a bowl or sink for a few minutes.

Rosewater (*ma' ward*) A distilled rosewater originating in the Middle East, it is made from the essence of distilled red and pink rose flowers. Even today the finest rosewater essence is produced in that area in the world. In the hot desert regions, fragrant rose varieties reach their par excellence. The returning Crusaders introduced the use of this essence in cooking into Europe from the Holy Land. In medieval Britain the rose aroma in food flourished, becoming popular in drinks, jams and sweets. Today, worldwide, especially in its land of origin, the essence is important in the preparation of desserts such as Turkish delight and other sweets, as well as in beverages. Always used very sparingly, it adds a mysterious touch to dishes. Rare is a home in the Middle East that does not always carry a bottle of rosewater in its larder. Rosewater is found in many supermarkets, in specialty food stores, and in Arab, Indian, Iranian and Turkish markets. Store in the refrigerator once the bottle is opened.

Saffron (*za'faran*) The dried stigma of the yellow crocus native to the Mediterranean. Employed when preparing food such as cheese, eggs, ice-cream, drinks, meat, pasta, sauces, soups, syrups and numerous sweets, it produces a strong yellow color and if fresh, imparts a unique flavor and a distinct aroma. Saffron can be purchased as a powder or in threads. However, the filaments are preferable—the powder, in many cases is adulterated. Before use, a few threads of saffron should be lightly toasted then crumbled and diluted in hot water, before adding to the dish being cooked. It is best, if possible, to add the saffron when the dish is almost done in order to preserve the color and flavor. Saffron is expensive and thus normally used sparingly. Most Middle Eastern and Indian supermarkets or grocery stores sell it. If saffron is properly stored in a cool dark place and in an airtight container, it can keep for at least three years. As with other spices, the flavor will lessen over time.

Sumac (*summaq*) The crushed dried berries of the fruit of the Mediterranean sumac, also spelled *sumach* or *sumak*, is widely used in Middle Eastern cuisine. This condiment, with its lemony flavor, is a favorite spice of Middle Eastern cooks. As a seasoning, it lends a tart taste to barbecues, chicken, curries, fish, salads, sauces, stews, stuffing and vegetables. In the eastern Arab countries and adjoining lands, it is also employed extensively with onions and salt as a savory spice for roasts. Arab gourmet cooks are convinced that there is no substitute for this tangy condiment. Sumac is found in Middle Eastern supermarkets and grocery stores (and online stores, see Resource Guide, page 154) and at spice or gourmet emporiums, such as Penzeys (www.penzeys.com). The shelf life of pure sumac stored in a cool place away from heat and in a sealed jar is about a year.

Tahini Also called *taheena* or *tahina*, tahini is the product of hulled and crushed sesame seeds. In consistency and appearance it is somewhat like peanut butter, but it has a more subtle taste. A delectable, nourishing, and wholesome thick paste with a nutty flavor, it is the mayonnaise of the Middle East. In the Middle East tahini is most closely associated with Classic Hummus Chickpea Purée (page 35) a dish now found in most parts of the world, Roasted Eggplant Purée (page 34), and Halawa, or halvah, a worldwide known confection. A tasty sesame seed paste, it comes in two types: light and dark. The light version is considered to have both the best flavor and texture. Tahini, derived from the Arabic *tahana* (to grind), has no cholesterol and is relatively sodium free. For the Arabs, it is a highly valued, protein-packed condiment, and with its many culinary and health attributes, it is a near perfect food. It has long been believed in the Middle Eastern lands that, when combined with legumes, tahini becomes the ultimate food.

While awaiting its next use, you may notice that the oil will separate and rise to the top of the tahini jar. A good tip is to always stir up the tahini in the jar before using it. Once only found in Middle East supermarkets and grocery stores, its popularity has garnered it shelf space in health food stores and in many general supermarkets.

Turmeric (*kurkum*) Before being ground to a powder, which is how it is most commonly known in the West, turmeric starts its life as an aromatic root, finger-like in appearance with a brown skin and bright yellow flesh, with a delicate and slightly peppery taste. After harvesting, the rhizomes are boiled; then dried and polished. Subsequently, they are either milled into powder or left whole and sold in that state, to be ground at time of use.

Turmeric is employed worldwide in the preparation of food, both at home and commercially. Due to its antibacterial properties, it was employed to preserve food long before the widespread use of refrigeration. It is much used in pickling, and for seasoning composite dishes. It goes well with all vegetables, especially with various types of beans and lentils, curries, cauliflower, devilled eggs, leafy green vegetables, potatoes and rice. Turmeric does not burn quickly and hence can be added at any point in cooking. The spice is also used to give color and flavor to marinades, salad dressings and soups. Turmeric is often substituted for the very expensive saffron. Ground turmeric lasts a long time—about two years—as long as it is stored in an airtight container in a cool place away from direct light.

Yogurt *(robe or laban)* Known commonly in the Greater Syria Region as *laban*, yogurt is the universal sauce of the eastern Arab World. Discovered some 5,000 years ago on the Mesopotamian plains, yogurt, for those wishing to cut down on the amount of fat, cholesterol and calories in their diets, is the near perfect food when made from skimmed milk. Brands labeled low fat and low-cholesterol can be substituted for mayonnaise, sour cream or similar products. Naturally, for the creamiest texture and best flavor, yogurt made from whole milk is superior, but the low-fat yogurts are very good substitutes for the full-fat type.

Besides its nutritious value, yogurt is a marvelously versatile and adaptable food. It adds richness, flavor and an appetizing aroma to a myriad of dishes. It blends well with cheese, eggs, grains, meats, fruits, vegetables, and makes an excellent marinade. I even use a couple of teaspoons to tenderize meat or poultry at times. Delicious when flavored with syrups, nuts, herbs and spices, it enhances and is enhanced by other foods. And on a hot summer day, nothing is more refreshing than an iced yogurt drink.

Plain yogurt is used for all the recipes in this book. Today plain yogurt is easy to find in any grocery store, but homemade yogurt is very easy to make, cost-saving, and fresh tasting. A recipe for making homemade yogurt can be found on page 31.

Za'tar This Arabic word is used to identify various types of thyme, much used in cooking in the Arab East, but more importantly it refers to a condiment that has been used as a staple in Middle East cuisine from medieval times. It is a mixture of various herbs and spices such as ground roasted chickpeas, marjoram, thyme or oregano, salt, toasted sesame seeds, but always with sumac being the main component. Each Arab country, even each large city, to some extent, has its own version of *za'tar*. As well, each rural family develops its own recipe for this tangy condiment.

Its uses are many and varied. It is often used to replace lemon and lime juices or vinegar, and is used as a seasoning, sprinkled on vegetables, salads, meatballs or kebabs or Creamy Yogurt Spread (page 29). Mixed with olive oil, it makes a great dip, especially with freshly baked bread. Nothing brings out the hunger pangs in the morning more than Mana'eesh bi Za'tar—za'tar mixed with olive oil and spread over rounds of dough then baked and eaten fresh out of the oven.

It's best to store za'tar in a dry area away from heat and light to maintain its shelf life of two years.

BASIC RECIPES

This section is the place to find recipes for popular condiments and pickles; Arabian Gulf Spice Mix, or Baharat (page 28), a quintessential spice blend; and foods, such as Homemade Plain Yogurt (page 31), that are enjoyed as are or, in some cases, as components in other dishes You will also find a recipe for preparing plain boiled rice (Saudi-Style White Rice, page 28)—a fixture of nearly every meal—and refreshing and creamy yogurt-based salads that are frequently served with meat, especially rich and fatty cuts. Also included is a recipe for Creamy Yogurt Spread (page 29), known as Labana, and for Labana Balls (page 29)—two thick, creamy cream cheeselike yogurt products that are extremely addictive and easy to make. Like several other dishes in this book, Creamy Yogurt Spread and Labana Balls have been adopted from their countries of origin, the Greater Syria area and Iraq, by the people of the Arab Gulf nations, where they are enjoyed throughout the day—at breakfast, as snacks and as part of a meal.

CRUNCHY PICKLED GARLIC
Ajar Thoom Al-'Ajam

An essential part of most meals in the Middle East, pickles are popular throughout the region. Over the years, the Arab Gulf countries have embraced the pickle-eating traditions of the Greater Syria region, Iraq and Iran, where pickled turnips, eggplants, cauliflower, carrots and especially, garlic, are the favorites. Of all of these, my favorite is pickled garlic, an exotic, tangy and spicy pickle that is Iranian in origin. Crunchy Pickled Garlic not only spices up a meal (it goes especially well with meat or chicken dishes), it also makes for a great appetizer. This recipe makes a large amount, but pickled garlic has amazing keeping powers! Culinary writers have said that pickled garlic improves with age—some make the unbelievable claim they will keep as long as fifteen years. I have stored pickled garlic for as long as 4 months in the refrigerator and was still eating from them long after. They stayed as tasty and crunchy as when I first made them. But fifteen years? This would be pretty hard to imagine because once one starts with one pickled clove of garlic, it will be difficult to resist a second and a third.

Makes 2-quarts (2 liters)
Prep time: 1 1/2 hours (and MUCH less with the help of friends or family)
Cooking time: 15 minutes
Maturing time: 3 days

2 lbs (1 kg) garlic, cloves separated and peeled
1 cup (250 ml) white vinegar
1 cup (250 ml) water
4 tablespoons sugar
1 tablespoon salt
1 tablespoon whole coriander seeds
12 peppercorns
6 whole cloves
2 teaspoons dried red pepper flakes
2 teaspoons ground turmeric
1/4 teaspoon dried tarragon
1/4 teaspoon dried marjoram
1/4 teaspoon dried thyme
Boiling water

1 Place all the ingredients in a large saucepan and bring to a boil. Cover and cook over medium-low heat for 8 minutes.
2 Immediately pour the garlic-vinegar mixture into a 2-quart (2-liter) heatproof jar and top off with boiling hot water. Cover with a tight-fitting lid and let stand in a cool, dark place for at least 3 days before serving. Store what is not used in its brine in the refrigerator for future use.

TANGY HOT TOMATO SAUCE

In the modern Arab Gulf countries, this spicy and hot sauce, a vegetarian delight, is served with all types of rice dishes or with cooked meats and vegetables. However, in the past, when most of the people in the Arab Gulf states were poor, it was served as a replacement for meat to give rice a delicious flavor. My first introduction to this sauce was at a hotel restaurant in Dubai where a number of dishes were placed on the table as appetizers. Adhering to the old Arab tradition of dipping and scooping bread into the dip-able dishes, we scooped away until we had finished off the delicious Tangy Hot Tomato Sauce even before the main course arrived.

Makes 1 1/4 cups (300 ml)
Prep time: 5 minutes
Cooking time: 15 minutes

4 tablespoons tomato paste
1 cup (250 ml) water
4 cloves garlic, crushed to a paste
   (see page 30)
1 teaspoon ground cumin
1/4 teaspoon ground red pepper (cayenne)
1 tablespoon vinegar
2 tablespoons extra-virgin olive oil
Salt to taste

1 Thoroughly combine all the ingredients in a small saucepan with a lid. Bring to a boil. Cover and cook over low heat for 10 minutes, stirring occasionally.
2 Remove from the heat and allow to cool. If the sauce is too thick, add a little water. (It should have the consistency of tomato sauce.) Store in a covered glass container in the refrigerator. It should be used within a week.

CREAMY GARLIC SAUCE Taratoor

This delicious garlic sauce—it enhances everything it touches!—was first prepared by peasants in the Greater Syria region. From there it was carried by the Phoenicians and later the Arabs to the Iberian Peninsula, and from there it moved up to southern France, where it is called *aioli*. This sauce and other similar garlic sauces are today an integral part of the Arab Gulf countries' cuisines. This sauce, an international favorite, goes great with all types of chicken, fish, meat and vegetable dishes. I especially enjoy it with barbecued fish. For those who fear too much garlic on the breath, this sauce may seem a little overpowering. Fear not—one taste will take your breath away! Even children will love it! (One of my grandchildren spreads this sauce on toast for his morning getter-upper.)

Makes about 1 cup (250 ml)
Prep time: 15 minutes

1 large head garlic, cloves separated and
   peeled
1 egg
1 teaspoon salt
1/2 cup (125 ml) extra-virgin olive oil
2 tablespoons freshly squeezed lemon juice

1 Process the garlic, egg and salt in a blender for a few moments. With the motor running, slowly pour in the oil. After all the oil is added, continue to blend for 1 minute.
2 Add the lemon juice and blend until a frothy sauce is formed. Place in a small serving dish or bowl and serve immediately.

ORANGE BLOSSOM SYRUP Sheera

This syrup is responsible for the divinely sweet taste of many Arab pastries. Also known as Qatar or Atar, it is used throughout the Middle East for the same purpose. Sheera is a sugar- and water-based syrup flavored with orange blossom water. As one travels westward in Arab North Africa the syrup used there for sweets, in most cases, is honey based, though it is also flavored with orange blossom water. For a change of taste, the orange blossom water can be replaced with rosewater. We usually have a few cups of this sweet syrup on hand in case someone in the family craves a waffle or pancake with a touch of the Arab Gulf.

Makes 2 1/2 cups (625 ml)
Prep time: 5 minutes
Cooking time: 10 minutes

2 cups (450 g) sugar
1 cup (250 ml) water
2 tablespoons freshly squeezed lemon juice
2 tablespoons orange blossom water

1 Place the sugar and water in a small saucepan. Cook over medium heat, stirring constantly, until the sugar is thoroughly dissolved.
2 Remove from the heat and stir in the lemon juice. Return to the heat and bring to a boil. Remove from the heat and stir in the orange blossom water. Allow to cool before using. Store leftover Orange Blossom Syrup in a glass jar in the refrigerator. It will last for an indefinite period of time, though it will become thicker over time.

> **NOTE:** If a less sweeter syrup is desired, use only half the sugar.

SAUDI-STYLE WHITE RICE
'Aysh Abyadh

Every time that I am invited for lunch or for dinner while in the Arab Gulf, there is almost a guarantee that 'Aysh Abyadh will be on the table. This dish is consumed almost daily and is served with all types of casseroles and stews such as Lamb and Okra Stew (page 90) as well as with barbecued meats, chicken and fish. Rice for the Arabs is as important as pasta is for the Italians and bread to the French. A basic side dish throughout the eastern Arab World, no meal would be complete without a steaming dish of white rice. One point to reinforce is that, personally, I strongly recommend eating this buttery rice with a spoon rather than a fork so that I can capture each grain ensuring that not one morsel has been wasted.

Makes 2 cups (450 g)
Prep time: 15 minutes
Cooking time: 40 minutes

1 cup (200 g) uncooked Basmati or other
   white long-grain rice, soaked for
   5 minutes, thoroughly rinsed and drained
   (see page 24)
1 teaspoon salt
Boiling hot water, about 4 to 6 cups
   (1 to 1.5 liters)
4 tablespoons butter, melted

1 Place the drained rice and salt in a medium saucepan with a lid. Pour in the boiling water to about 2 inches (5 cm) over the rice. Bring to a boil, cover, and cook over low heat for 8 minutes. Drain in a sieve and rinse with cold water for 1 minute.
2 In the same saucepan pour 2 tablespoons of the butter. Add the drained rice and pour the remaining 2 tablespoons of the butter evenly over top. Cover and cook over very low heat for 30 minutes, or until the rice is fully cooked—when the kernels can be easily pressed between the fingers—stirring a number of times.

ARABIAN GULF SPICE MIX
Baharat

Spice mixtures are being used extensively in Arab Gulf cooking to flavor and season all types of meat, chicken and fish dishes, soups and stews. I remember the first time I walked through the souk of Abu Dhabi, and I ventured upon the spice section of the open market not by sheer chance but rather by following the aroma of the array of spices. The most popular spice blend—Baharat, is an all-in-one mixture of various spices, the most popular being a mix of allspice, pepper, cardamom, cloves, coriander, cumin, nutmeg and paprika. However, every region has its own blend based on regional and sometimes personal preferences. Thus, other herbs and spices such as cassia bark, chili peppers, cinnamon, dried limes, ginger, mint, savory and others are also often used. Instead of measuring spices for various dishes, Baharat is a time-saver, having the spices already mixed and measured when getting ready to prepare a meal. In the past and even to some extent today, the spices used to prepare Baharat would be purchased whole then pulverized at home with a pestle and mortar. Today's ground spices are a God-send, lessening work-time in the kitchen and making the preparation of Baharat fast and easy. Even though Baharat can be purchased already ground and mixed, there is a drawback. Spices bought this way, over a period of time usually lose some of their flavor and aroma. Personally, I usually buy the spices ground and then mix them saving me the time to do other things. I enjoy Baharat sprinkled over a hard-boiled egg making it difficult for me to reconsider going back to the old standard salt and pepper.

Makes 1 cup (100 g)
Prep time: 10 minutes

2 tablespoons ground dried limes (sumac may be substituted)
2 tablespoons ground black pepper
2 tablespoons ground cumin
2 teaspoons paprika
2 tablespoons ground coriander
2 tablespoons ground cinnamon
1 tablespoon curry powder
2 teaspoons ground ginger
2 teaspoons ground cloves
2 teaspoons ground cardamom
2 teaspoons freshly grated nutmeg

1 Combine all the ingredients in a mixing bowl.
2 Transfer to a small glass container with a tight-fitting lid and store in a cool, dark place. It will keep for up to 6 months but will begin to lose its aroma and potency even after several weeks.

CREAMY YOGURT SPREAD Labana

Labana, also known as yogurt spread, has a soft cream cheese texture. It is widely sold readymade in the Arab Gulf countries and in large cities in North America. It seems that wherever the Arabs emigrate Labana follows them. Zanakeel Laban, which consists of Labana formed into balls and preserved in olive oil, is a good way to preserve Labana for long periods. Both forms are simple to prepare and are excellent appetizers and fillings for sandwiches. Labana is great spread on toast. A delicious way to serve the Labana or Zanakeel Laban is with a dish of olives and freshly cut vegetables on the side. These along with a good hot loaf of Pita Bread (page 122) make for a true and traditional Arab breakfast. From the days of my childhood until the present it has been my favorite early morning food. The bag used to hold the yogurt to drain off its excess liquid should be a medium-size fine-weave white cotton bag that can be purchased in any kitchenware department. Or, even better, you can improvize at home by cutting a white cotton pillowcase down to the size needed to make your own bag. Any type of plain yogurt can be used, though the more fat the yogurt contains the tastier the Labana and Labana Balls will be. However, if using a lower fat yogurt, the healthier the Labana and Labana Balls will be.

Makes 1 cup (225 g) Labana or about 20 Labana Balls
Prep time: 10 minutes
Drying time: 2 days

4 cups (1 kg) store-bought or Homemade Plain Yogurt (page 31)
3/4 teaspoon salt
Za'tar, to sprinkle on top
Extra-virgin olive oil, to drizzle on top

1 To prepare the Labana: Place the yogurt in a medium bowl and stir in the salt. Pour the seasoned yogurt into a small fine-weave white cotton bag and tie with a string. Suspend the tied bag over a receptacle for 2 days, allowing the water to drip out, or until the contents are firm. Or you can place the yogurt in a triple or quadruple-layered pouch made with cheese-cloth that is gathered together at the top with a string.
2 Remove the Labana from the bag and place them in a small bowl. Cover and refrigerate and use as needed.
3 To serve, remove required amount then spread evenly on a small plate. Sprinkle with a little of the *za'tar* and the olive oil just before serving.

Variation

LABANA BALLS
Zanakeel Laban

Prep time: 20 minutes
Drying time: 8 hours

1 To prepare the Zanakeel Laban: Place 1 heaping tablespoon of the Labana in the palm of your hand, then roll into a ball. Place on a small tray. Repeat to make 20 balls.
2 Allow to stand overnight uncovered at room temperature to allow them to dry out further. If you like, you may loosely drape thin netting over the balls. (This process of overnight airing will allow the balls to bind better—if the balls retain moisture they are likely to crumble in the oil.) Then place in sterilized jars and cover with olive oil. Seal and store refrigerated for future use. They will keep indefinitely.
3 Always serve the balls with a little of their olive oil.

FRONT AND BACK: Creamy Yogurt Spread and Labana Balls

CREAMY CUCUMBER AND YOGURT SALAD Khiyar bi Laban

During the hot summer on our prairie homestead, my mother usually made this dish once or twice a week as a cooling lunchtime treat. We often ate it as a side dish with all types of main courses, especially with meat and rice dishes. At other times we ate it as a light late-night snack before retiring for the evening. What a surprise for me when lunching in Muscat at the home of a friend on a very hot late spring day to find my host place before me a cooling dish of Khiyar bi Laban, almost the same as my mother's dish. A smooth yet crunchy yogurt salad, it epitomizes the best in taste when combining yogurt and garlic together. Today, versions of this dish using a variety of fresh vegetables are found in all the Arab Gulf countries and the bordering states.

Serves 4 to 6
Prep time: 15 minutes
Refrigeration time: 2 hours

One 8-in (20-cm) cucumber, peeled and chopped
2 cups (500 g) store-bought or Homemade Plain Yogurt (page 31)
2 cloves garlic, crushed to a paste (see below)
1 tablespoon finely chopped fresh mint leaves
1/2 teaspoon salt
1/4 teaspoon ground black pepper

1 Combine all the ingredients in a serving bowl.
2 Refrigerate, covered, for 2 hours before serving.

> **HOW TO MAKE GARLIC PASTE**
> **To create garlic paste using a mortar and pestle**, place peeled whole garlic cloves into the bowl of a mortar. Begin pounding straight down over the garlic, smashing the cloves. Then pound in a circular fashion, until the smashed cloves come together and begin to form a smooth paste.
> **To create garlic paste using a garlic press**, crush the garlic in the press. Then, working on a cutting board, place the side of a chef's knife on the crushed garlic and press down firmly, moving the side of the blade across the garlic as you press. Repeat until the garlic has a paste-like consistency. Or, you may press on the crushed garlic with the tines of a fork to smooth it into a paste.

CORIANDER AND YOGURT SALAD
Salatat Kuzbara

Salatat Kuzbara is one of the most popular yogurt salads in the Middle East and the Arab Gulf. It is usually served as a side dish to accompany lamb dishes and no roasted lamb can be served without it. The first time that I enjoyed this dish was some forty years ago when I was invited to a Palestinian-Canadian's home for a feast, which had roasted lamb as the centerpiece of the meal. From that day I made sure that Salatat Kuzbara was on the menu every time I served meat, especially any fatty type. The salad's flavor eases the heavy taste left by the fat. Fresh coriander leaves (cilantro) serve as an aromatic stimulant to this yogurt-based salad.

Serves 6
Prep time: 15 minutes
Refrigeration time: 1 hour

1/2 bunch fresh coriander leaves (cilantro) (about 1/4 lb/125 g), de-stemmed, thoroughly washed and drained
4 cups (1 kg) store-bought or Homemade Plain Yogurt (page 31)
3 cloves garlic, crushed to a paste (see left)
1 teaspoon salt
1/2 teaspoon black pepper
1/2 teaspoon dried mint leaves

1 Finely chop the coriander leaves. (You should have about 2 cups/125 g.)
2 Thoroughly combine all the ingredients in a serving bowl. Cover and chill before serving.

homemade plain yogurt
Robe

In the Arab Gulf countries Robe is a traditional part of the everyday meal enjoyed at both lunch and dinner. There, as well as in many other parts of the world, people believe that yogurt is good for the health and contains healing properties. And well they have a point. A milk product curdled by the actions of cultures and having the consistency of custard, yogurt is almost a medicinal food. It contains a digestive enzyme, which helps to keep one healthy. In my youth, yogurt was typically placed on the table with almost every meal, as a side dish or as an ingredient in a main dish. It was as if it had to be there to complete the meal and to provide the healthy essentials of good eating. Perhaps, mom and dad did not know the specific medicinal curative attributes that modern day research is now providing, but what they did know was that it was a cure-all, the same idea passed down as timeless tradition. Before the discovery of oil and the appearance of modern supermarkets, Robe was traditionally made at home. Today store-bought yogurt is common on many tables in the Arab World. Yet, there are adamant traditionalists who prefer to make it at home because it is simple to make and more correctly, authentic. Amazingly, it is made in the same fashion as it has been for centuries and centuries. In fact, a while back while in Kuwait City, I attended a luncheon honoring the recipient of a second PhD in biology. When asked about the uniqueness of his intelligence, he denied being different saying that he was the same as anyone else because when he made yogurt he too put his finger in the milk to test the temperature. Times may have changed but traditions, to some extent, still continue.

> **TIP:** Keep in mind that the more fat content the milk has, or the "starter" yogurt, that you use to make yogurt, the richer and creamier the yogurt will be. And remember! Always set aside part of the yogurt for the next batch to use as a starter.

Makes 6 cups (1.5 kg)
Prep time: 5 minutes
Cooking time: 15 minutes
Standing time: 20 minutes (to allow the boiled milk to cool to lukewarm)
Resting time: 8 hours

6 cups (1.5 liters) milk, any type
3 tablespoons store-bought or homemade plain yogurt (starter from a previous batch or purchased)

1 Bring the milk to a boil in a medium saucepan with lid, over medium heat, uncovered. (Be careful—the milk will quickly rise to the top of the pot once hot). Lower the heat to medium-low and simmer uncovered for 3 minutes. Remove from the heat.

2 Allow to cool to lukewarm temperature, about 110° to 115°F (43° to 46°C). (You will know that the milk has cooled enough if you can keep your little finger in the milk to the count of ten.)

3 Using a wooden spoon, thoroughly stir in the yogurt (starter) then cover with the saucepan lid. Wrap with a heavy towel and allow to stand for 8 hours in a warm place. Do not disturb.

4 Refrigerate overnight before serving or using in another recipe.

CHAPTER 1

APPETIZERS AND SNACKS

With the advent of petroleum wealth and the influx of expatriates from the four corners of the world, there has been an explosion of appetizers on the Arab Gulf table. Of course, long before oil was discovered, the inhabitants of the Arabian Peninsula had their own simple appetizers, such as roasted chickpeas, nuts, olives, raisins and, above all, dates, which were offered for snacks or served as appetizers.

From among the expatriates who came to work in the Arab Gulf countries' large hotels or to open restaurants, those from the Greater Syria area have had the biggest impact on cooking in the Arab Gulf. The most successful were the Lebanese whose dishes, especially their appetizers, known as *mazza* (also *maza* or *mezze*) have now, to a great extent, become part of the food fare in most of the Arab Gulf lands. Among the favorites are Roasted Eggplant Purée or Baba Ghanouj (page 34) and Red Bell Pepper Dip with Pine Nuts (page 43), nearly a given with any mazza order. The Lebanese have been so successful in spreading their smorgasbord of appetizers served on small dishes (as well as other foods) that today, in the Arab Gulf nations, the dishes from Syria, Palestine and Jordan are collectively called "Lebanese food."

These Lebanese appetizers as well as those brought in by the Iranian, Iraqi and Indian workers are now so ingrained in Arab Gulf kitchens that many of the young believe them to be the native dishes of their homeland. For example, Arab Gulf menus include Aromatic Chickpea Fritters (Baqoura, page 39), an appetizer originating in India, while Stuffed Grape Leaves (page 36) are popular in every Middle Eastern country. However, the new appetizers from non-Arab Gulf lands are not adopted as is. Over the years Arab cooks have added different spices and elaborate garnishes, resulting in appetizers unique to the Gulf countries.

ROASTED EGGPLANT PURÉE

Baba Ghanouj

In Arabic, the name of this dish means "spoiled old daddy." As the story goes, the woman who first prepared Baba Ghanouj made it to pamper her old and toothless father. This vegetarian dish from the Greater Syria region is a must when serving *mazza* in the Arab Gulf—so much so that any appetizer table at a feast or dinner party is not complete without it. Garnished with parsley and tomatoes, its appearance is as good as its garlicky and smoky taste. The Arab Gulf's version slightly varies from that of its home of origin in that a little coriander and cumin are added to spice it up. A few years ago, while in Abu Dhabi, I was sitting in a restaurant with a number of colleagues. I was amazed at the number of appetizer dishes that had been placed on our table—at least thirty. However, someone called the waiter over to complain. I was shocked. With a full medley of appetizers sitting before us, he could not find the Baba Ghanouj!

Serves 6 to 8
Prep time: 20 minutes
Cooking time about 1 1/2 hours

1 large eggplant, about 2 lbs (1 kg), pierced
    with a fork on all sides
2 cloves garlic, crushed to a paste (see
    page 30)
1 teaspoon salt
1/2 teaspoon ground black pepper
1/4 teaspoon ground cumin
1/4 teaspoon ground coriander
4 tablespoons freshly squeezed lemon juice
4 tablespoons tahini (sesame paste)
4 tablespoons extra-virgin olive oil, plus
    extra for drizzling
1/2 cup (25 g) finely chopped fresh parsley,
    for garnish
1 small tomato, finely chopped, for garnish

1 Preheat the oven to 350°F (175°C).
2 Place the eggplant on a baking pan. Bake for 1 1/2 hours, turning frequently, until tender when a small knife is inserted easily and the skin is crisp. Allow to cool, remove and discard the skin. Mash the pulp, in a mixing bowl, with a fork or potato masher. (Do not use a blender or food processor; these will render the pulp too fine.) Set aside.
3 Place the remaining ingredients, except the parsley and tomato, in a blender and blend for a few moments, adding a little water if too thick. (The ideal consistency is that of heavy cream or corn syrup.)
4 Add the blended ingredients to the bowl with the mashed eggplant and stir to thoroughly combine. Spread evenly on a platter. Garnish with the parsley and tomato before serving.
5 A little extra olive oil can be drizzled over the top just before serving, if desired.

classic hummus chickpea purée

Hummus

This very tasty and healthy appetizer has spread from the Greater Syria region to around the world. Known simply as "hummus" in the West (*hummus* means "chickpeas"), the same dish is known in Lebanon, Syria, Jordan and Palestine as *hummus bi-tahini* or "hummus with tahini." The Arab Gulf version is unique due to the addition of cumin, coriander and ground red pepper, making it a bit spicier. Popular with vegetarians, it is often sold in health food stores, prepared and ready to eat. However, no real comparison can be made between the homemade version and the store-bought. Pre-made, ready-to-go hummus lacks the luster and flavor of the freshly made version and, best of all, it is very simple to prepare.

Serves 8
Prep time: 15 minutes

2¹/2 cups (500 g) drained cooked or canned cooked chickpeas (see page 17 for canned/dried equivalents)
4 tablespoons tahini (sesame paste)
4 tablespoons freshly squeezed lemon juice
4 tablespoons water
2 cloves garlic, crushed to a paste (see page 30)
¹/2 teaspoon salt
Generous pinch of ground cumin
Generous pinch of ground coriander
Pinch of ground red pepper (cayenne)
4 tablespoons extra-virgin olive oil
1 tablespoon chopped fresh parsley
¹/4 teaspoon paprika, for garnish

1 Place the chickpeas, tahini, lemon juice, water, garlic, salt, cumin, ground coriander, ground red pepper and 2 tablespoons of the olive oil in a blender. Blend until the mixture is a thick paste. (If a thinner consistency is desired, add more water.)
2 Spread in a shallow platter and refrigerate for at least 1 hour. Just before serving, garnish with the chopped parsley, then sprinkle with the remaining 2 tablespoons of oil and the paprika.

STUFFED GRAPE LEAVES

Waraq 'Inab Mihshi

Known to the Greeks as *dolmath*, the Turks *dolma*, the Iranians *dolmeh*, and the Arabs *mahshi*, stuffed vegetables have been enjoyed in the Middle East and the Balkans for centuries. It is, however, the stuffed leaves of the grape that are the most commonly preferred in the eastern Mediterranean countries and Iran. The slight tartness in the taste of the grape leaf enhanced with the ingredients in the stuffing produce such an exquisite taste that even though a little extra work, time and patience may be needed to prepare this appetizer, you may well end up making them over and over again. In the Arab World, the Syrians, Lebanese, Palestinians, Iraqis and Iranians have been rolling grape leaves for centuries and it was they who introduced them to the Arab Gulf. Stuffed grape leaves have become so popular in the Arab Gulf that almost every hotel that serves Arab food will have them on their menus. With time, these stuffed leaves took on a delicious character of their own in their new home, a source of pride in the Arab Gulf. Basmati rice is the preferred staple for the stuffing as opposed to the standard short grain rice and the Gulf's version includes onions, tomatoes and cumin, enhancing the taste of the leaves with a well-spiced stuffing. To enjoy them at their utmost, they should be eaten hot. As with any stuffed vegetables with rice, Arabs enjoy their stuffed grape leaves accompanied by Creamy Cucumber and Yogurt Salad (page 30) or with Homemade Plain Yogurt (page 31). Stuffing grape leaves may seem a bit complicated to the uninitiated. The trick is to lay the leaves flat and to keep the stuffing from falling out by turning in the sides of the leaves in as you roll them.

**Serves about 6 as an entrée
   and 12 as an appetizer**
Soaking time: 20 minutes
Prep time: 45 minutes
Cooking time: 1 hour

One 1-lb (500-g) jar preserved grape leaves
1 lb (500 g) ground lamb or beef
1 cup (200 g) uncooked Basmati or other
   white long-grain rice, soaked for 5 minutes,
   thoroughly rinsed and drained (see page 24)
2 onions, very finely chopped
2 tomatoes, finely chopped
4 cloves garlic, crushed to a paste (see page 30)
1/2 cup (50 g) finely chopped green onions
   (scallions)
2 tablespoons finely chopped fresh coriander
   leaves (cilantro)
4 tablespoons extra-virgin olive oil
1 teaspoon ground black pepper
1 teaspoon ground cumin
1/2 teaspoon allspice
2 teaspoons salt
2 cups (500 ml) tomato juice mixed with
   1 teaspoon dried oregano
Water

1 Remove the preserved grape leaves from the jar, unroll them and place them in a large pan with boiling hot water. Let them soak for 5 minutes, drain well, and then soak two more times in fresh hot water, each time for 5 minutes, draining well after each soaking. (This triple-soaking process will remove the salt from the leaves.) Drain and set aside.
2 Prepare the stuffing by combining all the remaining ingredients, except 1 teaspoon of the salt, the tomato juice and water.
3 To stuff and roll up the leaves, follow the illustrated steps on opposite page.
4 Place any remaining leaves on the bottom of a medium saucepan with a lid. Arrange the rolls, seam side down, over the leaf-lined bottom of pot placing the rolls tightly side by side in crisscrossing layers. Sprinkle the remaining 1 teaspoon of salt over the top of the rolled grape leaves. Pour the tomato juice over the rolls. Cover with an inverted plate. Pressing down on the plate, add enough water to barely cover the plate. Bring to a boil, then cover with the saucepan lid. Cook over medium-low heat for 1 hour or until the meat and rice are done. Carefully remove the stuffed grape leaves with a fork. Serve hot as an appetizer or as a main dish.

Stuffing and Rolling the Grape Leaves

1 Take a leaf and spread it out on a cutting board with the wide part of the leaf towards you and the veins facing upward. With a knife, trim, if necessary, any remaining stems. If the leaf is torn, patch it with a part of another damaged leaf.

2 Place 1 to 2 tablespoons of the stuffing, depending on the size of the leaf, at the base of the leaf, just above where the stem was removed. Using your fingers, spread the stuffing out to create a 1/2-inch (1-cm)-thick band of stuffing. Do not extend the stuffing all the way to edge of the leaf; you will need to wrap the leaf up and around the stuffing.

3 Fold the stem end of the leaf up and over the filling and then fold both sides of the leaf toward the middle.

4 Tightly roll up the leaf, making sure to tuck in the sides as you roll. Repeat with the remaining grape leaves and filling. Once you get the hang of the rolling technique, it goes much faster.

NOTE: Grape leaves, which are the leaves of cultivated or wild grapes, are typically preserved in brine and stored in jars. They are imported to the Arab Gulf from other surrounding countries where grapes are grown. All over the world, they can be purchased from Middle Eastern and Mediterranean grocery stores. Stuffed grape leaves are popular especially in the Middle Eastern countries, the Balkans and Greece. I have a vine of wild grapes that produces enough leaves in the summer for our needs and enough to freeze for our winter supply. If you have access to fresh grape leaves, you can use them instead of the preserved type. Simply use 1 lb (500 g) and soak the leaves in boiling water for 10 minutes to soften them. Drain and set aside, and proceed with the rest of the recipe.

spiced chickpea kebabs

Kabab Al-Nikhi

Like numerous other dishes now common in the Arab Gulf countries, this dish likely originated in the Indian sub-continent, being very similar to an Indian-Pakistani snack called *shami* kebab. The Arab Gulf version is made without meat and, of course, contains just the right taste of Arabian Gulf Spice Mix (Baharat) (page 28). Wholesome and tasty, these kebabs can be served as a main dish, side dish or for snacks. I was first introduced to these kebabs at a local restaurant in Dubai. I ordered them assuming that I would be enjoying spicy meat kebabs made with chickpeas. Needless to say, when I took my first bite, I realized that I was enjoying something quite different. I suddenly realized that vegetarians could enjoy what meat-eaters take pleasure in and without the meat. These kebabs are made in the shape of balls and the trick to this recipe is to try to drop the dough into the oil in that fashion.

Makes about 18 small kebabs
Prep time: 15 minutes
Cooking time: 40 minutes

Oil, for deep-frying
1 cup (200 g) drained cooked or canned
   chickpeas (see page 17 for canned/dried
   equivalents)
1 small onion, chopped
1 small tomato, chopped
1/4 cup (35 g) fresh or frozen green peas,
   thawed and drained
1/4 small red bell pepper, deseeded and
   chopped
1 teaspoon baking powder
1/4 cup (30 g) all-purpose flour, plus more
   if needed
3/4 teaspoon salt
1/2 teaspoon ground cumin
1/2 teaspoon Arabian Gulf Spice Mix
   (Baharat) (page 28)
2 tablespoons finely chopped fresh
   coriander leaves (cilantro)
1 large egg
Creamy Garlic Sauce (page 27) or Tangy Hot
   Tomato Sauce (page 27), for serving

1 Place all the ingredients, except the oil, in a food processor and process into a soft dough, adding a little water or more flour if necessary. (The dough should be soft enough for spooning—almost like a very thick batter.) Make sure that the chickpeas are fully ground into the dough.
2 Pour about 1 1/2 inches (3.75 cm) of oil (enough to submerge the kebabs) into a medium saucepan and set over medium-high heat. Heat the oil to a minimum temperature of 345°F (175°C) and no higher than 375°F (190°C), checking with a deep-frying or candy thermometer. If you do not have a thermometer, drop a small piece of bread in the oil. If the bread browns quickly (1 minute or less), the oil is the right temperature. Alternatively you can throw a drop of water in the oil. If the water sizzles upon contact, the oil is ready.
3 As a test, gently drop 1 heaping tablespoon of the dough into the oil. If the kebab breaks up in the oil, add an additional egg or more flour to the dough to bind it. Deep-fry until golden brown, about 8 minutes, turning the kebab over once. If the kebab does not break up, continue to deep-fry the remainder of the dough in batches of four to six. While deep-frying, between batches, re-check the temperature to make sure it's between 345° and 375°F (175° and 190°C). (You may need to let the oil re-heat between batches.)
4 Remove with a slotted spoon or tongs and drain on paper towels. Serve warm with the Creamy Garlic Sauce (page 27) or Tangy Hot Tomato Sauce (page 27).

Makes about 24 fritters
Prep time: 20 minutes
Resting time: 1 hour
Cooking time: 30 minutes

Oil, for deep-frying

Fritter Dough
1¹/₂ cups (115 g) chickpea flour
10 green onions (scallions), trimmed and
    finely chopped
1 cup (255 g) canned stewed tomatoes
1 potato, peeled and grated
1 large egg, beaten
2 teaspoons baking powder
¹/₂ teaspoon baking soda
1 teaspoon salt
1 teaspoon ground cumin
¹/₂ teaspoon Arabian Gulf Spice Mix
    (Baharat) (page 28)
¹/₄ teaspoon ground red pepper (cayenne)
¹/₂ cup (125 ml) water

1 Combine all the ingredients for the Fritter
Dough in a mixing bowl, and mix thoroughly
to create a smooth batter. Add a little more
water or chickpea flour, if necessary, to create a pancake batter-like consistency. Cover
and allow to stand at room temperature for
1 hour.
2 Pour about 2 inches (5 cm) of oil into a
medium saucepan and set over medium-
high heat. Heat the oil to a minimum temperature of 345°F (175°C) and no higher
than 375°F (190°C), checking with a deep-
frying or candy thermometer. If you do not
have a thermometer, drop a small piece of
bread in the oil. If the bread browns quickly
(1 minute or less), the oil is the right temperature. Alternatively you can throw a
drop of water in the oil. If the water sizzles
upon contact, the oil is ready.
3 Gently drop tablespoons of the Fritter
Dough into the hot oil and deep-fry the fritters in batches until they turn golden brown,
turning them over once. Do not overcrowd
the pan. While deep-frying between batches,
re-check the temperature to make sure it's
still between 345° and 375°F (175° and
190°C). (You may need to let the oil re-heat
between batches.) Remove with a slotted
spoon and drain on paper towels. Serve
warm as an appetizer or as a main course.

AROMATIC CHICKPEA FRITTERS
Baqoura

Chickpeas for the Arabs are synonymous with health and pleasure. In the Eastern Arab
World, peasants are convinced that chickpeas have qualities that give them the essential
energy necessary for their lives of toil. In the North African countries, where they too are
employed extensively in cooking for their taste and dietary benefits, many there also believe that chickpeas increase the energy, and even sexual desires, of both men and women.
The sixteenth-century North African Arab writer Shaykh 'Umar Abu Muhammad suggested
chickpeas as a cure for impotence and a first-rate sexual stimulant. One way or another, this
pulse has its benefits and it is up to whoever eats Baqoura to decide the value of the chickpeas. These chickpea fritters, popular in Oman, most likely originated in India where they
are known as Pakora. The Indian version includes hot chili peppers, at times, replacing the
ground red pepper and cumin or curry, while the Arab Gulf fritter is made distinct by its use
of Arabian Gulf Spice Mix (page 28). No matter what type, they should be eaten immediately
once they are fried to maintain their crunchy exterior and soft interior. These can be served
as a main dish along with Creamy Cucumber and Bell Pepper Salad (page 46).

Makes 1¹/2 cups (375 g)
Prep time: 15 minutes
Chilling time: 1 hour

¹/2 cup (125 g) tahini (sesame paste)
¹/2 cup (125 g) store-bought or Homemade
    Plain Yogurt (page 31)
4 tablespoons freshly squeezed lemon juice
3 cloves garlic, crushed to a paste
    (see page 30)
2 tablespoons very finely chopped fresh
    parsley
1 teaspoon ground coriander
¹/2 teaspoon salt
¹/4 teaspoon ground black pepper
Generous pinch of ground cumin
A few sprigs of fresh parsley, for garnish

1 Place all the ingredients, except the parsley, in a food processor and process for 1 minute, adding a little water if a smoother consistency is desired. Spread evenly on a platter. Garnish with the parsley and chill in the refrigerator.
2 Serve as a dip with raw vegetables, Wafer-Thin Bedouin Pancakes (page 120) or other breads or even with crackers.

YOGURT AND TAHINI DIP WITH FRESH HERBS

Originally a Sudanese dish, Yogurt and Tahini Dip is now a national dish in Qatar. The slightly nutty and smooth flavor along with the punch of garlic goes great especially with Wafer-Thin Bedouin Pancakes (page 120) or any type of crusty bread. But it is the good-old standby, Pita Bread (page 122) that serves best as the scooping spoon for this creamy yogurt dip. In one of the restaurants in Muscat, a colleague and I ordered a number of appetizers for our lunchtime meal, among them Yogurt and Tahini Dip. To show my colleague that despite my life in Canada, many miles from the Arabian Peninsula, I was proficient in eating the dip in true Arab fashion I proudly exhibited my method of ripping a piece of Arabic bread, folding and scooping up the Yogurt and Tahini Dip. As I focused on perfecting what I was doing, little did I notice that Haytham was busy taking an excess amount and spreading it over an entire piece of bread and eating it like a rolled up sandwich. When I looked at him with surprise, he said, "How can anyone satisfy the craving for this dip with a small piece of bread?"

deviled eggs, arabian-style

Baydh Mahshi

This Saudi Arabian dish, which likely came into the country by the way of expatriates from the West, can be served as a main dish, side dish or as an appetizer. The addition of yogurt as well as spinach gives this Saudi version its distinct flavor and appearance. The lettuce leaves are not merely garnish; they should be used to scoop up the eggs and eaten along with them.

Makes 16 deviled eggs
Prep time: 30 minutes
Cooling time: 10 minutes
Cooking time: 10 minutes

1/2 lb (250 g) fresh spinach, preferably baby leaf, thoroughly washed, drained and chopped (remove stems if using large spinach leaves)
2 tablespoons water
8 large eggs, hard-boiled
2 tablespoons finely chopped green onions (scallions)
4 tablespoons store-bought or Homemade Plain Yogurt (page 31)
3 tablespoons extra-virgin olive oil
2 tablespoons freshly squeezed lemon juice
1 teaspoon Dijon mustard
1/2 teaspoon salt
1/2 teaspoon ground black pepper
Lettuce leaves, for garnish

1 Place the spinach and water in a medium skillet and set over medium-low heat. Cook for 10 minutes. Remove and set in a colander to drain and cool for about 10 minutes. You should have about 1/2 cup (110 g) cooked spinach.
2 Slice the eggs in half lengthwise and carefully remove the cooked yolk, taking care not to break the whites.
3 Thoroughly mash the yolks with the spinach and the rest of the ingredients, except the lettuce leaves, in a bowl. Stuff the white halves with the mixture, using enough to spread it across the entire surface of the whites and to form a dome over the whites to bring the eggs back to their original shape. Line a serving platter with the lettuce leaves. Arrange the eggs on the lettuce leaves and chill before serving.

sesame seed sticks

Asabi' Simsim

From the days of *The One Thousand and One Arabian Nights*, and even before, sesame seeds have been a part of Arab cuisine—used in everything from appetizers to main dishes and to desserts. Numerous sweets, especially those of Arab North Africa, include the seeds as an important ingredient or for a garnish. However, the origin of these popular Bahraini-style sesame seed sticks is more than likely from immigrants from the Indian sub-continent. It was in Bahrain that I had my first taste of crunchy Sesame Seed Sticks served alongside Chicken Noodle Soup (page 62), a classic pairing. Granted, the soup was appetizing, but the sticks provided a nutty sesame flavor that seemed to be the yin and yang for both dishes. Excellent for serving at any time of the day, the sticks can be eaten as light snacks in the same way as pretzels or crackers. Sesame sticks make for a great dipping stick when serving Red Bell Pepper Dip with Pine Nuts (page 43) or Yogurt and Tahini Dip with Fresh Herbs (page 40) and, of course, any type of soup.

Makes 2 dozen
Prep time: 35 minutes
Cooling time: 5 minutes
Cooking time: 35 minutes

Oil, for deep-frying

Sesame Seed Dough
1 cup (140 g) sesame seeds
1/2 cup (60 g) all-purpose flour
2 large eggs
1 1/2 teaspoons baking powder
1/2 teaspoon salt
1/2 teaspoon ground black pepper
1/2 teaspoon ground caraway
1/4 teaspoon ground coriander
1/4 teaspoon freshly grated nutmeg
Generous pinch of ground red pepper
   (cayenne)
2 tablespoons water, plus more if needed

1 Place the sesame seeds in a medium skillet and toast over medium-low heat for about 2 minutes, or until they just begin to slightly brown. Immediately remove from the skillet and allow the sesame seeds to cool. Place them in a coffee grinder and finely grind. Set aside.
2 Combine all the ingredients for the Sesame Seed Dough in a mixing bowl and thoroughly mix. Knead, adding more water if necessary, until a soft, smooth and elastic dough is formed. Break off small, walnut-size pieces of dough and roll them between your hands to form finger-shaped sticks. Set aside on a tray.

3 Pour about 1 1/2 inches (3.75 cm) of oil into a medium saucepan and set over medium-high heat. Heat the oil to a minimum temperature of 345°F (175°C) and no higher than 375°F (190°C), checking with a deep-frying or candy thermometer. If you do not have a thermometer, drop a small piece of bread in the oil. If the bread browns quickly (1 minute or less), the oil is the right temperature. Alternatively you can throw a drop of water in the oil. If the water sizzles upon contact, the oil is ready.
4 Working in batches, deep-fry the sticks fritters until they turn golden brown, about 6 to 7 minutes, turning them over once. Remove with a slotted spoon or tongs and drain on paper towels. While deep-frying, between batches, re-check the temperature to make sure it's still between 345° and 375°F (175° and 190°C). (You may need to let the oil re-heat between batches.) They can be served hot or at room temperature. They are the best served the same day they are made.

> **NOTE:** If the sesame seeds are to be stored for a long period of time they should be refrigerated. They will keep up to six months in a refrigerator or up to a year in the freezer.

Sesame Seed Sticks

RED BELL PEPPER DIP WITH PINE NUTS Muhammara

The culinary art of Syria's second largest city, Aleppo, in my view the best in the Middle East, did not develop by accident but took shape century after century as culture after culture flowed through the city. Along the same lines, the countries of the Arab Gulf are on the same path of reaching a high level of cuisine thanks to the arrival of others who bring with them their culinary skills and traditions. Muhammara, a tasty well-known Aleppo dish, is now part and parcel of the *mazza* table in Arab Gulf restaurants and homes. This tangy and crunchy red pepper-based dip, which adds color to any table, is also a popular addition to buffets and feast dinners. It goes well with Baked Lamb Kebabs with Aromatic Spices (page 86) and any type of grilled meat or fish.

Serves 6 to 8
Cooking time: 20 minutes
Prep time: 30 minutes   **Cooling time:** 30 minutes
Refrigerating time: 2 hours

4 large red bell peppers
1¹/2 cups (225 g) finely ground walnuts
1 tablespoon pomegranate syrup dissolved in 2 tablespoons water
2 tablespoons freshly squeezed lemon juice
¹/2 teaspoon salt
¹/2 teaspoon ground coriander
¹/2 teaspoon ground cumin
¹/2 teaspoon ground red pepper (cayenne)

For garnish
2 tablespoons toasted pine nuts
4 tablespoons pomegranate seeds
4 tablespoons finely chopped fresh parsley
2 tablespoons extra-virgin olive oil

1 Turn the broiler to high and set the oven rack 3 to 5 inches (7.5 to 12.75 cm) from the heat source. Place the pepper in the oven and broil for about 15 to 20 minutes, turning them over a number of times until the skin blisters on all sides. Remove from the oven and allow to cool.
2 Remove the skin and seeds and discard. Mash the roasted pepper flesh with a potato masher or process it in a food processor for 1 minute. Transfer to a mixing bowl. Add the rest of the ingredients and mix well.
3 Spread on a platter, cover with plastic wrap and refrigerate for about 2 hours.
4 Just before serving, garnish with the pine nuts, pomegranate seeds and parsley and drizzle on the olive oil. Serve with crackers or Pita Bread (page 122).

CHAPTER 2
SALADS

Being an arid region, vegetables—especially those very perishable, water-loving types, such as cucumbers and tomatoes—have not long been a part of Arab Gulf cooking. Only when immigrant groups from other parts of the world, in particular from the Greater Syria area, North Africa, Iran and Iraq, and even Europe, started flooding into the area in the era of oil, was a taste and demand for salads created. Once the demand was there, the means, such as irrigation, was provided, thanks partially to oil wealth.

The "greening" of the desert has provided most of the vegetables, and fruits, needed in the Arab Gulf countries. There is little need today for ships or trucks to bring these ingredients from the Greater Syria area, Iraq and beyond. Countries like the United Arab Emirates, which once imported almost all its fruits and vege-tables, now sells vegetables to other countries. Today, a visitor to the large urban centers in the Arab Gulf countries can enjoy salads from the four corners of the globe. One can dine on newly created salads that have been prepared to suit the varied tastes of travelers searching for fine food. In the hands of Arab Gulf chefs and home cooks, these salads have been transformed into something even more delicious than the original. The popular cucumber and yogurt salad has been enhanced with red bell pepper and ginger, transforming it into something even more delicious than the original (see Creamy Cucumber and Bell Pepper Salad, page 46). A simple but delicious salad of diced vegetables tossed with a tahini dressing, originating in the Greater Syria area, has become a favorite salad of the Gulf by way of simply adding more spices (see Diced Vegetable Salad with Tahini Dressing, page 52).

During my numerous visits to the Arab Gulf countries I was often surprised to find that dishes like Tabbouleh (page 53) and various yogurt salads were much tastier than those that I had eaten in Syria and Lebanon. Though clearly influ-enced by the ex-pats' cuisines, the people of the Gulf countries have truly made these imported dishes their own in wonderful and distinct ways.

CREAMY CUCUMBER AND BELL PEPPER SALAD
Salatat Khiyar wa Filfil bi-Laban

Kuwait was one of the first Arab Gulf countries to produce oil in commercial quantities and hence lured thousands of workers from the Indian sub-continent. These workers, along with the centuries-old sea trade with India, greatly influenced the Kuwaiti kitchen. Included among the dishes from the Indian sub-continent is this creamy cucumber-yogurt salad. Arabs are creative with their yogurt dishes. Some say that each dish made with yogurt can have five different versions. Such is the case with yogurt-based salads. I was used to the basic version, what my mother made—yogurt and cucumbers with a touch of garlic in it. So it was, when in Kuwait and being presented with this salad at one of Kuwait City's fine dining restaurants, that I was mildly surprised to find onions, bell peppers and ginger included in a dish that had been transformed from its traditional version to one much more elaborate. This goes well with Roast Chicken with Saffron Rice Stuffing (page 73) or simply with any dish that includes rice because there is something so good about yogurt and rice joining forces on the dinner table. Ask any Arab!

Serves 4 to 6
Prep time: 15 minutes
Cooking time: 15 minutes
Chilling time: 2 hours

4 tablespoons extra-virgin olive oil
1 large onion, minced
1 red bell pepper, deseeded and finely chopped
2 cloves garlic, crushed to a paste (see page 30)
1 teaspoon dried mint leaves
1/2 teaspoon ground ginger
1/2 teaspoon salt
1/2 teaspoon ground black pepper
2 cups (500 g) store-bought or Homemade Plain Yogurt (page 31)
1 cucumber, about 8-in (20-cm) long, peeled and chopped

1 Heat the oil in a medium skillet over medium-low heat. Sauté the onion and bell pepper for 10 minutes or until the onion becomes limp, but not brown. Transfer the onion and bell pepper to a serving bowl.
2 Allow to cool and then stir in the remaining ingredients. Chill in the refrigerator for 2 hours before serving.

Serves 4 to 6
Prep time: 30 minutes

4 large tomatoes, diced into ¹/₂-in (1.25-cm)
  cubes
4 tablespoons chopped fresh coriander
  leaves (cilantro)
1 small jalapeño or other fresh finger-length
  green chili pepper of your choice, finely
  chopped

Dressing
4 tablespoons freshly squeezed lemon juice
4 tablespoons extra-virgin olive oil
1 tablespoon finely chopped fresh basil
  leaves or 1 teaspoon dried basil leaves
¹/₂ teaspoon salt
¹/₄ teaspoon ground black pepper

1 Gently toss the tomato, coriander and chili
pepper in a salad bowl.
2 Combine the ingredients for the Dressing
in a small bowl. Add the Dressing to the bowl
with the vegetables, gently toss to combine,
and serve.

ZESTY TOMATO AND FRESH CORIANDER SALAD
Salatat Banadura bi Kuzbara

This Kuwaiti salad, also popular in Yemen, was most likely introduced to Kuwait by the Palestinian community work-ing there. Light and tangy and infused with the taste of fresh coriander leaves (cilantro), it is refreshing yet subtly spicy hot. Nothing beats the taste of fresh coriander leaves with tomatoes. My first encounter with this salad took place years ago when a friend of the family prepared it as a side dish to accompany the Palestinian chicken dish Musakhkhan. She explained that tomatoes tend to cut the taste of fat in poultry and meats and that this salad is an essential component when any heavy meal is served. I took her words to heart and have been a committed enthusi-ast of this salad whenever I serve stuffed or barbecued lamb or chicken. This versatile salad goes well with any main dish, especially meat and barbecued chicken, all types of kebabs, most rice dishes and a good number of stews.

spicy eggplant salad
Salatat Badhinjan bil-Filfil

Today, almost every special occasion dinner in the Arab Middle East includes at least one or two eggplant dishes. For the Arabs, the eggplant is the queen of versatility—it can be an ingredient in appetizers, salads, main dishes and even desserts. By far, the eggplant, which historically was introduced to the western world by the Arabs with their conquest of the Iberian Peninsula and Sicily, is at the top of an Arab's list of favorite foods. This Saudi Arabian recipe is one of the multitudes of eggplant dishes that can be made from this widely used vegetable. It is a hot and spicy salad with a vinegar-based sauce and is ideal when served with meat-based main dishes such as Baked Lamb Kebabs with Aromatic Spices (page 86), Batter-Fried Meatballs (page 81) and Lamb in a Savory Sauce with Pita Bread (page 78). When preparing the eggplant, allow an hour to let the salted eggplant sit. It is important to allow the excess water from the eggplant slices to drain; otherwise, the eggplant will discolor in the course of cooking. A good trick is to allow it to sit salted in a strainer with a heavy weight placed on top—a medium saucepan filled with water serves as a good weight.

Serves 6
Prep time: 25 minutes
Resting time: 1 hour
Cooking time: 25 minutes
Chilling time: 30 minutes

1 large firm eggplant (about 2 lbs/1 kg), peeled and cut in half lengthwise
1¹/2 teaspoons salt
²/3 cup (160 ml) oil, for frying, plus more if needed
4 firm tomatoes, sliced in rounds about ¹/4-in (6-mm) thick
2 jalapeños or other fresh finger-length green chili peppers of your choice, sliced into thin rounds
4 tablespoons vinegar
2 cloves garlic, crushed to a paste (see page 30)
¹/2 teaspoon ground black pepper
¹/2 teaspoon ground cumin
2 tablespoons finely chopped fresh coriander leaves (cilantro), for garnish

1 Slice the eggplant halves into ¹/4-inch (6-mm)-thick half-rounds. Place the eggplant in a strainer, sprinkle evenly with 1 teaspoon of the salt and place a heavy weight on top. Let stand for 1 hour.

2 Heat the oil in a large skillet over medium heat and fry the eggplant slices until they turn golden brown and become soft and translucent (about 8 to 10 minutes), turning the pieces over once and adding more oil if needed. Drain on paper towels, and then place evenly on a serving platter. Do not discard the cooking oil.

3 In the same skillet, fry the tomato slices over medium heat, 2 minutes on each side, adding more oil if necessary. Spread the tomato slices evenly over the eggplant slices. In the same skillet, over medium-low heat, fry the chili pepper for about 5 minutes, or until brown, adding more oil if needed. Spread over the fried tomato slices.

4 Combine the vinegar, garlic, pepper, cumin and the remaining ¹/2 teaspoon of the salt in a small bowl, and then sprinkle evenly over the vegetables. Garnish with the chopped coriander leaves and chill in the refrigerator before serving.

WARM AND SPICY POTATO SALAD

It was only in the twentieth century, when potatoes were introduced on a large scale into the Arab Gulf region by expatriates, that they began to appear in Gulf dishes. Today the potato is an important part of the cooking region. This warm potato salad is one of the most popular among them. Traditionally, in Arab Gulf cooking only two or three spices were used for a certain dish, typically pepper, coriander and cumin. Now, due to the influence of other cuisines, a greater number of spices may be used in a dish, sometimes as many as a half-dozen, though usually in lesser amounts. The use of a good number of spices in this salad, which can be found in all the Arab Gulf countries, is an indication that it likely originated somewhere in the Indian sub-continent and was introduced to the Arab Gulf countries by the expatriates of that region. Though the people of the Gulf are enamored with the spices of India, and the hot spicy foods Indian ex-pats brought with them, they still prefer their foods a little less spicy.

Serves 6
Prep time: 1 hour 10 minutes
Cooking time: 20 minutes

4 large potatoes, boiled until cooked but still firm
4 tablespoons oil
1 teaspoon cumin seeds
2 onions, finely chopped
1 teaspoon ground cumin
1 teaspoon ground coriander
1/2 teaspoon dried red pepper flakes
1/2 teaspoon ground turmeric
1 teaspoon salt
1 tablespoon freshly squeezed lemon juice

1 Peel the boiled potato and dice into 1-inch (2.5-cm) cubes.
2 Heat the oil in a large skillet over high heat. Add the cumin seed and stir-fry for about 10 seconds. Immediately add the onion and sauté over medium-low heat for 10 minutes. Stir in the remaining spices, salt and potato cubes. Gently stir the potato cubes until they are coated with the spices and mixed with the onion.
3 Place on a serving platter, sprinkle with the lemon juice and serve immediately.

FRESH CUCUMBER AND TOMATO SALAD WITH SUMAC

Salatat Summaq

Salatat Summaq, traditionally one of the summer salads of Iraq, has traveled to the Arab Gulf countries and settled there. A refreshingly tangy tasting salad, it features as its major ingredient, sumac, a Middle Eastern spice par excellence. The sumac berry bush has grown wild throughout the Arab East for centuries and the spice has been used extensively in the eastern Arab World and the bordering countries since ancient times. Its taste is more tart than lemony, though I have used it occasionally in place of lemon juice in some recipes. The addition of the crushed dried red berry to foods adds a tart and tangy, snappy taste not only to salads, but also to chicken and meat dishes. This salad can be served with any type of meat-based dish as well as in or alongside Spicy Falafel Patties (page 108) or Barbecued Chicken Slices (page 66) sandwiches.

Serves 6
Prep time: 20 minutes

2 medium cucumbers, about 6 to 7-in (15 to 18-cm) long, quartered lengthwise
1 large tomato, quartered
1 onion, preferably Spanish, cut in half and very thinly sliced

Sumac Dressing
3 tablespoons extra-virgin olive oil
2 tablespoons sumac
3/4 teaspoon salt
1/2 teaspoon ground black pepper

1 Thinly slice the cucumber crosswise and place in a salad bowl.
2 Slice the tomato quarters into 1/4-inch (6-mm)-thick sections. Add the tomato and the onion to the bowl with the cucumber.
3 Combine the ingredients for the Sumac Dressing in a small bowl. Add the Sumac Dressing to the bowl with the vegetables, toss gently to combine, and serve.

ORANGE AND OLIVE SALAD

The modern evolvement of Saudi Arabia has transformed not only the country's infrastructure but also the cuisine of the country. On a typical Saudi table you're likely to find a good number of foods from many parts of the world, including this salad which has its origin in Morocco. Some years back a Saudi Arabian student and his wife invited us for a meal. One of the dishes was an orange and olive salad. He was surprised when I told him that I had eaten virtually the same salad in Morocco. The Moroccans, who are proud of their cuisine, open restaurants in any part of the world where they settle. No doubt one of these enterprising Moroccans introduced this dish to Saudi Arabia. So embedded was this salad in the country's repertoire of foods that the student truly believed it to be indigenous to his own country. The olives that I have used in this recipe are brine-cured. I usually use the Greek Kalamata olive, but any brine or oil-cured pitted black olives will do.

Serves 4
Prep time: 25 minutes

4 large oranges, peeled and separated into segments
1/2 cup (50 g) brine or oil-cured, pitted and halved black olives
1 small onion (preferably Spanish), thinly sliced
6 Romaine lettuce leaves, rinsed and well-drained

Dressing
1/2 teaspoon salt
1/2 teaspoon ground black pepper
2 tablespoons freshly squeezed lemon juice
2 tablespoons extra-virgin olive oil

1 Cut the orange segments into small pieces.
2 Combine the orange segments, olives and onion in a mixing bowl. Set aside.
3 Combine the ingredients for the Dressing in a small bowl. Add to the bowl with the oranges and gently toss to combine.
4 Place the lettuce leaves on a serving plate. Spread the orange and olive salad over the top of the leaves and serve.

REFRESHING GREEN SALAD
Salatat Khadra

Simple and quick to prepare, this salad is very popular among the nationals of Saudi Arabia. Traditionally it is made with cucumbers, tomatoes and parsley and is mixed with just salt and lemon juice. My version, however, differs slightly when it comes to the dressing. I like to add garlic and oil to give this basic salad a little more complexity. On a hot summer day, Salatat Khadra is especially refreshing alongside Barbecued Chicken Slices (page 66) or simply on its own. A good way to eat this is to scoop it up with Wafer-Thin Bedouin Pancakes (page 120) or basic Pita Bread (page 122).

Serves 4
Prep time: 25 minutes

2 cucumbers (each about 7-in/18-cm long)
   or 1 English cucumber, cut in half
   lengthwise
2 tomatoes, quartered and thinly sliced
2 cups (100 g) chopped fresh parsley

Dressing
2 cloves garlic, crushed to a paste
   (see page 30)
2 tablespoons freshly squeezed lemon
   juice
2 tablespoons extra-virgin olive oil
1/2 teaspoon salt
1/4 teaspoon ground black pepper

1 Slice the cucumber halves crosswise into thin half-rounds.
2 Place the cucumber, tomato and parsley in a large salad bowl. Set aside.
3 Combine the ingredients for the Dressing in a small bowl. Pour the Dressing over the vegetables and toss gently before serving.

DICED VEGETABLE SALAD WITH TAHINI DRESSING

It was in Doha, Qatar's capital city, while enjoying a buffet dinner that a Lebanese chef suggested we try this salad that had been made under his watchful eye. Never in my life had I been so happy to take someone's advice! Versions of this salad from the Greater Syria region are now found in all the Arab Gulf countries. This dish can be served as a side salad or as a dip. It goes especially well with all types of Falafel and complements any type of barbecued meat. Personally, I find it to be, probably due to its tahini dressing, a fine salad served with fried fish.

Serves 4 to 6
Prep time: 30 minutes

2 tomatoes, diced into 1/4-in (6-mm) cubes
1 cucumber, about 6 to 8 in/15 to 20 cm long, diced into 1/4-in (6-mm) cubes
1/2 cup (50 g) finely chopped green onions (scallions)
2 tablespoons finely chopped fresh coriander leaves (cilantro)
2 cloves garlic, crushed to a paste (see page 30)
4 tablespoons freshly squeezed lemon juice
4 tablespoons tahini (sesame paste)
3 tablespoons water
1/2 teaspoon salt
1/2 teaspoon ground black pepper
1/4 teaspoon ground cumin
Generous pinch of ground cardamom
Generous pinch of ground red pepper (cayenne)

1 Place the tomato, cucumber, chopped green onion and coriander leaves in a salad bowl.
2 Place the remaining ingredients in a blender, then blend for 1 minute. Pour over the vegetables and toss to combine.
3 Serve this salad as a side dish or as a sandwich filler along with Spicy Falafel Patties (page 108). (If Falafel patties are served in Pita Bread (page 122) pockets, as sandwiches, place two heaping tablespoons of this salad in each sandwich.)

Serves 8   **Soaking time:** 10 minutes
Prep time: 40 minutes

1/2 cup (115 g) medium bulghur, soaked for
    10 minutes in warm water
2 large bunches fresh parsley (about 1 lb/500 g
    total), thoroughly washed and drained
4 tablespoons finely chopped fresh mint leaves
1 bunch green onions (scallions) (about
    1/4 lb/125 g), trimmed and finely chopped
2 tomatoes, finely chopped
Lettuce leaves, to line salad bowl or serving
    platter

Dressing
4 tablespoons extra-virgin olive oil
4 tablespoons freshly squeezed lemon juice
1 teaspoon salt
1/2 teaspoon ground black pepper

1 Drain the soaked bulghur in a fine-meshed
sieve, pressing out the excess water with a
large spoon. Chop the parsley as fine as you
can. (You should have about 4 cups/200 g of
finely chopped parsley.)
2 Combine the bulghur, parsley, mint, green
onion and tomato in a large bowl.
3 Combine the ingredients for the Dressing in
a small bowl. Add the Dressing to the bowl with
the bulghur and vegetables. Toss and serve on
a serving platter lined with the lettuce leaves.

TABBOULEħ

Tabbouleh, sometimes spelled Tabboula, Tabouli, Taboola or Tabboola, has been the
quintessence of all salads in the Middle East for untold centuries. Today, its popularity
has spread to the Arab Gulf nations, where it has become one of the region's most fully
integrated non-Gulf dishes. No *mazza* table would be complete without at least one
Tabbouleh salad bowl and the Lebanese restaurants throughout the Arab Gulf region
each boast that they make the best. In homes, it is served with almost every dinner or
may be enjoyed simply as a snack. Arab folklore propounds that the parsley-bulghur ratio
used in this salad indicates the economic standing of the host: more parsley to bulghur,
the higher the economic indicator; if more bulghur, then the host is on the lower economic
scale. Yet, no matter at what level, this lemony and tangy salad has become a Gulf favorite.
Instead of using a fork to eat tabbouleh, try scooping it up with a leaf of lettuce to ensure
not one drop of dressing is lost. Preparation time for salads is usually not very long. However, to make the best Tabbouleh, one must take care and patience to chop the parsley as
fine as possible. It is said that those who have perfected Tabbouleh are those who chop
the parsley the finest. The recipe that follows is for a traditional Tabbouleh—the type to be
found in Syria and Lebanon, and one that is most likely to be found in the West. In the Arab
Gulf countries, creative cooks have put a Gulf twist on the traditional Tabbouleh by including, at times, chopped fresh coriander leaves, a little sumac and pomegranate syrup. When
you tire of the traditional Tabbouleh, try the Gulf version, which is included as a variation.

Variation

GULF-STYLE
TABBOULEħ

1 To make Arab Gulf-Style Tabbouleh,
place the bulghur and vegetables (minus
the lettuce leaves) in a bowl, but reduce
the amount of bulghur to 1/4 cup (60g).
Replace the chopped green onion with
1/3 cup (50 g) finely chopped onion (from
about 1 small onion). Add 4 tablespoons
finely chopped coriander leaves. Toss
to combine.
2 Combine the ingredients for the
Dressing in a small bowl, but reduce the
amount of lemon juice to 2 tablespoons.
Add 1 teaspoon pomegranate syrup and
1 tablespoon sumac. Toss and serve.

CHAPTER 3
SOUPS

The desert lands of the Arabian Peninsula did not, in the past, allow for the cultivation of fruits and vegetables. For this reason, most of the soups of the region were meat-based, in particular, lamb and, along the coastline, fish-based. With the influx of expatriates from all around the world came new herbs, chili peppers and spices as well as fruits and vegetables, which have given rise to the many tasty and enjoyable soups one finds in the Arab Gulf countries today. Seemingly unsophisticated yet delectable, the traditional, once simpler soups of the Arab Gulf have been adapted and revamped, mostly by chefs in posh hotel restaurants, into hearty soups, designed for the palates of tourists who now visit these once desert countries. Spicy Broad Bean Soup (page 57) and Chicken Noodle Soup (page 62) are two good examples of the new soups that now claim a place in the regional cuisine.

Today, Gulf soups are tasty (and often slightly spicy hot), wholesome meals unto themselves. All that is needed to complete this one-dish repast is Wafer-Thin Bedouin Pancakes (page 120), Sesame Seed Sticks (page 42) or Pita Bread (page 122) and, if more is needed, perhaps a simple salad.

Even though restaurant chefs have "upgraded" the basic varieties of Arab Gulf soups, the traditional simmering pots of aromatic soups are always welcome for all strata of society. Chicken, fish, lamb, chickpeas, fava beans and lentils are the meat and pulses mostly used. Most are simple to prepare, inexpensive, filling, and do not require exotic ingredients. Herbs and spices give them their zest and tang while the meat gives them a rich taste. And for the thousands of low-paid workers flooding the Arab Gulf nations, these nourishing soups of the Arab Gulf satisfy their hunger at very little cost. In my innumerable trips to the Arab Gulf countries, I have enjoyed soups that have their origin in a great number of countries from around the world. One of these occasions was in one of the plush restaurants in Dubai where I enjoyed a mouth-watering lentil soup (see Spiced Lentil Soup with Lemon, page 59), which the chef had made his own through the addition of spices. I went on and on to a friend about the fineries of soups and the reason why we partake in their pleasure—after all, from among the volume of dishes offered on this restaurant's menu, I had chosen a lentil soup rather than roasted lamb or grilled chicken. Simply put, "Soup tends to calm the nerves and relieve hunger while awakening the appetite."

NOODLE SOUP WITH TOMATOES AND FRESH GREEN CHILI PEPPER

Hasa' Al-She'reya

This spicy noodle soup is a favorite meal on a cold winter day in the Arabian Peninsula. In Saudi Arabia, from where this recipe hails, spices, in many cases, are used in their whole form rather than being ground. They are placed in a spice bundle made with cheesecloth, which is then removed from the food after cooking. However, I prefer to put the spices directly in the soup. It seems to me that they give the soup more tang and almost the same taste. In Arabic, depending on the country or region, soups are called *hasa'* or *shawraba*. Hasa' is used more in Iraq but shawraba is found in the Greater Syria area; both hasa' and shawraba are used in the Arab Gulf countries.

Serves 6
Prep time: 20 minutes
Cooking time: 1 hour 45 minutes

1 lb (500 g) stewing cut of lamb or beef (such as boneless lamb shoulder or bottom round beef steak), cubed
8 cups (2 liters) water
Two 14.5-oz (411-g) cans stewed tomatoes
2 teaspoons salt
1 small jalapeño or other fresh finger-length green chili pepper of your choice, deseeded and finely chopped
1 teaspoon ground black pepper
1 teaspoon ground cardamom
1 teaspoon dried tarragon
1/2 teaspoon ground ginger
3 1/2 oz (100 g) dried vermicelli or very thin spaghetti, broken into small pieces (about 1 cup/100g)

1 Bring the meat and water to a boil, in a large saucepan with a lid, uncovered. Cover and cook over medium-low heat for about 1 hour.
2 Add the remaining ingredients, except the vermicelli, then cover the saucepan and cook over medium-low heat for 30 minutes, or until the meat is tender. Stir in the vermicelli and cook for another 10 minutes. Serve hot.

spicy broad bean soup

Fool Nabed

In the Egypt of the Pharaohs, both rich and poor loved broad beans (fava) and from that era this bean has graced the tables of the inhabitants of the Nile Valley. Because of its popularity, the Egyptians made use of it in appetizers, soups, salads and main dishes. One of these creations is the Spicy Broad Bean Soup, which is now popular in Kuwait and most of the Arab Gulf countries, where cooks have added extra herbs and spices to give it a "Gulf" flair. The puréed consistency makes for a smooth, thick and hearty soup while the spices enhance not only the taste but its aroma as well. It is preferable to use dried broad beans for this recipe as those in the can become too soft during the cooking process.

Serves about 6
Soaking time: 24 hours
Prep time: 25 minutes
Cooking time: 1 hour 30 minutes

1$\frac{1}{2}$ cups (300 g) dried large broad (fava) beans, soaked for 24 hours, skinned, and split (see tip)
8 cups (2 liters) water
4 cloves garlic, crushed to a paste (see page 30)
2 teaspoons salt
1 teaspoon ground black pepper
1 teaspoon ground cumin
$\frac{1}{2}$ teaspoon ground coriander
Generous pinch of ground red pepper (cayenne)
4 tablespoons extra-virgin olive oil
4 tablespoons freshly squeezed lemon juice
2 tablespoons finely chopped fresh coriander leaves (cilantro), for garnish

1 Bring the beans and water to a boil in a large saucepan with a lid. Cover and simmer over medium-low heat for 1$\frac{1}{2}$ hours, or until the beans are tender, adding more water if necessary to keep the beans covered.
2 Transfer the cooked fava beans and their liquid to a blender. Purée and return to the saucepan. Add the remaining ingredients, except the lemon juice and coriander leaves. Stir to combine. Bring to a boil, reduce the heat to low, and cook for another 5 minutes. Transfer to a serving bowl and stir in the lemon juice. Sprinkle the chopped coriander leaves over the soup and serve.

FAVA BEAN TIPS: Large dried fava beans, which are about $\frac{1}{2}$ x $\frac{3}{4}$ inches (1.25 x 2 cm), can be found in most Mediterranean and Middle Eastern grocery stores and supermarkets. The outer pods are already removed, but a thin skin still needs to be removed. After soaking the beans and draining them, place a pod between two fingertips and squeeze. The skin will slip right off. For the rare time when it does not slip off, use the tip of a small knife to loosen the skin. When the skin is removed, the beans will automatically split lengthwise. Sometimes you may be able to find dried broad beans that have been skinned and split, eliminating the entire procedure of soaking, draining and skinning. However, if you use these beans you will need to increase the cooking time since you will not have soaked them before cooking them.

CREAMY TOMATO AND CHICKPEA SOUP

Shawrabat Al-Nikhi

The first time I enjoyed a version of this soup was in an Indian restaurant in Dubai, the industrial heart of the United Arab Emirates. It is a traditional dish in the Arab Gulf area that is likely to have been brought from the Indian sub-continent in medieval times long before the discovery of oil. Costing very little to make, it was a poor man's food par excellence. Today, it is embellished with a few more ingredients, such as tomatoes, reflecting the modern affluence of the Arab Gulf countries today. Chickpeas are the basis of numerous scrumptious dishes, including this soup. After working all day, coming home to the aroma of this chickpea soup is a great source of comfort to an empty stomach. Shawrabat al-Nikhi has a velvety texture while its flavor is a wonderful combination of chickpeas and tomatoes accented with the bright flavor of fresh coriander leaves (cilantro).

Serves 8
Prep time: 25 minutes
Cooking time: 40 minutes

4 tablespoons extra-virgin olive oil
4 tablespoons finely chopped fresh
  coriander leaves (cilantro)
2 onions, minced
4 cloves garlic, crushed to a paste
  (see page 30)
2 cups (400 g) drained cooked or canned
  chickpeas (see page 17 for canned/
  dried equivalents)
6 cups (1.5 liters) water
2 cups (450 g) stewed tomatoes (about
  1 1/2 14.5-oz/411-g cans)
1 1/2 teaspoons salt
1 teaspoon ground cumin
1/2 teaspoon ground black pepper
1/2 teaspoon ground turmeric
Generous pinch of ground red pepper
  (cayenne)

1 Pour the oil into a large saucepan with a lid and place over medium heat. Add the coriander leaves and onion and sauté for 10 minutes, uncovered.
2 Add the remaining ingredients, stir, and bring to a boil. Cover and cook over medium heat for 25 minutes.
3 Remove from the heat and allow to cool slightly. Purée, then return to the saucepan, adding more water if desired. Reheat and serve.

spiced lentil soup with lemon

Shawrabat 'Adas

Growing up during the Great Depression on the arid plains of southern Saskatchewan, I remember the countless lentil soups and stews that our family consumed almost every day. My parents had brought lentil seeds with them when they immigrated to Canada, and in the dry dusty soil of the prairies this hardy plant grew and thrived. No one else in that part of the country was familiar with lentils and we, like our fellow Arab immigrants, kept it well hidden. Being foreigners with inferiority complexes, we ate our delicious lentil dishes hidden in our home, safe from the prying eyes of neighbors. Not so any longer. The Arabs are proud of their lentils, especially in soup form. In almost all of Dubai and Abu Dhabi's posh restaurants, Shawrabat 'Adas with red lentils, a local favorite, is included on their menus. Wholesome and healthy, this soup is found not only in the Arab Gulf countries but also in a variety of versions in the countries stretching from North Africa and the Mediterranean to the Indian sub-continent. Most of the varieties, including this one, made in the Arab Gulf countries use more herbs and spices than other Arab countries. Squeezing a few drops of lemon in the soup gives it a nice added zesty flavor.

Serves 8   **Prep time:** 20 minutes
Soaking time: 5 minutes
Cooking time: 1 hour 20 minutes

1 cup (200 g) red split lentils
2 large onions, minced
4 cloves garlic, crushed to a paste (see page 30)
4 tablespoons uncooked Basmati or other white long-grain rice, soaked for
   5 minutes, thoroughly rinsed and drained (see page 24)
1¹/2 teaspoons salt
1 teaspoon ground cumin
1 teaspoon ground coriander
¹/4 teaspoon ground red pepper (cayenne)
8 cups (2 liters) water
4 tablespoons extra-virgin olive oil
2 tablespoons freshly squeezed lemon juice
4 tablespoons finely chopped fresh coriander leaves (cilantro), for garnish
6 lemon or lime wedges, for serving

1 Place the lentils with half of the chopped onion, garlic, rice, salt, cumin, ground coriander, ground red pepper and water in a large saucepan with a lid. Bring to a boil, then cover and cook over medium-low heat for 1 hour, stirring occasionally. Add more water if a thinner consistency is desired.
2 In the meantime, heat the oil in a small skillet over medium heat. Add the remaining half of the onion and fry for 10 minutes, stirring occasionally. Add the fried onion and the lemon juice to the soup, stir, and then transfer to individual serving bowls. Sprinkle the chopped coriander leaves over the top and serve with the lemon or lime wedges on the side.

hearty meat and bulghur soup

Hasa' Al-Jareesh

This soup is a Saudi creation. Its main ingredient is *jareesh*, a variety of cracked wheat available all over the Arab Gulf area. Jareesh can be purchased internationally in some locations. Bulghur, on the other hand, is a commodity that is available almost anywhere and is a fine replacement for jareesh. Unexcelled as a nourishing eatable, bulghur has more food energy than corn meal; more iron than rice; less fat than uncooked wheat; six times more calcium than corn meal and three times more than rice; and more vitamins than barley, cornmeal or rice. This is one of the main reasons why this soup is popular when breaking the fast during the holy month of Ramadan. Another reason is simply because it tastes so good.During my youthful years on our farm my mother used bulghur in so many dishes that I thought it was the most important food in the world. As the years slipped by and I grew older, I found that none of my schoolmates had ever seen, let alone eaten, what some call "Middle Eastern rice." Fast-forward to today, and a good number of people in the Western world think of bulghur as a perfect health food. And this all happened during my lifetime.

Serves 8   **Prep time:** 20 minutes
Cooking time: 1 hour 30 minutes

4 tablespoons extra-virgin olive oil
1 lb (500 g) stewing lamb or beef (such as boneless lamb
   shoulder or bottom round beef steak), cut into small pieces
1 large onion, minced
8 cups (2 liters) water
Two 14.5-oz (411-g) cans stewed tomatoes
¹/2 cup (125 g) coarse bulghur
2 teaspoons salt
1 teaspoon Arabian Gulf Spice Mix (Baharat) (page 28)
¹/2 teaspoon ground black pepper
¹/4 teaspoon dried red pepper flakes
¹/2 teaspoon ground cinnamon, for garnish

1 Heat the oil in a large saucepan with a lid over medium-low heat, and then sauté the meat for 5 minutes, uncovered. Add the onion and sauté for another 8 minutes. Add the water and bring to a boil.
2 Lower the heat to medium-low and cook for 30 minutes. Stir in the remaining ingredients, except the cinnamon, and bring to a boil. Cover and cook over medium-low heat for 50 minutes. Transfer to a serving bowl and sprinkle the cinnamon over the top. Serve piping hot.

AROMATIC BARLEY AND LENTIL SOUP

The use of barley in soups is popular in the Arab Gulf countries. Yet, the use of this grain in soups is not generally found in the modern cuisines of the other Arab lands. However, lentils are another story. They were an affordable food that nourished the peasant classes, and were, and still are a common pulse throughout the Arab World. In the eastern Arab World, where lentils have been consumed for centuries, the number of soups and stews made from this pulse are legion. Flavorful and hearty with a meaty taste, these dishes and countless other lentil dishes, prepared with meat or without, are all mouth-watering. The combination of barley and lentils in this traditional Arab Gulf soup makes for a nourishing and affordable meal for anyone.

Serves about 6
Prep time: 15 minutes
Cooking time: 1 hour 15 minutes

3 tablespoons oil
1 large onion, finely chopped
2 cloves garlic, crushed to a paste (see page 30)
2 tablespoons finely chopped fresh coriander leaves (cilantro)
1/4 cup (55 g) dried barley
1/4 cup (50 g) dried brown or green lentils
4 cups (1 liter) water
3/4 teaspoon salt
1/2 teaspoon dried basil leaves
1/2 teaspoon ground turmeric
1/4 teaspoon ground black pepper
1/4 teaspoon ground coriander
Generous pinch of ground red pepper (cayenne)
1/2 cup (100 g) drained cooked or canned chickpeas (see page 17 for canned/dried equivalents)

1 Heat the oil in a large saucepan with a lid over medium heat. Add the onion and fry for 8 minutes, uncovered. Add the garlic and coriander leaves and fry, stirring frequently, for 3 minutes.
2 Add the remainder of the ingredients and bring to a boil. Cover and cook over low heat for 1 hour, stirring occasionally. Add more water if a thinner consistency is desired. Serve hot.

> **NOTE:** In the Middle East, barley is considered the grain of the poor. A wholesome grain, barley adds fiber to hot and cold dishes as well as a delightful nutty flavor and a pleasant chewy texture. It can be purchased in many supermarkets in two varieties: hulled (its fibrous outer hull is removed, leaving the bran and germ) and pearled (the bran removed and polished). Barley can be used in soups, salads, stews, pilafs, breads, cookies, muffins and as a cereal. When hulled it should be cooked for about 90 minutes; when pearled, for 60 minutes.

MIXED VEGETABLE PURÉED SOUP Shawraba

A wide range of soups made from lamb or chicken to lentils or vegetables form part of Oman's daily cuisine. Because Oman is more fertile than the other Arab Gulf countries, its traditional cuisine includes more vegetables as exemplified in this soup. It is especially when breaking the fast during Ramadan that a variety of soups, such as Shawraba, grace the tables of homes and restaurants alike. From the humble to the elaborate, varieties of soups nourish the inhabitants of the region, sometimes simply as a one-dish meal. This tasty Omani soup is a fine example of one of these many other varieties. For those who enjoy a thick and smooth soup, this is the one to try.

Serves from 6 to 8
Prep time: 25 minutes
Cooking time: 1 hour 45 minutes

1/4 cup (1/2 stick/60 g) butter
1 large onion, minced
2 potatoes, peeled and chopped
1 carrot, peeled and chopped
1 green or red bell pepper, deseeded and chopped
1 cup (100 g) chopped cabbage
2 tomatoes, chopped
4 cups (1 liter) meat or vegetable stock
4 tablespoons oatmeal, mixed with 2 cups (500 ml) water
2 teaspoons dried thyme
1 1/2 teaspoons salt
1/2 teaspoon ground black pepper
1/2 teaspoon ground cumin
1/2 teaspoon ground coriander
1/4 teaspoon ground cardamom
1/4 teaspoon ground red pepper (cayenne)
2 tablespoons freshly squeezed lemon juice

1 Melt the butter in a large saucepan with a lid, over medium heat, uncovered. Add the onion and sauté for 10 minutes. Add the potato, carrot, bell pepper, cabbage, tomato and meat or vegetable stock. Bring to a boil, cover and cook over medium-low heat for 1 hour, stirring occasionally. Remove from the heat and allow to cool.
2 Purée the saucepan contents in a blender, then return the puréed vegetables to the saucepan. Stir in the remainder of the ingredients, except the lemon juice. Bring to a boil, cover, and simmer over medium-low heat for about 20 minutes, stirring occasionally. Stir in the lemon juice and serve hot.

NOODLE SOUP WITH LAMB AND SPINACH

Shawrabat Sabanikh

During my youthful years I had no use for the spinach that flourished in our hand-watered garden. My mother always told me to eat spinach if I wanted to grow into a healthy man. As I grew up I came to know Popeye the Sailor man and his spinach. Now that I think of it, everyone thinks world cultures are poles apart, but when it comes down to facts they are not very much different. What did Popeye and my mother have in common? She only had a slight knowledge of Western culture and literature. Most of her stories came from *The Arabian Nights*. This soup, which features spinach as one of its main ingredients, was a common way to enjoy spinach in our home. This soup will appeal to those who love their healthy leafy greens. Not only nutritious, this aromatic soup from the Arab Gulf region is wonderfully flavored with an enticing assortment of spices and fresh dill. Besides being served as a soup, it can also be served as a main dish along with Saudi-Style White Rice (page 28).

Serves 8
Prep time: 45 minutes
Cooking time: 2 hours 40 minutes

1 lb (500 g) lamb shoulder steak or chop
1/2 teaspoon ground black pepper
1/2 teaspoon ground cinnamon
1 large onion, minced
4 cloves garlic, sliced
10 cups (2.25 liters) water
1 1/2 teaspoons salt
4 tablespoons extra-virgin olive oil
1 small bunch fresh dill (about 1 oz/30 g), washed, drained and finely chopped
1 lb (500 g) fresh spinach leaves, thoroughly washed, drained, de-stemmed and chopped
2 oz (50 g) dried vermicelli or very thin spaghetti, broken into pieces (about 1/2 cup/50 g)
1/2 cup (100 g) drained cooked or canned chickpeas (see page 17 for canned/dried equivalents) (optional)
1 teaspoon ground cumin
1 teaspoon ground coriander
3 tablespoons freshly squeezed lemon juice

1 Place the lamb, pepper, cinnamon, half of the minced onion, half of the garlic slices, and water into a large saucepan with a lid. Bring to a boil, then cover and cook over medium-low heat for 2 hours. Add the salt and cook for a few more minutes. Remove the meat with a slotted spoon and de-bone. Discard the bones but reserve the broth. Cut the meat into small pieces and set aside.
2 Heat the oil in another large saucepan with a lid over medium heat. Add the remaining minced onion and garlic slices and cook for 5 minutes, uncovered, while stirring frequently. Stir in the dill and spinach and cook, covered, over low heat for 10 minutes. Add the reserved broth, meat and remaining ingredients, except the lemon juice. Bring to a boil, cover, and cook over medium-low heat for 15 minutes, adding more water if necessary. Stir in the lemon juice and serve hot.

Serves 8
Prep time: 30 minutes
Cooking time: 1 hour 20 minutes

1 small bunch fresh coriander leaves
  (cilantro) (about ¼ lb/125 g), de-
  stemmed, thoroughly washed and drained
1 lb (500 g) bone-in chicken pieces
2 onions, minced
4 cups (1 liter) chicken stock
4 cups (1 liter) cold water
1½ teaspoons salt
1 teaspoon ground black pepper
2 tablespoons butter
3½ ounces (100 g) dried vermicelli or very
  thin spaghetti, broken into small pieces
  (about 1 cup/100 g)
½ teaspoon ground cardamom
2 tablespoons freshly squeezed lemon juice
8 lemon or lime wedges, for serving

1 Finely chop the coriander leaves and set aside. (You should have about 2 cups/125 g).
2 Place the chicken, onion, coriander leaves, chicken stock, water, salt and the pepper into a large saucepan with a lid. Bring to a boil, then cover and cook over medium-low heat for 1 hour.
3 Melt the butter in a medium skillet over medium heat. Add the vermicelli and quickly fry it just until it browns. Add the vermicelli and cardamom to the saucepan. Cook for another 5 minutes over medium-low heat and stir in the lemon juice. Serve hot with the lemon or the lime wedges.

> **TIP:** The two tablespoons freshly squeezed lemon juice can be replaced with lime juice for a slightly different sour note to the soup. Medieval Arabic culinary texts describe many of their chicken-based dishes, such as this soup, as being flavored with lime juice, one of the most popular souring agents used for chicken during that period.

chicken noodle soup
Shawrabat Dajaj

This simple soup found in the United Arab Emirates and, no doubt in other Arab Gulf countries, is often made during Ramadan. It is a heavenly soup for those who are enamored with the taste of fresh coriander leaves (cilantro). A very easy soup to prepare, it could very well have been brought to the Gulf nations by expatriates. It has the imprints of Moroccan cooking, except for the initial frying process, which is not usually practiced in Moroccan kitchens.

RICHLY SPICED SEAFOOD SOUP

Shawrabat Samak

Fish soups similar to this one have been in the Arabian (aka Persian) Gulf region for hundreds of years. I relished such a soup made with *hamour* (grouper) and shrimp in one of the restaurants in Dubai's Heritage Village. This, along with other soups on the menu that we subsequently tried, diffuse the aura of what Dubai has now become—an international drawing point for not only tourism, business and trade, but also for cuisine. I have never forgotten the aroma and flavor of these soups. As I sat at home in the cold winter days of Toronto, miles and miles away from Dubai and the rest of the Arab Gulf, I longed for these soups and, therefore, created my own versions. The spices and shrimp in this soup blend well with the tasty hamour making this dish a succulent treat.

Serves 8
Prep time: 30 minutes
Cooking time: 40 minutes

4 tablespoons extra-virgin olive oil
1 onion, minced
1 small jalapeño or other fresh finger-length green chili pepper of your choice, finely chopped
4 cloves garlic, crushed to a paste (see page 30)
1 tablespoon peeled and grated fresh ginger
2 teaspoons salt
1 teaspoon ground turmeric
1/2 teaspoon ground cumin
1/2 teaspoon ground coriander
1/2 teaspoon ground black pepper
6 cups (1.5 liters) water
4 tablespoons tomato paste, diluted in 1 cup (250 ml) water
1/2 lb (250 g) fresh grouper (hamour) fillet, 1/2-in (1.25-cm) thick, cut into small pieces (substitute with cod or haddock)
1/2 lb (250 g) fresh shrimp, peeled, de-veined and tails removed
4 tablespoons finely chopped fresh coriander leaves (cilantro)

1 Heat the oil in a large saucepan with a lid over medium heat. Add the onion and the chili pepper and sauté for 10 minutes, uncovered. Add the garlic and ginger and cook for 3 minutes, stirring frequently.
2 Add the salt, turmeric, cumin, ground coriander, pepper, water and diluted tomato paste, and bring to a boil. Stir in the fish and shrimp, and cover. When it has come to a boil, lower the heat to medium and cook for 20 minutes. Stir in the coriander leaves and serve.

CHAPTER 4
chicken dishes

In the Arab Gulf countries, chicken dishes are almost as popular as meat dishes, especially in the cities. Chicken cooks faster for the fast pace of urban life and is available in various cuts and quite versatile. Granted, it is an inexpensive meat and is affordable for both the haves and have-nots. One chicken, when cooked in stews and soups, can feed a family for a few days. In towns and urban households, where raising chickens is permitted, a by-product such as eggs can provide for the family as well.

Chicken is also a part of the traditional street food offerings in all of the Arab Gulf cities. No traveler walking through the streets of an Arab Gulf city will deny being enticed by the intoxicating smell of Shawarma—layers of thin chicken or lamb slices barbecued on a huge rotating spit that are thinly shaved and served with a salad in pita bread, providing for a spicy combination of textures and tastes.

The kitchens in the Arab Gulf countries are filled with chicken recipes. Such chicken dishes as Roast Chicken with Saffron Rice Stuffing (page 73), Baked Chicken with Almonds and Rice (page 67), Aromatic Chicken and Rice with Almonds and Raisins (page 74), Lemony Chicken Stew (page 75), Tender Chicken with Creamy Milk Rice (page 68) and endless types of other chicken dishes are served in all parts of these countries. Chicken dishes from around the globe are found in the large cities such as Dubai and Abu Dhabi as well. It is fair to say that the chicken dishes of the world have come to the Arab Gulf.

BARBECUED CHICKEN SLICES

Dajaj Shawarma

A delicious dish that can be made from beef, lamb or chicken, Shawarma is famous across all the Middle East, and has become an Arab Gulf food par-excellence. To some extent, it has also become known in most countries of the world—usually as a fast-food barbecued meat dish. I remember a few years back while in Abu Dhabi, day after day enjoying Shawarma sandwiches in a restaurant run by a Lebanese proprietor. The sandwiches that he served, due to the addition of spices such as Baharat, were much tastier than those I had savored in Beirut and Damascus. When I asked a long time Lebanese resident in Abu Dhabi why the Shawarma was so tasty in his Gulf state, he responded, "It's the use of Baharat—that's what makes the difference!" He smiled continuing, "Of course, the Shawarma maker's other secrets help." Even though Shawarma originated in Turkey and has been popular in the Greater Syria area for decades, in the United Arab Emirates it had been perfected, based upon Arab Gulf tastes, no doubt because of the intense competition with foods from other lands. While this homestyle version of Shawarma, cooked in the oven cannot be compared to the highly aromatic Shawarma prepared on a huge rotating spit at restaurants or by street vendors, it is absolutely mouth-watering and delicious (and will satisfy your hankering for Shawarma without having to leave your home!). A simple salad, such as Refreshing Green Salad (page 51), is all that you need to serve alongside this satisfying dish.

Serves 4 to 6
Prep time: 20 minutes
Marinating time: 8 hours
Cooking time: 1 hour

2 lbs (1 kg) boneless chicken pieces, sliced
  into 1/2-in (1.25-cm)-wide strips
4 tablespoons freshly squeezed lemon juice
4 tablespoons extra-virgin olive oil
1 teaspoon salt
1/2 teaspoon ground black pepper
1/2 teaspoon paprika
1 teaspoon Arabian Gulf Spice Mix (Baharat)
  (page 28)

1 Place all the ingredients in a casserole dish. Turn the chicken pieces until thoroughly coated, cover, and refrigerate overnight.
2 Preheat the oven to 350°F (175°C).
3 Bake the chicken, uncovered, for 1 hour, or until the chicken is done. (When done, the chicken pieces will be white at their center and the meat will break apart easily with a fork.)
4 Serve with Saudi-Style White Rice (page 28) as a main dish, or as a sandwich in Pita Bread (page 122) or on top of a bed of Diced Vegetable Salad with Tahini Dressing (page 52).

BAKED CHICKEN WITH ALMONDS AND RICE

Al-Mandi

In Saudi Arabia, poultry and meat are cooked in many ways, and one of the most popular is *al-mandi*. An al-mandi dish refers, traditionally, to an ancient method of cooking chicken or lamb where it is placed in a large pot and mixed with rice, spices and water. The pot is then placed in a deep hole with hot coals, and is completely covered while the food cooks. While its method in the modern age has changed, its flavor is almost the same. The almonds that garnish the rice bring a unique flavor to the dish and upscale presentation, suitable for any dinner table. Serve with Creamy Cucumber and Yogurt Salad (page 30) or Coriander and Yogurt Salad (page 30) and Tangy Hot Tomato Sauce (page 27).

Serves 4
Prep time: 15 minutes
Soaking time: 5 minutes
Cooking time: 1 hour 25 minutes
Standing time: 30 minutes

1¹/2 lbs (750 g) chicken legs with skin on
2 cloves garlic, crushed to a paste
  (see page 30)
1 teaspoon salt
1 teaspoon Arabian Gulf Spice Mix (Baharat)
  (page 28)
¹/4 teaspoon ground cumin
¹/4 teaspoon ground coriander
¹/4 teaspoon ground black pepper
¹/4 teaspoon ground red pepper (cayenne)
2¹/4 cups (565 ml) water
1 onion, finely chopped
2 tablespoons butter
1 cup (200 g) uncooked Basmati or
  other white long-grain rice, soaked for
  5 minutes, thoroughly rinsed and drained
  (see page 24)
4 tablespoons blanched whole almonds,
  toasted, for garnish
4 to 6 lime wedges, for serving

1 Preheat the oven to 350°F (175°C).
2 Place the chicken legs, garlic, salt, Arabian Gulf Spice Mix, cumin, coriander, pepper, ground red pepper, water and half of the chopped onion in a large saucepan and bring to a boil. Simmer over medium-low heat for 15 minutes, then remove from the heat. Remove the chicken legs and set the saucepan with the broth aside (do NOT discard the broth). Place the chicken legs in a greased 9 x 13 x 2 inch (23 x 33 x 5 cm) baking pan. Cover with foil and bake for 40 minutes.
3 While the chicken is baking, melt the butter in a medium skillet over medium heat. Add the other half of the onion and fry for 10 minutes. Place the fried onion and rice in the saucepan with the reserved broth and bring to a boil over high heat. Cover and cook over medium-low heat for 12 minutes. Stir occasionally to ensure the rice does not stick to the bottom of the pan. Remove from the heat, cover, and allow to cook in its own steam for 30 minutes.
4 Spread the rice on a platter and place the baked chicken legs on top. Garnish with the almonds and serve with the lime wedges.

GARLICKY CHICKEN KEBABS
Dajaj Kabab

Kebabs, with their barbecuing aroma filling the streets of the old parts of the cities in most of the Middle East and North Africa, are usually made of lamb and, at times, beef. The same is true for the Arab Gulf countries except that ground chicken made into kebabs, likely of Indian origin, have become a specialty in that region. The ground chicken lends a flavor of its own and is simple to prepare and delicious to eat. Once walking with my family in the streets of Muscat, Oman's beautiful and spotless capital, we stumbled upon a fine Omani restaurant that had chicken kebabs on its menu. After ordering and then relishing these kebabs, I asked the owner, who was also the chef, about the ingredients he used to make such succulent patties. He openly divulged his secret spice combination proud of the fact that these kebabs were one of his best sellers. When I returned home, I created my own version, which I now often prepare to the delight of my family and friends. Serve with Creamy Cucumber and Yogurt Salad (page 30) or Homemade Plain Yogurt (page 31) and with Crunchy Pickled Garlic (page 26). I've also found that Creamy Garlic Sauce (page 27) makes a great dipping sauce for Kebabs.

Serves 4 to 6
Prep time: 25 minutes
Frying time: 40 minutes or
   Baking time: 50 minutes

2 lbs (1 kg) ground chicken
4 tablespoons all-purpose flour
1 onion, chopped
1 small jalapeño or other fresh finger-
   length green chili pepper of your
   choice, chopped
4 cloves garlic, crushed to a paste
   (see page 30)
1 cup (50 g) finely chopped fresh
   coriander leaves (cilantro)
1 large egg
2 teaspoons sumac
1 1/2 teaspoons Arabian Gulf Spice Mix
   (Baharat) (page 28)
1 teaspoon salt
1/2 teaspoon ground black pepper
Oil, for deep-frying

1 Place all the ingredients, except the oil, into a food processor and process for 2 minutes. The texture should be similar to mashed potatoes. If the mixture is too soft, add more flour; if it's a little stiff, add some water. Form into 2 to 3-inch (5 to 7.5-cm) patties.

2 Pour about 2 inches (5 cm) of oil (enough to submerge the patties) into a medium saucepan and set over medium-high heat. Heat the oil to a minimum temperature of 350°F (175°C) and no higher than 375°F (190°C), checking with a deep-frying or candy thermometer. If you do not have a thermometer, drop a small piece of bread in the oil. If the bread browns quickly (1 minute or less), the oil is the right temperature. Alternatively you can throw a drop of water in the oil. If the water sizzles upon contact, the oil is ready.

3 Deep-fry the patties, about 4 at a time, until golden brown, about 8 minutes total. Turn the patties mid-way through frying. Remove with a slotted spoon and place on paper towels to absorb any excess oil. Place on a serving dish and serve immediately.

4 Alternatively, these patties can be baked in the oven. Preheat the oven to 350°F (175°C). Place the patties on a greased baking sheet and bake for 50 minutes or until the tops turn golden brown. Remove and serve immediately.

Garlicky Chicken Kebabs

TENDER CHICKEN WITH CREAMY MILK RICE Saleeq

This time-honored Saudi Arabian main dish is rarely found in the restaurants of that country. It is traditionally served in the homes, especially when entertaining guests. In Arab tradition, hospitality is one of the bases of life that has been practiced in the Arabian Peninsula since the beginning of history and continues until our times. It is a usual practice when preparing dishes such as Saleeq to cook more than what the family needs in order to be prepared for unexpected guests. According to many Saudis, this dish of chicken and rice cooked in milk originated in the Hijaz area of Saudi Arabia, specifically Mecca, and was prepared at weddings. It is usually made in a gigantic pot to accommodate a large number of guests. These guests, whether friends or family, eventually moved to other areas of the country and brought with them this creamy rice and chicken dish that they had tasted in the Hijaz. It is also a popular dish to be served during the holy month of Ramadan. For a good combination meal, try serving this with Creamy Cucumber and Bell Pepper Salad (page 46).

Serves 6 to 8
Prep time: 30 minutes
Soaking time: 5 minutes
Cooking time: 1 hour 30 minutes

1 whole chicken (about 4 lbs/
   1.75 kg), cleaned and cut into 8
   pieces
2 small onions
1¹/2 teaspoons salt
4 cardamom pods, preferably black
1 large cinnamon stick
5 cups (1.25 liters) water
2 teaspoons dried thyme leaves
1 teaspoon ground coriander
¹/2 teaspoon ground cumin
¹/2 teaspoon ground black pepper
2 cups (400 g) uncooked Basmati
   or other white long-grain rice,
   soaked for 5 minutes, thoroughly
   rinsed and drained (see page 24)
2 cups (500 ml) milk
3 tablespoons butter, melted and
   kept warm

1 Place the chicken, onion, ¹/2 teaspoon of the salt, cardamom pods, cinnamon stick and water into a large saucepan with a lid. Bring to a boil, then cover and cook over medium heat for 25 minutes. Remove the chicken pieces, reserving 4 cups (1 liter) of the resulting chicken broth, adding enough water to make 4 cups (1 liter) if necessary. Allow the chicken to slightly cool, and place in a 2-quart (2-liter) casserole dish with a cover.

2 Preheat the oven to 350°F (175°C).

3 Rub the chicken with the remaining 1 teaspoon of salt and the thyme, coriander, cumin and black pepper. Cover and bake for 30 minutes. Remove the cover and continue to bake until the chicken browns.

4 In the meantime, transfer the reserved chicken broth into another large saucepan with a lid. Stir in the rice and bring to a boil. Cover, turn the heat to low, and simmer for 15 minutes. Stir in the milk and increase the heat to medium-low. Cook uncovered until all the liquid is absorbed, stirring a number of times. Transfer to a serving platter and drizzle on the butter. Place the chicken pieces on top and serve.

TANDOORI CHICKEN, OMANI-STYLE

Tandoori Chicken takes its name from *tandoor*, a type of oven originating in the Indian sub-continent. Tandoori Chicken is so popular today in Oman that it has come to be considered a traditional Omani dish. A tandoor, also called *tanoor*, is a clay oven pit that is filled with red-hot charcoal. Meat, chicken or, at times, other foods are marinated and lowered into it. The intense charcoal heat usually seals in the juices of the food, making it tasty and tender while at the same time, the smoke that permeates the food gives it a unique flavor. Today, these clay ovens are found throughout India, Iran and all across the countries of the Middle East. Although the twenty-first century does not normally provide for a tandoor in the modern kitchen, this recipe produces flavorful, succulent and tender chicken, thanks especially to its yogurt-based marinade. This oven-baked version is a near perfect substitute to the Tandoori Chicken I enjoyed in the Indian restaurants of Oman, which cooked the dish in their own tanoors. If you're planning to serve an appetizer with this dish, try Classic Hummus Chickpea Purée (page 35) or Roasted Eggplant Purée (page 34).

Serves 4 to 6
Prep time: 20 minutes
Marinade time: 4 hours
Cooking time: 1 hour

2 lbs (1 kg) boneless, skinless chicken
 breast, cut into bite-sized pieces
2 tablespoons finely chopped fresh
 coriander leaves (cilantro)
Tangy Hot Tomato Sauce (page 27),
 for serving

Marinade
1 cup (250 g) store-bought or Homemade
 Plain Yogurt (page 31)
4 cloves garlic, crushed to a paste (page 30)
3/4 teaspoon salt
1/2 teaspoon ground turmeric
1/2 teaspoon ground ginger
Generous pinch of freshly grated nutmeg
Generous pinch of ground black pepper
Generous pinch of ground cinnamon
Generous pinch of ground cardamom
Generous pinch of ground cumin
Generous pinch of ground red pepper
 (cayenne)
4 tablespoons oil

1 Preheat the oven to 350°F (175°C).
2 Place the ingredients for the Marinade in a mixing bowl. Mix thoroughly.
3 Place the chicken in a 2-quart casserole dish with a cover. Pour over the Marinade and mix well. Allow to marinate in the refrigerator for at least 4 hours, turning the chicken pieces over a few times.
4 Sprinkle the coriander leaves over the chicken and bake, covered, for 1 hour. Remove the cover and brown under the broiler. Serve with some Tangy Hot Tomato Sauce.

Serves 6
Prep time: 40 minutes
Soaking time: 5 minutes
Cooking time: 1 hour 40 minutes

2 lbs (1 kg) bone-in chicken pieces, cut into
    2 to 4-in (5 to 10-cm) sections
1 teaspoon salt dissolved in 4 cups (1 liter)
    water
1 cup (200 g) uncooked Basmati or
    other white long-grain rice, soaked for
    5 minutes, thoroughly rinsed and drained
    (see page 24)
4 tablespoons oil
1 large onion, thinly sliced
1 cup (250 g) store-bought or Homemade
    Plain Yogurt (page 31)
1 tablespoon peeled and grated fresh ginger
1/2 teaspoon ground cardamom
1 teaspoon salt
1 teaspoon ground black pepper
1/2 teaspoon ground cinnamon
1/2 teaspoon ground cumin
Generous pinch of saffron dissolved in
    1/2 cup (125 ml) water

1 Place the chicken and the salted water into a medium saucepan with a lid and bring to a boil. Cover and cook over medium-low heat for 30 minutes. Remove the chicken with a slotted spoon and set aside. Add the rice to the saucepan with the chicken broth and bring to a boil. Cook, uncovered, over medium-low heat for 10 minutes. Drain the rice and set aside.
2 Heat the oil in a small skillet over medium-low and sauté the onion for 10 minutes. Transfer to a 2-quart (2-liter) casserole dish with a cover.
3 Preheat the oven to 350°F (175°C).
4 Combine the yogurt with the remaining ingredients, except the dissolved saffron, in a large mixing bowl. Add the chicken pieces and gently turn the chicken to coat evenly. Place the chicken and any remaining yogurt mixture over the cooked onion in the casserole. Cover with the cooked rice. Drizzle the dissolved saffron all across the top of the rice. Cover and bake for 40 minutes, or until the rice is done. Serve directly from the casserole.

SAUDI-STYLE CHICKEN 'N RICE
Zourbian

This Saudi Arabian dish is tasty and wholesome and quite simple to prepare. If desired, lamb may be used as a substitute for the chicken. It is also popular in Yemen and, when made with lamb, serves as part of the traditional bridal festivities. I have prepared it both with chicken and lamb and have found both versions delectable. Yet I tend to lean toward using chicken because, as the old adage goes, "Chicken and rice, makes everything nice!" Serve Crunchy Pickled Garlic (page 26) alongside Zourbian for an added zest to the meal.

GULF-STYLE PASTA WITH CHICKEN

Quazi Macarona Saleeq

Not many associate pasta with Arab cooking, yet, long before the Italians fell in love with pasta and surpassed other peoples in its use, the Arabs were enjoying it. Evidence has come to light that a type of pasta was eaten in ancient Mesopotamia at the dawn of civilization. And in medieval Arabic culinary texts, a type of pasta noodle was used in certain dishes. Then, for centuries, pasta dishes faded into the back burner, until now, when expats from Italy, and other pasta-loving countries, have come to the Arab Gulf countries, either for work, business or tourism. Though pasta dishes continue to exist in the entire Arab World from east to west, they tend to have, generally, an "Italian touch" to them. However, I discovered a unique pasta dish popular in Saudi Arabia but unknown in the other Arab countries. Gulf-Style Pasta with Chicken, in my view, can match the best that Italy has to offer. (Don't tell the Italians this!) Serve with Roasted Eggplant Purée (page 34) or Creamy Cucumber and Bell Pepper Salad (page 46).

Serves 8
Prep time: 40 minutes
Cooking time: 1 hour 30 minutes

1/2 cup (125 ml) oil, plus extra for deep-frying the potatoes
2 lbs (1 kg) bone-in chicken pieces
4 tablespoons tomato paste, dissolved in 1 cup (250 ml) water
1/2 cup (125 g) store-bought or Homemade Plain Yogurt (page 31)
1/4 teaspoon ground red pepper (cayenne)
1 1/2 teaspoons salt
3/4 teaspoon ground black pepper
3/4 teaspoon ground cumin
3/4 teaspoon ground cinnamon
1/2 lb (250 g) ground beef or lamb
1 large onion, minced
2 potatoes, peeled and thinly sliced
8 oz (250 g) dried spaghetti, broken into about 2-in (5-cm) pieces
2 large hard-boiled eggs, sliced
4 tablespoons finely chopped fresh coriander leaves (cilantro), for garnish
Oil, for deep-frying

1 Heat 4 tablespoons of the oil in a large skillet with a lid over medium and fry the chicken for 8 minutes, uncovered, turning the pieces over once and adding more oil if needed. Remove the skillet from the heat and set aside.

2 Combine the dissolved tomato paste, yogurt, ground red pepper, 1 teaspoon of the salt, 1/2 teaspoon of the pepper, 1/2 teaspoon of the cumin and 1/2 teaspoon of the cinnamon in a small bowl. Pour this yogurt mixture over the chicken in the skillet.

3 Cover the skillet and cook over low heat for 40 minutes, or until the chicken is done, adding a little water if necessary to ensure there remains a sauce. (When done, the meat will easily pull away from the bones and will break apart easily with a fork.) Remove the chicken pieces with a slotted spoon and set aside, keeping the sauce in the skillet. Keep the chicken and the sauce warm.

4 Heat the remaining 4 tablespoons of oil in a medium skillet. Add the ground meat, onion, remaining 1/2 teaspoon of salt, remaining 1/4 teaspoon of pepper, remaining 1/4 teaspoon of cumin and remaining 1/4 teaspoon of cinnamon. Fry over medium-low heat for 12 minutes, or until the meat is cooked, stir-ring frequently. (The meat will turn a brownish color when done.) Set aside but keep warm.

5 Cut the potato slices into 1/4-inch (6-mm)-wide sticks.

6 Pour 1 1/2 inches (3.75 cm) or more of oil (enough to submerge the potato) into a medium saucepan and set over medium-high heat. Heat the oil to a minimum temperature of 345°F (175°C) and no higher than 375°F (190°C), checking with a deep-frying or candy thermometer. If you do not have a thermometer, drop a small piece of bread in the oil. If the bread browns quickly (1 minute or less), the oil is the right temperature. Alternatively you can throw a drop of water in the oil. If the water sizzles upon contact, the oil is ready. Deep-fry the potato, in two batches, until light brown. Remove with a slotted spoon and set on paper towels to drain. Set aside but keep warm.

7 Cook the spaghetti according to instructions on the package. Drain and keep warm.

8 Place the spaghetti on a serving platter and arrange the chicken pieces on top. Pour the sauce over the chicken pieces and then decoratively place the meat, potato and egg over top. Sprinkle on the chopped coriander leaves and serve.

ROAST CHICKEN WITH SAFFRON RICE STUFFING

Dajaj Mahshi

Stuffed chicken with rice is the most typical and preferred way of stuffing chicken in the entire Middle East. Versions of this type of stuffing can be found in all parts of the Arabian Peninsula. It is widely served at family and other special gatherings. In my version, which I first tried in the United Arab Emirates and then later in other Arab Gulf countries, I've made a few delicious changes: I've increased slightly the amount of traditionally used spices; added rosemary, sage and cardamom to the basting sauce; included raisins, almonds, cashews and pine nuts to the stuffing. The key to making moist and tender Dajaj Mahshi is to baste every twenty minutes, without fail. For those who enjoy a splash of lemon on their chicken, serve with lemon wedges, allowing each person to squeeze as much lemon as they like over the chicken. In the Gulf region this dish is usually served with Homemade Plain Yogurt (page 31). Other good side dishes would be Zesty Tomato and Fresh Coriander Salad (page 47) and Creamy Cucumber and Bell Pepper Salad (page 46).

Serves 6   **Prep time:** 40 minutes
Soaking time: 5 minutes
Cooking time: 2 hours 30 minutes

1 whole chicken (about 4 to 5 lbs/1.75 to 2.25 kg)
3 tablespoons all-purpose flour mixed with 2 teaspoons salt and a generous pinch of ground red pepper (cayenne)

¹/4 cup (¹/2 stick/60 g) butter, melted

Stuffing
¹/3 cup (80 ml) extra-virgin olive oil
¹/2 lb (250 g) ground beef
1 onion, minced
4 tablespoons slivered almonds
4 tablespoons raw, whole cashews
4 tablespoons pine nuts

¹/2 cup (100 g) uncooked Basmati or other white long-grain rice, soaked for 5 minutes, thoroughly rinsed and drained (see page 24)
4 tablespoons raisins
¹/2 teaspoon salt
¹/2 teaspoon ground cinnamon
¹/2 teaspoon ground black pepper
¹/4 teaspoon ground cardamom
¹/4 teaspoon ground cloves
1¹/2 cups (375 ml) water

Basting Mixture
¹/2 teaspoon ground cinnamon
¹/2 teaspoon ground black pepper
¹/4 teaspoon ground cardamom
¹/4 teaspoon ground cloves
¹/2 teaspoon dried rosemary
¹/2 teaspoon dried sage
Pinch of saffron
1¹/2 cups (375 ml) boiling hot water

1 Thoroughly clean the chicken then rub with the flour mixture, both inside and out. Place the chicken in a medium roasting pan with a cover and set aside

2 To make the Stuffing: Heat the oil in a large saucepan over medium-low heat, then sauté the meat for 8 minutes. Stir in the onion and sauté for 5 minutes. Stir in the almond, cashew and pine nut and sauté for 3 minutes. Stir in the rice, raisin, salt, cinnamon, pepper, cardamom, clove and water and bring to a boil. Reduce the heat to medium-low and cook for 10 minutes, stirring a few times. Allow to cool.

3 Combine all the ingredients for the Basting Mixture in a small bowl. Set aside.

4 Preheat the oven to 350°F (175°C).

5 Stuff the chicken, including the neck opening, then sew the openings closed and baste all over with the melted butter. Bake, covered, for 2 hours, or until the chicken is well cooked, basting every 20 minutes with the basting mix. (When done, the meat should pull easily from the bones.) For a roasted chicken with golden brown color, bake uncovered during the last 20 minutes. Serve the chicken with its stuffing while hot.

AROMATIC CHICKEN AND RICE WITH ALMONDS AND RAISINS

Kabsa

One of Saudi Arabia's most celebrated and traditional dishes, Kabsa is found today not only in the Arab Gulf countries but beyond in the Greater Syria region. It consists of long-grain rice, Basmati being the most common, along with vegetables, a number of spices and meat, either lamb or beef, chicken, fish or shrimp. Kabsa's flavor derives primarily from the mixture of its spices and, of course, the accompanying condiments. The cook can either prepare the spice mixture at home or can purchase pre-mixed Kabsa spices from a Middle Eastern food store. Though the latter method reduces the preparation time for making the dish, this pre-mix may also affect the cook's preference for certain spices. I was introduced to this dish by a Saudi Arabian couple, students at the University of Toronto who had invited us for a family meal—my first introduction to Saudi Arabian cooking. When it was presented at the table, my first reaction was that it resembled the Spanish paella. I was told by my host that the recipe for Kabsa had been passed down in the family for generations. I felt honored to have been part of their history. Serve with Creamy Cucumber and Yogurt Salad (page 30).

Aromatic Chicken and Rice with Almonds and Raisins

Serves 6
Soaking time: 2 hours
Prep time: 30 minutes
Cooking time: 1 hour 30 minutes
Standing time: 30 minutes

4 tablespoons raisins, for garnish
2¹/₂ lbs (1.25 kg) bone-in chicken pieces
¹/₂ cup (125 ml) extra-virgin olive oil
1 large onion, minced
2 cups (450 g) stewed tomatoes (about
   1¹/₂ 14.5-oz/411-g cans)
6 cloves garlic, crushed to a paste
   (see page 30)
2 teaspoons salt
1 teaspoon ground coriander
1 teaspoon ground black pepper
¹/₂ teaspoon ground cinnamon
¹/₂ teaspoon ground cumin
¹/₄ teaspoon ground cardamom
Generous pinch of saffron dissolved in
   2 tablespoons of water
1 large carrot, peeled and grated
1¹/₂ cups (300 g) uncooked Basmati or
   other white long-grain rice, soaked for
   5 minutes, thoroughly rinsed and
   drained (see page 24)
4 tablespoons slivered almonds, for
   garnish

1 Place the raisin in a small bowl and cover with water to soak. If you have time, do this a couple of hours before preparing the rest of the dish (see note).

2 Cut the chicken pieces into 2 to 4-inch (5 to 10-cm) sections. Harder to cut pieces, such as legs, can be left whole.

3 Heat the oil in a large saucepan with a lid over medium heat and sauté the onion for 6 minutes, uncovered. Add the chicken, tomato and garlic and sauté for 8 minutes, stirring frequently and turning the chicken over a few times. Add enough water to cover the chicken. Stir in the salt, coriander, pepper, cinnamon, cumin, cardamom, dissolved saffron and carrot. Bring to a boil, cover, and simmer over medium-low heat for 50 minutes, or until the chicken is cooked. (When done, the meat will easily pull away from the bones.) Remove the chicken with a slotted spoon, reserving the sauce in the saucepan. Set aside but keep warm.

4 Measure out the reserved sauce and if less than 3 cups (750 ml), add enough water to make 3 cups (750 ml). Return the sauce to the saucepan, add the rice, and bring to a boil. Cover and cook over medium-low heat for 12 minutes, stirring 2 or 3 times to ensure that the rice does not stick to the

bottom of the saucepan, and re-cover the saucepan after each stir. Turn off the heat and, with the pan covered, allow the rice to cook in its own steam for another 30 minutes.

5 Place the rice on a serving platter and arrange the pieces of chicken on top. Drain the raisin. Garnish with the raisin and almond and serve.

Lemony Chicken Stew
Dajaj Murraq

Murraq is a very popular stew in the United Arab Emirates and its origin goes back to the Bedouin, being one of their most famous dishes. A traditional dish once served on a large platter and eaten by hand (scooped up with pieces of thin bread), it is today enjoyed in most homes in the nation. Today, however, in many of the homes of the affluent it is scooped up with a spoon. Murraq can be made with lamb or chicken and can be either a main or side dish. During Ramadan, it is one of the most popular dishes because of the various nutrients included in its ingredients thus making it filling and healthful. One of the great advantages of this dish is that the vegetables and spices used to create it can be adjusted according to personal taste. Customarily, Murraq is served with side plates of sliced limes, dates, radishes, green onions (scallions) and slices of onions. Nothing is as good as the smell of a home-cooked stew and Murraq bears witness to this fact. To serve at its best, accompany Murraq with Saudi-Style White Rice (page 28) and Fresh Cucumber and Tomato Salad with Sumac (page 49).

Serves 6 to 8
Prep time: 45 minutes
Cooking time: 1 hour 20 minutes

1/2 cup (125 ml) oil
1 whole chicken (about 4 lbs/1.75 kg), cut into 8 serving pieces
2 large onions, minced
4 cloves garlic, crushed to a paste (see page 30)
1 cup (50 g) finely chopped fresh coriander leaves (cilantro)
2 1/2 teaspoons Arabian Gulf Spice Mix (Baharat) (page 28)
4 tomatoes, finely chopped
4 potatoes, peeled and cut into 1/2-in (1.25-cm) cubes
2 carrots, peeled and finely chopped
6 cups (1.5 liters) water, plus more if needed
2 1/2 teaspoons salt
1 teaspoon ground turmeric
3 tablespoons freshly squeezed lemon juice

1 Heat the oil in a large saucepan with a lid over medium heat. Add the chicken, onion, garlic, coriander leaves and Arabian Gulf Spice Mix and fry for 8 minutes, uncovered, turning the chicken over often. Stir in the remaining ingredients, except the lemon juice, and bring to a boil.
2 Cover and cook over medium-low heat for 1 hour or until the chicken is well cooked, adding more water if necessary to ensure there is enough water to cover the chicken. (When done, the meat should pull easily from the bones.) Stir in the lemon juice and serve immediately.

CHAPTER 5

MEAT DISHES

Arab cuisine was born in the tents of the Bedouin—a nomadic people who ate what they could carry with them as they moved throughout the deserts, migrating with the seasons. To survive the harsh elements of the desert, for millennia, the Bedouin tribes of the Arabian Peninsula relied heavily on a diet of meat, in the main lamb, but often also camel meat. Most tribes, accompanied by their flocks of sheep and, of course, camels, moved from one grazing ground to the next following vegetation for their livestock. Since vegetables and grains were largely unavailable in these barren lands, meat subsequently became virtually the only staple in the desert nomad's diet. Other products produced by their animals, like butter, milk and especially yogurt, were used to enhance any type of meat dish. To complement their meat and dairy products, dates and, at times, barley, rice and wheat, when available, were added to their daily food.

Although the variety of foods was minimal, Bedouin dishes were delicious and satisfying. Coupled with the Arabs' renowned hospitality, dining, even in a tent atop the desert sands, was a truly unforgettable gastronomic experience. Under the protection of the tent, there one would enjoy Thick and Rich Lamb Pottage (page 85), Tender Beef Simmered in Yogurt (page 83), and the timeless dish of Lamb in a Savory Sauce with Pita Bread (page 78). These dishes in their more simple forms were enjoyed in the Arabian Peninsula long before the rise of Islam. Ingrained in Arab culinary tradition, these dishes continue as part of the national heritage of the modern Arab Gulf, changing only slightly by way of some spices or better cuts of meat. These traditional dishes are an inherent part of the Arab Gulf and are an important connection to the proud past of the Gulf's now modern countries. Descendants of these nomadic tribes in the region have not forgotten the traditions of their forefathers. And, as in the past, meat remains a central part of the diet. Even though meat dishes are today enhanced with the availability of many more ingredients, spices and fresh herbs, and are complemented by fresh vegetables, meat is still a prominent part of lunch and dinner and, at times, breakfast. Barbecued, roasted and as the prime ingredient in soups and stews, meat is always on the dining tables of the Arab Gulf, reaching its epitome in the region's most famous meat dish—Kharouf Mihshee (whole roast stuffed lamb), the king of dishes served at important feasts. Whole roasted lamb, serving up to twenty-five people or more, isn't practical for most home cooks, so, in place of this classic dish, I've included two other princely dishes suitable for a celebration or simply a special dinner—Aromatic Roast Leg of Lamb (page 84) and Stuffed Lamb or Veal (page 88).

LAMB IN A SAVORY SAUCE WITH PITA BREAD Thareed

This dish, which consists of lamb in a savory sauce over Pita Bread (page 122), is like an Arab Gulf version of Irish beef stew over biscuits. Perhaps the Irish picked up this way of serving stew from the Spanish Moorish slaves when the ships of the Armada were wrecked on Irish shores. Or perhaps it was brought back to the country with returning Crusaders. *Thareed* dishes are found in the medieval Arab culinary texts and commonly contain broken pieces of bread drenched in a rich broth or sauce with meat and vegetables. This Bedouin dish was cooked in the Arabian Peninsula long before Islam. According to the Prophet Muhammad, Thareed was considered a dish superior to other foods and, in fact, it is said that his great-grandfather, Hashim, was the first to make the dish. It continued to be eaten throughout the Arab lands and, later, with conquests and time, it reached the tables of Moorish Spain. Thareed has continued to be popular until our times in one version or another throughout the Arab World. It is traditionally made with lamb, but beef or chicken can be used as substitutes.

Serves 6 to 8   Prep time: 40 minutes
Cooking time: 2 hours

4 tablespoons oil
1 onion, minced
4 cloves garlic, crushed to a paste (see page 30)
1/2 jalapeño or other fresh finger-length green chili pepper of your choice, finely chopped
3 tomatoes, finely chopped
2 tablespoons tomato paste dissolved in 1/2 cup (125 ml) water
2 tablespoons finely chopped fresh coriander leaves (cilantro)
2 teaspoons salt
2 teaspoons Arabian Gulf Spice Mix (Baharat) (page 28)
1/4 lemon, finely chopped
4 cups (1 liter) water
3 lbs (1.5 kg) boneless leg of lamb, cut into 1 to 2-in (2.5 to 5-cm) pieces
1/2 lb (250 g) carrots, peeled and cut into 1/4-in (6-mm)-thick rounds
1/2 lb (250 g) zucchini, cut into large chunks
2 store-bought or homemade Pita Bread (page 122), toasted and broken into pieces

1 Heat the oil in a large saucepan with a lid over medium-low heat. Add the onion, garlic, and chili pepper and cook, uncovered, for about 10 minutes or until they begin to brown. Add the tomato, dissolved tomato paste, and coriander leaves, and cook for 10 minutes. Stir in the salt, Arabian Gulf Spice Mix and chopped lemon.
2 Add the water and bring to a boil. Add the lamb, cover, and cook for 1 hour over medium-low heat, stirring a few times and adding extra water if necessary. Add the carrot and zucchini, cover, and continue to cook for another 30 minutes, stirring frequently and adding extra water if necessary.
3 Cover the bottom of a large serving bowl with the bread. Pour the meat and vegetable mixture over the bread and serve.

GOLDEN MEAT TURNOVERS
Samboosak ma' Laham

Samboosak (also Samboosa, Sanbusaj or Sanbusak), a type of fried savory turnover stuffed with meat, chicken or vegetables, is particularly popular in Saudi Arabia, where it is often prepared during Ramadan when breaking the fast. A beloved finger food for many centuries, they found their way from the Indian sub-continent, where they are known as *samosa*, to the countries of the Arab World and beyond. In the early ninth century, their popularity as a delicious convenient food reached such heights that Arab poets lauded their wondrous attributes, calling them the "tastiest food for the hasty diner." I consider them to be the epitome of lunch and snack foods, putting sandwiches to shame. According to food historian Clifford Wright, these little pies moved west from the Middle East as the Arabs expanded their empire appearing nowadays in new cultural contexts as Italian *calzones* and Spanish *empanadas*. The dough for this turnover is spiced especially for this type of Samboosak. Other more basic and versatile Samboosak dough recipes, such as that used for Spicy Vegetarian Turnovers (page 116), can be used interchangeably with many types of filling.

Golden Meat Turnovers

Shaping the Turnovers

1 Working on a lightly floured surface, roll 4 of the dough balls into thin circles about 3 to 4 inches (7.5 to 10 cm) in diameter. Keep the remaining dough balls covered with a damp towel while you work.

2 Place 1 tablespoon of the Filling in the center of each circle. Lift the dough up and over the Filling to create a half-moon shape. With wet fingers, firmly pinch the sides together in the same way as when pinching pie dough together. Go around the edge a second time to create a good seal. You may press the edge with fork tines for a decorative touch, if you wish.

3 Set the stuffed turnovers on a baking pan or tray and keep covered with a damp towel so that they don't dry out as you work. If you stack the turnovers, place waxed paper or plastic wrap between the layers so that they do not stick together. Repeat with the remaining dough balls and Filling, re-flouring your work surface if the dough balls begin to stick.

Makes 30 to 40 turnovers
Prep time: 1 hour
Resting time: 3 hours plus 10 minutes
Cooking time: 40 minutes

Oil, for deep-frying

Dough
3 cups (360 g) all-purpose flour, plus more if needed
1 teaspoon poppy seeds
1/2 teaspoon ground fennel seed
1/2 teaspoon salt
1/4 cup (1/2 stick/60 g) butter, melted
1/4 oz/7 g (1 envelope) active dry yeast dissolved in 1/2 cup (125 ml) warm water and 1 tablespoon sugar and allowed to stand for 10 minutes
1/2 cup (125 ml) water, plus more if needed

Filling
4 tablespoons extra-virgin olive oil
1 lb (500 g) ground beef or lamb
2 onions, minced
4 cloves garlic, crushed to a paste (see page 30)
1 teaspoon ground black pepper
1 teaspoon ground cumin
1 teaspoon salt

1 To make the Dough: Place the flour, poppy seeds, fennel and salt in a mixing bowl. Stir until well mixed, and then make a well in the center. Pour the butter, yeast mixture and water in the well. Knead the mixture until a

dough forms, adding extra flour or water if necessary. The consistency should be similar to bread dough—that is, soft, smooth and elastic. Cover and allow to stand in a warm place for 2 hours.

2 Form the Dough into 30 to 40 small balls. Cover the dough balls with plastic wrap or tea towel and allow to stand for 1 hour.

3 To make the Filling: Heat the olive oil in a medium skillet over low heat and add the rest of the ingredients. Cook for 12 minutes, stirring occasionally. Set aside to cool.

4 To form the turnovers: Follow the illustrated steps above.

5 Pour about 1 1/2 inches (3.75 cm) of oil into a medium saucepan and set over medium-high heat. Heat the oil to a minimum temperature of 345°F (175°C) and no higher than 375°F (190°C), checking with a deep-frying or candy thermometer. If you do not have a thermometer, drop a small piece of bread in the oil. If the bread browns quickly (1 minute or less), the oil is the right temperature. Alternatively you can throw a drop of water in the oil. If the water sizzles upon contact, the oil is ready.

6 Deep-fry the *Samboosak* 4 to 5 at a time until golden brown, about 2 to 3 minutes, turning them over once. Remove with a slotted spoon or tongs and set on paper towels to drain. Serve warm.

hearty lamb stew with vegetables

Marqoq

This dish is popular in Kuwait and in fact, in all the Arab Gulf countries. Of Bedouin origin, it can be cooked, depending on personal likes and availability with different types of meat and various types of vegetables. Nourishing and full of flavor, it makes a great family meal. No need to worry if there are leftovers as the stew can be reheated and it will be as tasty as the first day it was prepared. This dish is easy to make, but does require some advance planning as the dumplings are made the night before. Though dried limes are traditional in this recipe, lemon juice can be substituted but it should be stirred in when the stew is done.

Serves from 8
Prep time: 50 minutes
Cooking time: 2 hours and 10 minutes
Standing time: 8 hours

1 cup (120 g) all-purpose flour, plus extra
    for sprinkling
2 tablespoons butter, melted
1/3 cup (80 ml) water, plus more if needed
2 1/4 teaspoons salt
2 lbs (1 kg) bone-in lamb shoulder steak or
    chop, or veal or baby beef shoulder steaks,
    cut into 3 to 4-in (7.5 to 10-cm) pieces
4 tablespoons oil
2 onions, minced
4 cloves garlic, crushed to a paste (see page 30)
4 potatoes, peeled and diced into
    1-in (2.5-cm) cubes
2 large green or red bell peppers, deseeded
    and quartered
4 tomatoes, quartered
1 teaspoon Arabian Gulf Spice Mix (Baharat)
    (page 28)
1/2 teaspoon ground black pepper
1/2 teaspoon ground coriander
1/4 teaspoon ground cardamom
1/4 teaspoon ground cinnamon
1/4 teaspoon ground red pepper (cayenne)
2 dried limes, pricked in a few places, or
    4 tablespoons freshly squeezed lemon juice

1 Place the flour, butter, water and 1/4 teaspoon of the salt in a mixing bowl. Knead into a smooth dough, adding a little more water if necessary. Working on a lightly floured surface, roll the dough out until it is about 1/4-inch (6-mm) thick. Cut into 2 to 2 1/2-inch (5 to 6.25-cm) circles and sprinkle with a little flour. Cover with a tea towel and allow to stand overnight.
2 Place the meat in a medium saucepan with a lid and cover with water to about 2 inches (5 cm) above the meat. Bring to a boil, cover, and cook over medium-low heat for 30 minutes.
3 In the meantime, heat the oil in a medium skillet over medium-low heat. Add the onion and cook for 10 minutes. Stir in the garlic and cook for 3 minutes, stirring frequently.
4 Add the cooked onion and the garlic, the remaining 2 teaspoons of salt, and the rest of the ingredients, except the dough circles and lemon juice, if using, to the saucepan with the meat. Bring to a boil, adding extra water if necessary. Cover and cook over medium-low heat for 1 hour or until the meat and the potatoes are well done. (When done, the meat can be pulled off the bone with a fork and the potato will easily breakup with a fork.)
5 Gently stir in the dough circles, adding more water if necessary, and cook over low heat for 15 minutes, or until the circles are cooked. Add the lemon juice, if using, gently stir and serve hot with Saudi-Style White Rice (page 28). If you've used dried limes, remove and discard them before serving.

NOTE: 4 tablespoons of lemon juice can be substituted but it should be stirred in when the stew is done.

BATTER-FRIED MEATBALLS

Qadi Qada

This tasty Saudi Arabian dish likely has a history that goes back hundreds of years. Included in the medieval culinary texts of the Arabs, are similar dishes that were cooked in the kitchens of caliphs in Baghdad in the ninth and tenth centuries. In the Arab Gulf, there are various types of meatballs and a range of meatball dishes. However, the way of preparing the meatballs in this recipe is somewhat different in that they have to be prepared in two different stages. The meatballs are first cooked then they are coated and fried—a favored method of preparing them in the medieval eastern Arab lands.

Serves 4 to 6
Prep time: 50 minutes
Cooking time: 1 hour and 20 minutes
Standing time: 2 to 3 hours plus
    10 minutes

3/4 cup (90 g) all-purpose flour
1 teaspoon baking powder
1/4 oz/7 g (1 envelope) active dry yeast
    mixed with 1 teaspoon sugar and
    1/4 cup (65 ml) warm water then allowed
    to stand for 10 minutes
2 large eggs, beaten separately
1 lb (500 g) ground lamb or beef
4 cloves garlic, crushed to a paste
    (see page 30)
1/2 cup (110 g) cooked long-grain white
    rice, mashed
1 teaspoon salt
1/2 teaspoon ground black pepper
1/2 teaspoon Arabian Gulf Spice Mix
    (Baharat) (page 28)
Generous pinch of ground red pepper
    (cayenne)
Oil, for deep-frying

1 Mix together the flour, baking powder, yeast mixture, 1 of the eggs and, if needed, a little water in a mixing bowl, to form a pancake-like batter. Cover with a tea towel and set aside for 2 to 3 hours.

2 Mix together the meat, garlic, rice, salt, black pepper, Arabian Gulf Spice Mix, ground red pepper and the remaining egg in another mixing bowl. Shape into walnut-size meatballs and place in a medium saucepan with a lid. Add enough water to cover the meatballs and bring to a boil. Cover and cook over medium-low heat for 40 minutes. Carefully remove the meatballs with a slotted spoon and set aside to cool.

3 Pour about 1 1/2 inches (3.75 cm) of oil (enough to submerge the meatballs) into a medium saucepan and set over medium-high heat. Heat the oil to a minimum temperature of 345°F (175°C) and no higher than 375°F (190°C), checking with a deep-frying or candy thermometer. If you do not have a thermometer, drop a small piece of bread in the oil. If the bread browns quickly (1 minute or less), the oil is the right temperature. Alternatively you can throw a drop of water in the oil. If the water sizzles upon contact, the oil is ready.

4 Dip the meatballs in the batter and gently drop them into the oil, one at a time, until the top of the oil is covered with meatballs, but not tightly packed. Deep-fry until light brown. Remove with a slotted spoon and set on paper towels to drain. Serve hot with Refreshing Green Salad (page 51) or Diced Vegetable Salad with Tahini Dressing (page 52).

MINI SAUDI PIZZAS 'Aysh Abu Laham

It is said that if all snack foods were ranked in order, open-faced pies would, without question, lead the list. Covered with an infinite combination of toppings, they are delicious, nutritious and simple to prepare. As a child, I will always remember the aroma flowing out of the kitchen when I returned home from school. The mouth-watering aroma of baking pies would increase my hunger pangs a hundred fold. No matter what type of pie mother was making that day, the smell from the kitchen would always ensnare me in its culinary bewitching web. And the aromas are no different than those of the meat pie-sellers in the souks of the Arab Gulf and the other Arab countries. The emanating whiffs of baked "mini pizzas" begin early in the morning and last until late in the day, enticing passers-by to eat one, whether hungry or not. What makes the Saudi version distinct is that the dough is mixed with spices such as cumin and caraway, and occasionally fennel, while the meat topping is mixed with tahini and garnished with poppy seeds. Traditionally, the dough is formed in the shape of a thick-bottomed pie shell and filled with a meat mixture and then topped with a tahini-based sauce. I opt to prepare the dish as individual-size "pizzas," allowing each person to enjoy his or her own. After preparing my own version of this Saudi Arabian pie, I believe it to be among those that top the list. In the words of my daughter, after we had devoured one of these large Saudi pies, "This is better than any pizza that I have tasted!"

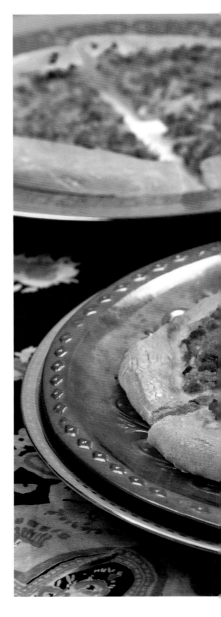

Serves 6
Prep time: 1 hour and 15 minutes
Standing time: 2 hours
Cooking time: 45 minutes

Dough
3 cups (360 g) all-purpose flour, plus more if needed
1/4 oz/7 g (1 envelope) active dry yeast mixed
    with 1/2 cup (125 ml) warm water and
    1 teaspoon sugar and allowed to stand for
    10 minutes
2 large eggs, beaten
1/4 teaspoon ground cumin
1/4 teaspoon ground caraway
1/2 teaspoon salt
1/4 cup (65 ml) extra-virgin olive oil, plus extra
    for brushing crust
1/2 cup (125 ml) water, plus more if needed

Topping
1/4 cup (65 ml) extra-virgin olive oil
1 lb (500 g) ground beef or lamb
2 onions, minced
2 cloves garlic, crushed to a paste (see page 30)
1/2 teaspoon ground black pepper
1 teaspoon salt
1 bunch green onions (scallions) (about 1/4 lb/
    125 g), trimmed and cut into short lengths
2 tomatoes, finely chopped
4 tablespoons tahini (sesame paste)
2 tablespoons freshly squeezed lemon juice
1/4 cup (65 ml) water
1 tablespoon poppy seeds, for garnish

1 To make the Dough: Place the flour in a mixing bowl and make a well in the center. Place the rest of the ingredients in the well. Knead well, adding a little water or flour if necessary to make a smooth but firm dough. Cover with a tea towel and let stand in a warm place for 2 hours, until it doubles in size.

2 Preheat the oven to 350°F (175°C).

3 To make the Topping: Heat the oil in a medium skillet over medium heat. Add the ground meat and fry for 5 minutes, stirring occasionally to break up any lumps. Stir in the onion, garlic, pepper and salt. Fry for another 8 minutes, stirring occasionally. Stir in the green onion and tomato. Remove from the heat and set aside. Mix the tahini, lemon juice and water in a small bowl. Pour the tahini mixture over the meat and onion mixture. Stir to combine. Separate the Topping into 6 equal amounts.

4 Separate the Dough into 6 equal-sized balls. Working on a very lightly floured surface, roll the each ball out into a circle about 1/8 inch (3 mm) thick. Place the circles on a greased baking tray. Pinch the edges of each circle to form a slightly raised edge. Spread the 6 Topping amounts on the 6 Dough circles, covering all of the Dough inside the fluted edges. Sprinkle with the poppy seeds and bake for 30 minutes. Brush the edges with a little extra olive oil and, for maximum enjoyment, serve immediately.

Mini Saudi Pizzas

NOTE: Poppy seeds add aroma and flavor to dishes. And in most Asiatic lands they have been and are still used for their medicinal properties. Originating in Asia, some say Greece, poppy seeds are used in both sweets, such as cakes, cookies and rolls, and non-sweet dishes, such as fish, noodles and various types of sauces. Since a good number of the inhabitants of the Arab Gulf countries have been traders since antiquity, they are likely to have been used in Gulf cooking for hundreds of years.

TENDER BEEF SIMMERED IN YOGURT   Laham bil Laban

On our farm my mother, at times, prepared dishes with yogurt, though her repertoire of yogurt-based dishes was limited. It was years later, when I traveled to the Arab Gulf countries, that I came to know a whole series of dishes in which yogurt was used as an ingredient along with many vegetables, chicken, fish and meat. (Arabs also use yogurt to tenderize meat.) The desert Arabs based their diets on what was available—their animals—and had developed the art of cooking milk and its products with all types of meats. This culinary art has not yet spread on a large scale in the Western world. Laham bil Laban is one of the Arab Gulf's dishes that originated with the Bedouin, thus making it an indigenous dish to the area. Its longevity attests to its delicious taste! The only change throughout the centuries has been the addition of chili peppers, ground coriander and dried mint leaves.

Serves about 4
Prep time: 20 minutes
Cooking time: 1 hour and 30 minutes

6 tablespoons extra-virgin olive oil
2 onions, minced
4 cloves garlic, crushed to a paste (see page 30)
2 lbs (1 kg) bottom round steak, sirloin steak or beef tenderloin, cut into 1-in (2.5-cm) cubes
1 small jalapeño or other fresh finger-length green chili pepper of your choice, finely chopped
1 teaspoon salt
1 teaspoon ground coriander
1 teaspoon ground black pepper
3 1/2 cups (875 ml) water
1 cup (250 g) store-bought or Homemade Plain Yogurt (page 31) mixed with 1/4 cup (65 ml) water, 1 teaspoon dried mint leaves and 1/4 teaspoon salt

1 Heat the oil in a medium saucepan with a lid over medium-low heat. Add the onion and cook for 8 minutes, uncovered. Add the garlic, meat and chili pepper, and cook for another 8 minutes, stirring frequently. Stir in the salt, coriander, black pepper and water, and bring to a boil.
2 Cover and cook over low heat for 1 hour or until the meat is done, stirring occasionally and adding more water if necessary to end up with a sauce the texture of yogurt.
3 Bring the yogurt to a boil in a small saucepan over medium heat, stirring constantly in one direction. Add the hot yogurt to the meat, cover, and simmer over low heat for 10 minutes, stirring frequently. Serve with Saudi-Style White Rice (page 28).

AROMATIC ROAST LEG OF LAMB
Fakhidh fil Furn

Among the Arabs, lamb is the king of meat. Everyone's favorite, it is the meat most offered to honored guests. The leg is the most cherished part of the animal and to offer it to guests is a noble act by the host. There must be hundreds of ways to roast legs of lamb but I'm partial to this Saudi Arabian method, which creates tasty and tender meat, thanks to the addition of yogurt. When I cook lamb this way, it is always a treat for our family and invited friends and colleagues. Once guests indulge in this version of roasted leg of lamb, they usually ask, while still in the midst of eating, "When are you going to make this again for us?" Serve with Creamy Cucumber and Yogurt Salad (page 30) and Crunchy Pickled Garlic (page 26).

Serves 6
Prep time: 1 hour 10 minutes
Refrigeration time: 1 hour
Standing time: 1 hour
Roasting time: 2 hours and 15 minutes

1/2 teaspoon ground cardamom
1/2 teaspoon ground cinnamon
6 cloves garlic, crushed to a paste (see page 30)
One 4 to 5-lb (1.75 to 2.25-kg) bone-in leg of lamb (butt portion) or 3 lbs (1.5 kg) boneless leg of lamb, scored in a number of places with 1-in (2.5-cm)-deep cuts
1 cup (250 g) store-bought or Homemade Plain Yogurt (page 31)
2 tablespoons freshly squeezed lemon juice
2 teaspoons salt
1 teaspoon Arabian Gulf Spice Mix (Baharat) (page 28)
1 teaspoon ground black pepper
1/4 teaspoon ground red pepper (cayenne)
Generous pinch of saffron dissolved in 2 tablespoons water
4 tablespoons extra-virgin olive oil
1 cup (250 ml) hot water
2 cups (240 g) all-purpose flour
1/2 cup (125 ml) warm water
1/2 cup (75 g) blanched whole almonds, toasted, for garnishing

1 Mix the cardamom, cinnamon and half of the garlic in a bowl. Rub the mixture into the cuts in the leg of lamb. Coat the entire leg of lamb with the yogurt and place in the refrigerator for 1 hour.

2 Mix together the remaining half of the garlic, lemon juice, salt, Arabian Gulf Spice Mix, black pepper, ground red pepper and dissolved saffron in another bowl. Coat the leg of lamb with this spice mixture and set aside at room temperature for 1 hour.

3 Place the leg of lamb in a medium casserole dish. Pour the oil and hot water around the lamb into the bottom of the casserole.

4 Preheat the oven to 350°F (175°C).

5 Make a dough with the flour and about 1/2 cup (125 ml) of warm water, or enough to make a dough similar to bread dough. Roll the dough out to a little larger than the size of the casserole. Place the dough across the top of the casserole and squeeze it all around the top edge to secure it and get a good seal. Roast for 2 hours.

6 Remove the dough and discard. (Be careful when removing the dough, a good deal of hot steam will escape.) Return the lamb to the oven and brown under the broiler.

7 Place the roasted lamb on a serving platter and garnish with the toasted almonds. I like to place oven-baked or deep-fried potato wedges around the meat when ready to serve.

Aromatic Roast Leg of Lamb

thick aND rich Lamb pottage
Harees

A very popular dish in all the Arab Gulf countries, pottage or Harees, is a food as old as time in the Arabian Peninsula. Pottage is a type of thick soup consisting of meat cooked with grains, rice or pulses. It can also be cooked without meat. Wheat is usually used instead of rice in preparing this dish, but this version calls for rice, which makes for a richer version. Whether made with wheat or rice, pottage is slowly cooked with lamb or chicken and spices resulting in a thick soup with a rich meaty flavor. All through the Middle Ages pottage was an easily available and inexpensive food for the poor. It was common for a peasant housewife to have a pot of pottage on the fire, at times, adding new ingredients as they became available. However, for the affluent there always have been pottage dishes, such as this one, that are made to gourmet taste. Harees is part and parcel of Arab Gulf cuisine and more generally is a common dish amongst almost all of the Arab tribes of the eastern Arab World. Of simple origin, but rich in taste, it is served at weddings, special occasions and daily during Ramadan. In the Greater Syria area a similar dish with the same name is made but with much less spices. In the Emirates, butter is added to top the dish before it is served. In Kuwait, cinnamon and sugar crown the melted butter. Many Arabs enjoy eating this rich delicacy by scooping it up with pieces of Pita Bread (page 122) or Wafer-Thin Bedouin Pancakes (page 120). I like to serve it with Homemade Plain Yogurt (page 31) and Crunchy Pickled Garlic (page 26).

Serves 8
Prep time: 45 minutes
Cooking time: 3 hours and 45 minutes
Soaking time: 4 hours
Standing time: 10 minutes

1¹/2 cups (300 g) uncooked Basmati or other white long-grain rice, thoroughly rinsed and drained (see page 24)
5 quarts (5 liters) water
2 lbs (1 kg) bone-in lamb shoulder or another bone-in cut of lamb (such as steaks, chops or shank), cut into pieces
¹/2 teaspoon ground cumin
¹/2 teaspoon ground coriander
¹/2 teaspoon ground ginger
¹/2 teaspoon ground cinnamon
¹/4 teaspoon ground red pepper (cayenne)
Generous pinch of freshly grated nutmeg
Generous pinch of ground cloves
Generous pinch of ground cardamom
2 teaspoons salt
3 tablespoons unsalted butter or Ghee (page 135), melted

1 Place the rice in half of the water (2¹/2 quarts /10 cups) and allow to soak for 4 hours.
2 Place the lamb, spices and the remaining water in a stockpot and bring to a boil. Cook over medium-low heat for about 2¹/2 hours, removing any froth that rises from the meat, or until the meat is very tender and falling off the bone, adding more water if necessary.
3 Add the soaked rice with its water, and the salt to the boiled lamb. Cook for another 1 hour, or until both the rice and lamb become mushy and similar in texture to a smooth porridge, stirring frequently and adding more water if necessary. Remove from the heat and allow to cool. Remove the bones and discard. Transfer the stockpot contents to a food processor and process to a paste. Return the paste to the stockpot and heat over low heat, stirring constantly, until heated through. Serve in individual serving bowls, drizzle the butter or Ghee over the top and before serving.

NOTE: The quantity of water used in this recipe looks enormous, but most of the water evaporates during cooking—in fact, you'll wonder where it all went.

Makes about 3 dozen
Prep time: 50 minutes
Baking time: 40 minutes

1 lb (500 g) ground lamb or beef
2 cups (450 g) mashed potatoes
1 small tomato, finely chopped
4 green onions (scallions), trimmed and
    finely chopped
1/3 cup (25 g) chickpea flour, plus more if
    needed
4 tablespoons finely chopped fresh
    coriander leaves (cilantro)
2 large eggs, beaten
1 1/2 teaspoons salt
1/2 teaspoon ground cumin
1/2 teaspoon ground coriander
1/2 teaspoon curry powder
1/2 teaspoon ground black pepper
2 tablespoons freshly squeezed lemon juice
2 tablespoons finely chopped fresh mint
    leaves
1 teaspoon sumac

1 Preheat the oven to 350°F (175°C).
2 Thoroughly mix together all the ingredients, except the mint and sumac, in a mixing bowl. The mixture should be the texture of ground hamburger. If it is too soft add a little flour; if too hard, add a little water. With moistened hands, form the mixture into patties that are 2 to 3-inches (5 to 7.5-cm) in diameter and 1/2-inch (1.25-cm) thick. Re-wet your hands every so often to keep the mixture from sticking to them.
3 Place on a greased baking sheet and bake for about 40 minutes, or until browned. Place on a serving platter and sprinkle with the mint leaves and the sumac before serving. Serve with Warm and Spicy Potato Salad (page 49) or Zesty Tomato and Fresh Coriander Salad (page 47).

> **NOTE:** If after making a kebab or two you notice that the kebabs are not holding their shape; add a little more flour to the mixture. If it is difficult to form them into smooth kebabs, add a little water to make them more pliable.

baked lamb kebabs with aromatic spices Kabab Mutabbal

The spicy dishes found in the Arab Gulf countries, in the main, originate in the Indian sub-continent. However, many of them have called the Arabian Peninsula home for hundreds of years. The products of strongly flavored aromatic bark, flowers, fruits, leaves or roots of mostly tropical plants and spices have been highly valued for thousands of years. With the exception of allspice, capsicums and vanilla, most of the remaining seasonings originated in China, India and the Near East, and were brought by sea and camel caravan to the Mediterranean region by the Arabs. For hundreds of years, the profits made from this commerce formed the basis of Middle Eastern empires and brought much wealth and new flavors to the Arabian Peninsula. New products meant new ideas and, no doubt, part of this was the development of these types of aromatic kebabs. It's not really clear which region of the Arab Gulf can take credit for creating them, but to be fair, it would only make sense that all of these countries stake their claim. After all, they make them, we claim them! When serving these kebabs, I like to set a dish of Yogurt and Tahini Dip with Fresh Herbs (page 40) on the table, allowing each person to either pour the dip over the kebabs or to dunk the bites of the kebabs into the dip.

SPICY MEATBALLS IN A CREAMY YOGURT SAUCE

Kabab bil Laban

Yogurt has been a cherished medicinal "super food" in the Middle Eastern and Central Asian lands since the dawn of civilization. Only lately has its image as a life-extender taken hold. Some call it "the miracle milk product"; others "a mystery food"; while the romantics call it "the elixir of life." Cooks from the Greater Syria area to the Indian sub-continent and much of Central Asia often use this healthy product in their meat dishes. For the Bedouin of the Arab Gulf, yogurt was a natural pairing with their meat dishes, serving both as a marinade and a sauce. Today, this Saudi Arabian dish is a fine example of how yogurt and meat together make for a delightful treat. Being a little more elegant, intricate and spiced (and spicy hot) than other meat-yogurt dishes such as Tender Beef Simmered in Yogurt (page 83), it has become part of the creative development of Saudi Arabian cuisine. For an appealing presentation, try to make the balls consistent in shape and size. This dish tastes great when served with Aromatic Baked Tomato Slices (page 127).

Serves 4
Prep time: 30 minutes
Cooking time: 35 minutes

1 lb (500 g) lean ground beef
1 onion, minced or grated
2 cups (100 g) finely chopped fresh parsley
1/4 teaspoon ground cumin
3/4 teaspoon salt
1/2 teaspoon ground black pepper
1/4 teaspoon ground coriander
1/4 teaspoon Arabian Gulf Spice Mix (Baharat) (page 28)
Generous pinch of ground red pepper (cayenne)
1 cup (250 g) store-bought or Homemade Plain Yogurt (page 31)
2 cloves garlic, crushed to a paste (see page 30)
4 tablespoons extra-virgin olive oil

1 Thoroughly mix together the meat, onion, parsley, cumin, 1/2 teaspoon of the salt, 1/4 teaspoon of the black pepper, coriander, Arabian Gulf Spice Mix and ground red pepper in a mixing bowl. Shape the mixture into small walnut-size meatballs and set aside.

2 Whisk the yogurt, the remaining salt and black pepper, and the garlic in another mixing bowl. Refrigerate until ready to use.

3 Heat the oil in a medium skillet with a lid over medium heat. Add the meatballs, cover, and reduce the heat to low. Cook for 30 minutes, gently stirring a number of times and adding a little more oil if needed. Arrange the meatballs on a serving platter and spread the yogurt mixture on top. Serve immediately.

STUFFED LAMB OR VEAL

Kaboorga

Stuffed meats and vegetables are considered to be the epitome of dishes throughout the Middle East and the neighboring countries. Besides stuffed lamb for which the Arabs are renowned, stuffed ribs are popularly prepared throughout the eastern Arab lands, especially during special occasions and milestone events. This Saudi Arabian version is a little different from those prepared in the Greater Syria area where the stuffing is usually rice, meat and chickpeas. In this recipe, you have the option of substituting lamb breast with veal breast or using veal ribs. Strangely, even though this dish, in my view, is a gourmet treat, I rarely found it on the menus in restaurants of the Arab countries. Almost everyone is familiar with its mouth-watering attributes yet there has been no demand to have it served in restaurants—perhaps due to the extra work involved in its preparation. Serve with Creamy Cucumber and Yogurt Salad (page 30) and Coriander and Yogurt Salad (page 30) as well as a side dish of Crunchy Pickled Garlic (page 26).

Serves 8 to 10
Soaking time: 5 minutes
Prep time: 45 minutes
Cooking time: 3 hours 15 minutes

4 tablespoons extra-virgin olive oil
1 cup (200 g) uncooked Basmati or
  other white long-grain rice, soaked for
  5 minutes, thoroughly rinsed and drained
  (see page 24)
3 onions, minced
2 green bell peppers, deseeded and finely
  chopped
6 cloves garlic, crushed to a paste
  (see page 30)
1/2 cup (50 g) pine nuts
1/2 cup (25 g) finely chopped fresh parsley
2 1/2 teaspoons salt
1 1/2 teaspoons ground black pepper
4 cups (1 liter) water
2 boneless breasts of lamb or veal, about
  5 lbs (2.25 kg) total, or 4 to 5 lbs (1.75 to
  2.25 kg) veal ribs
2 cups (450 g) canned stewed tomatoes
  (about 1 1/2 14.5-oz/411-g cans)
4 tablespoons finely chopped fresh
  coriander leaves (cilantro)
1 teaspoon dried oregano
1 teaspoon Arabian Gulf Spice Mix (Baharat)
  (page 28)
2 tablespoons pomegranate syrup
1/4 teaspoon ground red pepper (cayenne)

Special tools
**Large Sewing Needle (about 2 1/2-in/6.25-cm
  long)**
Thread

1 Heat the oil in a large skillet with a lid over medium heat and stir in the rice, onion, green bell pepper and half of the garlic. Sauté, uncovered, for 10 minutes, stirring frequently. Add the pine nut, parsley, 1 teaspoon of the salt, 1/2 teaspoon of the black pepper and 2 cups (500 ml) of the water. Bring to a boil. Cover and cook over medium-low heat for 10 minutes, stirring occasionally to ensure that the rice mixture does not stick to the bottom of the skillet.

2 In the meantime, trim large amounts of excess fat off the lamb or veal breasts or veal ribs. Leave a little fat here and there to keep the meat juicy. Then stuff and season the meat, following the illustrated steps on the facing page.

3 Preheat the oven to 350°F (175°C).

4 Combine the remaining 2 cups (500 ml) of the water with the stewed tomato, coriander leaves, oregano, Arabian Gulf Spice Mix, pomegranate syrup and ground red pepper in a bowl. Pour this mixture over the meat. Cover and bake for 2 1/2 hours, basting occasionally with the juice. Remove the cover and bake for another 30 minutes, or until the meat is well done. Serve with the pan juices over the meat and the rice.

Stuffing the Lamb or Veal

1 Form a pocket with the lamb or veal breasts using a 2 to 3-inch (5 to 7.5-cm) needle and nylon thread (or any sturdy thread). Sew the two breasts of lamb or veal together, leaving an opening on one end. (If you think that your thread is not sturdy enough, sew twice.)

2 If you're using veal ribs, make a pocket by separating the ribs from the outer meat. Use a sharp knife to separate the outer layer ribs from the inside layer of meat. Carefully cut between the two layers to form a pocket. Or, if you buy your meat from a Middle Eastern market, ask the butcher to do this for you.

3 Stuff the pocket with the rice mixture.

4 Sew the open end closed.

5 Place in a large roaster with a cover. Rub all over with the remaining half of the garlic, the remaining 1 1/2 teaspoons of salt and the remaining 1 teaspoon of black pepper.

SAVORY LAMB TARTARE
Kufta Nayya

This dish originated in the mountain villages of Lebanon where raw meat dishes are a delicacy. However, it is not surprising to find Kufta Nayya as part of hotel buffets and restaurants in the Arab Gulf countries as it makes for a great gourmet appetizer. The lean lamb, infused with fresh mint and parsley along with spices, has a near melt-in-the mouth texture when served with a drizzle of olive oil over the top. Almost every Lebanese food menu I was presented with on my visits to the Arab Gulf countries, from Kuwait to Oman, included Kufta Nayya as an appetizer. The Arab Gulf version, as compared with my memory of first eating it at the source, in a Lebanese village, seems to be slightly more spiced. For those who enjoy Western-style tartare, the fresh greens in this version give it a surprising punch.

Serves 8
Prep time: 35 minutes

1 lb (500 g) lean boneless leg of lamb, cut into small pieces
1 cup (50 g) finely chopped fresh parsley
4 tablespoons finely chopped fresh mint leaves
4 tablespoons finely chopped fresh coriander leaves (cilantro)
1 teaspoon salt
1/2 teaspoon ground black pepper
1/4 teaspoon allspice
1 small onion, preferably Spanish, minced
2 green onions (scallions), trimmed and finely chopped, for garnish
Extra-virgin olive oil, for drizzling on top
Fresh mint leaves (optional)

1 Place the lamb, parsley, mint, coriander, salt, black pepper and allspice in a food processor. Process into a smooth paste. Transfer to a mixing bowl and thoroughly mix in the onion. Spread evenly on a platter. Sprinkle with the green onion and olive oil and serve immediately.
2 The dish is excellent when served with Pita Bread (page 122), Crunchy Pickled Garlic (page 26) or any other type of pickle and fresh mint leaves. When lamb tartare is being scooped with small pieces of Pita Bread, a fresh mint leaf is placed on the tartare before placing it in the mouth.

> **TIP:** To ensure you get the freshest meat possible, the main ingredient required for a good Nayya, a visit to a good butcher shop is a good idea.

LAMB AND OKRA STEW
Khoresh Bamieh

Okra stews are found in many versions from North Africa to Iran and beyond. This version carries an Iranian name and is found in the Arab Gulf countries. Iran's location at the very center of the Silk Road, gave it a strategic position at a point of confluence between East and West and between the ancient and medieval worlds. This made it an ideal transition point for products being traded between the Orient and the West for thousands of years. Many of these products were introduced into what was then Persia from China and India in ancient times then carried to the Iberian Peninsula by the Arabs after the rise of Islam. Of course, the nearby Arab Gulf countries were also much influenced by Iranian trading. In addition, on a continuing basis, Iranians have worked and settled in the Arab Gulf countries, leading to home-grown versions of popular Iranian dishes, such as Khoresh Bamieh. This Iranian-inspired dish is popular in all of the Arab Gulf countries.

Serves 6
Prep time: 25 minutes
Cooking time: 1 hour and 15 minutes

1 lb (500 g) fresh or frozen okra
1/4 cup (1/2 stick/60 g) butter
1 lb (500 g) stewing lamb, such as boneless lamb shoulder, cut into 1/2-in (1.25-cm) cubes
1 medium onion, finely chopped
2 cloves garlic, crushed to a paste (see page 30)
1 jalapeño or other fresh finger-length green chili pepper of your choice, finely chopped
2 cups (450 g) canned stewed tomatoes, (about 1 1/2 14.5-oz/411-g cans)
2 1/2 cups (625 ml) water
1 teaspoon ground turmeric
1 teaspoon salt
1/2 teaspoon ground black pepper
1/2 teaspoon ground cumin
2 tablespoons freshly squeezed lemon juice

1 If you're using fresh okra, snip off the hard tips. If you're using frozen okra, do not defrost it. Leave it in the freezer until ready to use.
2 Melt the butter in a medium saucepan with a lid over low heat. Add the lamb and sauté over medium heat, uncovered, for 10 minutes. Add the onion, garlic and chili pepper and sauté for another 10 minutes, stirring a few times. Add the stewed tomato and water and bring to a boil. Cover and cook over medium heat for 30 minutes.
3 Gently stir in the remaining ingredients, except the okra and lemon juice. Add the okra and bring to a boil. Cover and simmer over medium-low heat for 30 minutes, adding a little more water if necessary. Gently stir in the lemon juice, then serve hot with Saudi-Style White Rice (page 28).

GRILLED LAMB CHOPS

Riyash Kharouf ma' Taratoor

The first time I tasted something somewhat similar to this type of lamb chop was in Lebanon where we were guests of a family that had once lived in Qatar. Our host told me that he had learned how to cook lamb chops in this fashion from a chef who worked at one of the tourist hotels in the country. He described to me how they were made and the ingredients used. Back home in Canada, the memory of tasty spiced lamb chops lingered and enticed me, over the years, to create several of my own versions, of which the following is one. I've provided instructions for broiling or grilling the chops—both yield delicious results. The best way to enjoy these chops is to serve them with Saudi-Style White Rice (page 28) and either Zesty Tomato and Fresh Coriander Salad (page 47) or Fresh Cucumber and Tomato Salad with Sumac (page 49).

Serves 4
Prep time: 15 minutes
Refrigeration time: 1 hour
Cooking time: 6 minutes
Resting time: 3 minutes

2 tablespoons extra-virgin olive oil
1/2 teaspoon salt
1/2 teaspoon dried oregano
1/2 teaspoon dried thyme
1/2 teaspoon dried basil leaves
1/2 teaspoon ground black pepper
1/4 teaspoon Arabian Gulf Spice Mix
   (Baharat) (page 28)
Twelve 1-in (2.5-cm)-thick lamb loin or rib
   chops, about 3 oz (75 g) each
Creamy Garlic Sauce (page 27)

1 Mix together the olive oil, salt, oregano, thyme, basil, black pepper and Arabian Gulf Spice Mix in a small bowl.
2 Rub both sides of the chops with the spice mixture. Cover and place the chops in the refrigerator for 1 hour.
3 To broil the chops, turn the broiler to high and set the oven rack 3 to 5 inches (7.5 to 12.75 cm) from the heat source. To grill the chops, preheat the grill to medium-high heat. Broil or grill the chops (if grilling place directly over the heat) for about 3 minutes on each side for medium-rare doneness.
4 Allow the chops to rest, covered with foil, for a few minutes before serving. Serve with the Creamy Garlic Sauce.

CHAPTER 6

SEAFOOD AND FISH DISHES

I have never heard of a person who has traveled to the Arab Gulf countries who has not tried the fish dishes of the region, usually made from very fresh fish—just out of the water. There are a good number of restaurants that have large fish tanks from which a customer can choose the fish of their choice and have it baked, fried or grilled—from tank to the frying pan, as the saying goes. As well, other restaurants buy their fish early in the morning just after the fishermen return with their catch of the day. Fresh fish and all types of creatures of the sea, for those living along the shores of the countries of the Arab Gulf, have, through the centuries, been part and parcel of Gulf cuisine. At one time the Arabian Gulf teemed with the natural creatures of the sea. However, today the catch is barely able to satisfy the demand. For this reason fish farming is becoming very popular. The millions of expatriates who have come to work in the region have greatly increased the demand for seafood, transforming it from being one of the least expensive foods in the Gulf area to almost a rich person's food.

However, in this area of the world, fish is still very important in the kitchen and social life of all the people. Often the inhabitants living on the Arabian Peninsula's shores, when they are honored with special guests, put before them a mouth-watering feast of fish, offering a varied range of fish dishes from which to choose. At such feasts there would be baked or grilled fish dishes, fish casseroles, fish patties, deep-fried fish, fish and seafood rice dishes, fish salads, fish soups and many, many more. The guest would notice that Arab Gulf cooks do not shy away from using the full selection of aromatic spices at their disposal when cooking seafood and fish; yet the use of spices in Arab Gulf seafood and fish dishes never overpowers the delicate flavor of the main ingredient.

Despite the huge demand for fish, there remain about 300 varieties of fish in the waters of the Arabian Gulf, and fresh fish remains a staple food along the shoreline of the Arabian Peninsula. Among the fish varieties most favored are barracuda, crab, kingfish, lobster, shrimp, red snapper, tuna and other types of the creatures of the sea. However, the fish that is in demand above all the rest is *hamour*, a type of grouper. Its firm white flesh absorbs the traditional spices used in the Gulf area better than most other fish. Prepared in a myriad of ways, hamour can be baked, grilled or added to soups or stews. Typically it is flavored with chili peppers and spices such as cardamom, coriander, cumin, black pepper, and turmeric or the spice blends such as Baharat or curry powder. Hamour is also called "gulf grouper" or the "brown spotted reef cod."

Serves about 6
Prep time: 25 minutes
Refrigeration time: 1 hour
Cooking time: 50 minutes

1¹/2 lbs (750 g) grouper (hamour) fillet,
    cut into 3 to 4-in (7.5 to 10-cm) pieces
    (substitute cod, haddock, halibut, sea
    bass, tilapia or other white firm-fleshed
    fish)
³/4 teaspoon salt
2 tablespoons freshly squeezed lemon juice
5 tablespoons (²/3 stick/70 g) butter
1 large onion, finely chopped
4 tablespoons finely chopped fresh
    coriander leaves (cilantro)
4 cloves garlic, crushed to a paste
    (see page 30)
1 teaspoon dried oregano
¹/2 teaspoon ground black pepper
4 tablespoons tomato paste, dissolved in
    2¹/2 cups (625 ml) of water
1 recipe Saudi-Style White Rice (page 28)
Several sprigs of fresh parsley, for garnish

fish fillets in an aromatic red sauce Yakhnat Samak

In Kuwait eating is not eating without fish. For centuries, pearl diving, trading and fishing were the mainstay of the Kuwaitis. The sea gave them their livelihood and the seafood dishes that they so highly relish. Almost twenty years ago while in Kuwait, during the second week of my trip, I experienced the graciousness that Arabs are so known for. (During my travels throughout the Arab Gulf countries, when I would be introduced to new friends or colleagues Arab hospitality kicked in—no matter where, no matter when, people I met would invite me for lunch or for dinner, and, in most cases, at lavish restaurants.) I had received an invitation to go the following day to one of Kuwait City's elegant eating places. Although each meal I ate was better than the previous, I longed for a simple stew, something almost home-cooked in the midst of urban dining. That next day I was lucky to have my dream fulfilled—placed before me was Yakhnat Samak, a stew of fish in a tomato-based sauce and a local favorite in Kuwait. For a satisfying meal, serve with Saudi-Style White Rice (page 28) or mashed potatoes.

1 Place the fish pieces in a casserole dish or large platter and sprinkle on the salt and lemon juice. Set in the refrigerator for 1 hour.
2 Melt the butter in a large skillet with a lid over medium-low heat. Add the onion, coriander leaves, garlic, oregano and black pepper and cook over medium-low heat, uncovered, for 10 minutes, stirring a number of times. Add the dissolved tomato paste and bring to a boil. Cover and simmer over low heat for 10 minutes. Add the fish pieces, bring to a boil, and turn the heat to low. Cover and simmer over low heat for 25 minutes.
3 Place the rice on a serving platter and arrange the fish pieces over the rice. Pour the sauce from the skillet over the fish and the rice. Garnish with the parsley.

GRILLED MARINATED FISH KEBABS

Tikat Hamour

"Let's have *hamour* again for dinner this evening. I love this fish! Let's order fried hamour!" My daughter seemed to have read my mind as we sat down in the Al-Areesh Restaurant in Dubai's Heritage Village planning to order our meal. The night before at the Fetafeet Restaurant overlooking the famous Dubai Creek crowded with dhows moving cargo and people between the two sides of the creek and beyond, we had enjoyed tasty grilled hamour, or grouper, the most favored fish in that part of the world. If the hamour is fresh, this dish is divine. These kebabs are typically served with lemon slices and Saudi-Style White Rice (page 28) or French fries. For a more complete meal, serve with Creamy Garlic Sauce (page 27) and Tabbouleh (page 53).

Serves 4
Prep time: 25 minutes
Marinating time: 1 hour
Cooking time: from 6 to 12 minutes

2 tablespoons freshly squeezed lemon
   juice
4 cloves garlic, crushed to a paste
   (see page 30)
1 teaspoon salt
2 teaspoons Arabian Gulf Spice Mix
   (Baharat) (page 28)
2 lbs (1kg) grouper (hamour) fillet or
   steak, cut into 1-in (2.5-cm) cubes
   (substitute swordfish, salmon, kingfish
   or halibut)

1 Combine the lemon juice with the garlic, salt and Arabian Gulf Spice Mix in a medium bowl. Add the fish cubes and gently turn the fish in the mixture to coat evenly. Let marinate in the refrigerator for 1 hour.

2 Preheat a grill to medium heat. Place the fish cubes on skewers and barbecue them directly over the heat, turning them a few times. The fish is done when it begins to brown nicely and flakes with a fork, about 6 to 9 minutes. Or, turn the broiler to high and set the oven rack in the middle position. Place the skewers on a sheet pan or broiler pan and broil in the oven until done, about 10 to 12 minutes.

LIGHTLY BREADED FISH IN A TANGY TOMATO SAUCE Salona

I first relished this traditional dish in one of the classy hotels that abound in Dubai, the United Arab Emirates' powerhouse. Like many of the other hotels in the city, it always featured on its menu a number of traditional Arab Gulf dishes and on that day it was Salona, a dish of fish in a thin tomato sauce that's between a soup and a stew. I had been told by a national in the city that Salona's sole disadvantage was that it was addicting. Suffice to say that thereafter whenever I found it on a restaurant menu, I ordered it. When served with cooked rice or mashed potatoes, Salona makes for a wholesome and tasty main course for a large family or a small gathering of friends.

Serves 8
Prep time: 45 minutes
Marinating time: 30 minutes
Cooking time: 1 hour

3 tablespoons freshly squeezed lemon juice
1 1/2 teaspoons salt
2 teaspoons Arabian Gulf Spice Mix
  (Baharat) (page 28)

3 lbs (1.5 kg) grouper (hamour) fillet, cut into
  large pieces (substitute cod, haddock,
  halibut, sea bass, tilapia or other white
  firm-flesh fish)
All-purpose flour, for dredging the fish
Oil, for frying
2 onions, minced
1/2 jalapeño or other fresh finger-length green
  chili pepper of your choice, finely chopped

4 cloves garlic, crushed to a paste
  (see page 30)
3 tomatoes, finely chopped
4 tablespoons tomato paste dissolved in
  1 cup (250 ml) water
2 tablespoons finely chopped fresh
  coriander leaves (cilantro)
1 lime, finely chopped
1 cup (250 ml) water

1 Combine the lemon juice, 1 teaspoon of the salt and 1 teaspoon of the Arabian Gulf Spice Mix in a small bowl. Rub the fish pieces with the mixture and let marinate in the refrigerator for 30 minutes.

2 Lightly dredge the fish pieces with the flour.

3 Pour 1 inch (2.5 cm) of oil into a medium saucepan with a lid and set over medium heat. When the oil is hot, shallow-fry the fish pieces, turning them over once, until light brown, about 8 minutes. Remove and drain on paper towels.

4 Remove all but 4 tablespoons of the oil from the saucepan. Add the onion and chili pepper and sauté over medium heat for about 10 minutes, or until they begin to brown. Add the garlic, tomato, the dissolved tomato paste and coriander leaves and cook, covered, over medium-low heat for 10 minutes, stirring a number of times. Stir in the chopped lime, the remaining salt and Arabian Gulf Spice Mix. Cook for another 3 minutes, stirring frequently. Add the water and bring to a boil. Cover and simmer over low heat for 10 minutes, adding a little more water if the sauce becomes too thick. Add the fried fish, cover, and simmer for another 5 minutes.

5 Carefully place the fish and sauce on a serving platter and serve.

Makes 20 fish cakes
Prep time: 45 minutes
Cooking time: 45 minutes

2 lbs (1kg) grouper (hamour) fillet, cut into
   3 to 4-in (7.5 to 10-cm) pieces (substitute
   cod, haddock, halibut, sea bass, tilapia or
   other white firm-fleshed fish)
1 large onion, minced
1 cup (90 g) fine bread crumbs
1/2 cup (25 g) chopped fresh coriander
   leaves (cilantro)
2 large eggs, beaten
4 cloves garlic, crushed to a paste
   (see page 30)
2 tablespoons freshly squeezed lemon juice
2 teaspoons baking powder
1 teaspoon salt
1 teaspoon Arabian Gulf Spice Mix (Baharat)
   (page 28)
1 teaspoon ground turmeric
1 teaspoon ground cumin
1/2 teaspoon ground black pepper
Oil, for deep-frying

1 Place the fish in a food processor and
process for 2 minutes, or until it has the
texture of pie dough. Transfer to a mixing
bowl. Add the rest of the ingredients, except
the oil, and mix thoroughly. Form the mixture into small cakes about 2 to 3 inches
(5 to 7.5 cm) in diameter. Set aside.
2 Pour 2 inches (5 cm) of oil into a medium
saucepan and set over medium-high heat.
Heat the oil to a minimum temperature of
345°F (175°C) and no higher than 375°F
(190°C), checking with a deep-frying or
candy thermometer. If you do not have a
thermometer, drop a small piece of bread
in the oil. If the bread browns quickly
(1 minute or less), the oil is the right temperature. Alternatively you can throw a drop
of water in the oil. If the water sizzles upon
contact, the oil is ready.
3 Deep-fry the fish cakes, a few at a time so
that they do not touch other, until golden
brown, about 8 to 10 minutes. Remove with
a slotted spoon and set on paper towels to
drain. They can be served hot or cold.

pERfECT fiSh CAKES
Samak Kufta

These tasty and flavorful fish cakes found in the United Arab Emirates are also popular in
other Arab Gulf countries. Samak Kufta is a unique combination of fish and complementing
ingredients that produce a mildly spicy fish cake. Although its texture is somewhat similar
to the Arab East's meat *kufta* (made with lamb or beef), the UAE's fish kufta differs with its
addition of garlic, lemon juice, turmeric and even breadcrumbs, reflecting the numerous
cultures of that area. The type of fish used to prepare these cakes varies from restaurant to
restaurant and from home to home. Serve Samak Kufta as snacks or along with a salad for a
delicious main meal.

kuwaiti fish curry

Samak Karee

This curry dish probably came to Kuwait from the Indian sub-continent, either with the Kuwaiti traders or with the thousands of workers lured to the Arab Gulf states by the petroleum industry. Curry dishes are today an integral part of the kitchens in all the Arab Gulf countries. They are as a rule not as hot as those in the Indian sub-continent, having been adapted to the tastes of the Gulf Arabs. Although many of the best restaurants in Kuwait include this dish on their menu, it is always best to seek out the smaller local establishments to try a more authentic version. In these smaller places, Samak Karee will more likely have the taste of the home-cooked version—one that would have been passed down through generations. The more expensive restaurants tend to tone down the spices to ascribe to the tastes of tourists. Serve with Saudi-Style White Rice (page 28) and Coriander and Yogurt Salad (page 30) as well as Crunchy Pickled Garlic (page 26).

Serves 4 to 6
Prep time: 35 minutes
Cooking time: 1 hour 10 minutes

1/2 cup (125 ml) oil
2 onions, sliced
6 cloves garlic, minced
1 small jalapeño or other fresh finger-length green chili pepper of your choice, deseeded and thinly sliced
1 tablespoon peeled and grated fresh ginger
3 tomatoes (about 1 lb/500 g), finely chopped
1/2 teaspoon salt
1 1/2 teaspoons curry powder
1/2 teaspoon ground cumin
1/4 teaspoon freshly grated nutmeg
1 1/2 cups (375 ml) water
2 lbs (1 kg) grouper (hamour) fillet, cut into 3 to 4-in (7.5 to 10-cm) pieces (substitute cod, haddock, halibut, sea bass, tilapia or other white firm-fleshed fish)

1 Heat the oil in a large skillet over medium-low heat. Add the onion, garlic, chili pepper and ginger and sauté for 12 minutes.
2 Stir in the tomato and simmer for 8 minutes.
3 Stir in the salt, spices and water. Cover and simmer for 20 minute.
4 Add the fish pieces, cover, and simmer over low heat for 25 minutes, or until the fish is done.

Serves about 6
Prep time: 20 minutes
Standing time: 2 hours

1 large onion, preferably Spanish,
  thinly sliced
2 tablespoons salt
One 6-oz (170-g) can light or dark
  tuna, drained and flaked with a
  fork
3 tablespoons freshly squeezed
  lemon juice
2 tablespoons extra-virgin olive oil
  (reduce to 1 tablespoon if using
  tuna packed in oil)
1 teaspoon ground cumin
1/4 teaspoon ground red pepper
  (cayenne)
2 teaspoons dried oregano
1 recipe Saudi-Style White Rice
  (page 28)

1 Thoroughly mix together the onion and the salt in a bowl. Cover with a cheese cloth or tea towel and allow to stand for 2 hours.
2 Wash the onion in water several times and drain after each washing, thoroughly draining the onion after the last washing. Place the drained onion in a mixing bowl. Add the remaining ingredients, except the rice, and mix thoroughly.
3 Spread the cooked white rice on a platter and cover evenly with the tuna mixture. Serve immediately.

εasy Tuna salad and rice,
omani-style

Mezroota

This simplified form of a light traditional Omani dish is usually eaten during the hot summer months. Traditionally, a type of dried Omani fish soaked in water is used and boiled with turmeric. However, tuna makes a great substitute. Don't be put off by the quantity of onions used in this dish; the process of salting them draws out their bitterness. In fact, when I was in Oman a woman told me that she always places the salted onions outside in the direct sun for two hours. She said the combination of the sun and salt cut down on the sharp taste of the onions. I do not know if this is folklore or true, but if you have sunny days you can try it!

SAUTÉED FISh FILLETS WITh LENTILS AND RICE

Makbous Samak

Besides roast lamb, the Arab Gulf countries are noted for their fish dishes. This tasty dish, popular in all the Arab Gulf countries, is an example of fish at its best. At times, it takes the place of roasted lamb for special occasions. This traditional dish is prepared with rice and either meat and/or seafood. Typically it is served from a large communal platter at wedding feasts and banquets. For a great tasting combination, pair this dish with Creamy Cucumber and Bell Pepper Salad (page 46).

Serves 8
Prep time: 30 minutes
Cooking time: 1 hour
Soaking time: 8 hours
Standing time: 30 minutes

6 tablespoons (3/4 stick/85 g) butter
2 cups (400 g) uncooked Basmati or other white long-grain rice, soaked for 5 minutes, thoroughly rinsed and drained (see page 24)
1/2 cup (100 g) brown lentils, soaked overnight in 5 1/2 cups (1.3 liters) water and drained (reserve the water)
1/2 teaspoon ground black pepper
1/2 teaspoon ground cumin
1/2 teaspoon ground ginger
Generous pinch of ground red pepper (cayenne)
2 1/2 teaspoons salt
4 lbs (1.75 kg) grouper (hamour) fillet, cut into 2-in (5-cm) pieces (substitute halibut, cod, haddock, sea bass or other white firm-fleshed fish)
1 teaspoon garlic powder
1/2 cup (125 ml) oil
4 onions, thinly sliced

1 Melt the butter in a medium saucepan with a lid over medium heat. Add the rice and stir constantly for 2 minutes. Add the lentils with their soaking water, black pepper, cumin, ginger, ground red pepper and 1 teaspoon of the salt and bring to a boil. Cover and cook over medium-low heat for 20 minutes, stirring a few times. Remove from the heat, stir, and cover. Allow the rice and lentils to cook in their own steam for 30 minutes.
2 In the meantime, sprinkle the fish pieces on both sides with the garlic powder and the remaining salt. Set aside.
3 Heat 4 tablespoons of the oil in a medium skillet over medium heat. Add the onion and sauté until golden brown. Set aside, but keep warm.
4 Heat the remaining oil in another medium skillet over medium heat. Add the fish and fry for about 8 minutes, turning over once or until done. (The fish will flake easily with a fork when done.) Do not overcook. Set aside.
5 Place the rice and the lentils on a serving platter and spread the onion evenly over the top. Place the fish pieces over the onion and serve.

FRIED FISH WITH SPICY RICE
Samak 'Aysh

Local and regional dishes are slowly creeping onto the menus of Dubai's large hotels and fine restaurants where they are often adapted by enthusiastic chefs for the tastes of tourists and to excellent results. By making local foods available to guests, they are insured an important place in Dubai's culinary world, and allow expatriates and visitors to get an authentic feel of Arabia. Unlike during the first years of Dubai's development, today, the aroma and taste of this Emirate's native foods have become a permanent feature on hotel and restaurant menus. This hot and spicy fish dish is an example of a local dish that is now served in restaurants and hotels. You may notice that this dish is somewhat similar to Lightly Breaded Fish in a Tangy Tomato Sauce (page 96). However, Samak 'Aysh has rice as an ingredient while the former is a stew served with rice. Cardamom-Scented Fruit Salad (page 136) is a welcome side salad with this hot and spicy fish dish.

Serves 6
Prep time: 50 minutes
Soaking time: 30 minutes
Marinating time: 30 minutes
Cooking time: about 1 hour
Standing time: 30 minutes

2 tablespoons freshly squeezed lemon juice
1 teaspoon salt
2 teaspoons Arabian Gulf Spice Mix (Baharat) (page 28)
2 lbs (1kg) grouper (hamour) fillet, cut into large pieces (substitute cod, haddock, halibut, sea bass, tilapia or other white firm-fleshed fish)
Oil, for deep-frying
All-purpose flour, for dredging the fish
1 onion, minced
1/2 jalapeño or other fresh finger-length green chili pepper of your choice, finely chopped
4 cloves garlic, crushed to a paste (see page 30)
2 tomatoes, finely chopped
4 tablespoons tomato paste dissolved in 1 cup (250 ml) water
2 tablespoons finely chopped fresh coriander leaves (cilantro)
1/2 lemon, finely chopped
4 cups (1 liter) water
2 cups (400 g) uncooked Basmati or other white long-grain rice, soaked for 30 minutes, thoroughly rinsed and drained (see page 24)

1 Combine the lemon juice, 1/2 teaspoon of the salt and 1 teaspoon of the Arabian Gulf Spice Mix in a small bowl. Rub the fish pieces with the mixture and let marinate in the refrigerator for 30 minutes.

2 Pour 2 inches (5 cm) of oil into a large skillet with a lid and set over medium-high heat. Heat the oil to a minimum temperature of 345°F (175°C) and no higher than 375°F (190°C), checking with a deep-frying or candy thermometer. If you do not have a thermometer, drop a small piece of bread in the oil. If the bread browns quickly (1 minute or less), the oil is the right temperature. Alternatively you can throw a drop of water in the oil. If the water sizzles upon contact, the oil is ready.

3 Roll the fish pieces in the flour, shake off excess flour, and deep-fry until light brown, about 10 minutes, turning over once. Remove the fish pieces with a slotted spoon and drain on paper towels. Set aside, but keep warm.

4 Remove all but 4 tablespoons of the oil from the skillet. Add the onion and the chili pepper and sauté over medium heat for about 10 minutes, or until they begin to brown. Add the garlic, tomato, dissolved tomato paste and coriander leaves and bring to a boil. Cook over medium-low heat for 10 minutes, stirring a number of times. Stir in the lemon, the remaining salt and Arabian Gulf Spice Mix, and cook for another 3 minutes, stirring frequently. Add the water and bring to a boil. Cover and simmer for 5 minutes. Stir in the rice, cover, and cook over medium-low heat for 20 minutes, stirring a number of times to ensure the rice does not stick to the bottom of the skillet. Remove from the heat and stir. Cover and allow to cook in its own steam for 30 minutes.

5 Place the rice on a platter and arrange the fish on top and serve.

Fried Fish with Spicy Rice

shrimp balls in a tangy sauce Chebeh Rubyan

In the Arab Gulf countries, various seafood dishes come in many varieties. Crowning these are those made with shrimp. During my many trips to that part of the world there literally was no shrimp dish that I did not like. Usually prepared from fresh shrimp and moderately spiced, in the main, they were tasty and wholesome. The unusual taste of pomegranate syrup mixed with Arabian Gulf Spice Mix and fresh coriander leaves is what gives these shrimp balls their unique taste. This dish, one of my favorites, is likely of Malaysian origin as Chebeh is an island off the east coast of Peninsular Malaysia. Since this is formally an East Asian recipe, rice flour is called for as an ingredient—rice flour being the prevalent flour in that region of the world. However other types of flour can be substituted, as noted in the recipe.

Serves 4
Prep time: about 45 minutes
Refrigeration time: 30 minutes
Cooking time: 1 hour 15 minutes

1 lb (500 g) medium-size (16 to 20 count) fresh shrimp, peeled and de-veined
4 tablespoons finely chopped fresh coriander leaves (cilantro)
1/2 teaspoon ground turmeric
1 teaspoon salt
4 tablespoons rice flour or cake or pastry flour
1 large egg, beaten
5 tablespoons (2/3 stick/70 g) butter
3 large onions, minced (3 cups/550 g)
1 teaspoon Arabian Gulf Spice Mix (Baharat) (page 28)
2 cloves garlic, crushed to a paste (see page 30)
2 tablespoons pomegranate syrup
1 cup (250 ml) water
1 cup (255 g) stewed tomatoes (about 2/3 of one 14.5-oz/411-g can)
Generous pinch of ground red pepper (cayenne)

1 Process the shrimp and coriander leaves into a paste in a food processor. Transfer the paste to a mixing bowl and add the turmeric, 1/2 teaspoon of the salt, rice flour and egg and mix thoroughly. Cover and place in the refrigerator.

2 Preheat the oven to 350°F (175°C).

3 To make the filling, melt 3 tablespoons of the butter in a medium skillet. Add 2 cups (370 g) of the minced onion and cook over medium-low heat for 10 minutes. Stir in 1/2 teaspoon of the Arabian Gulf Spice Mix and remove from the heat.

4 To make the sauce, melt the remaining butter in a medium saucepan. Add the remaining onion and cook over medium-low heat for 10 minutes. Add the remaining salt and Arabian Gulf Spice Mix, and the rest of the ingredients. Reduce the heat to low, cover, and cook for 10 minutes. Transfer to a 9 x 13 x 2-inch (23 x 33 x 5-cm) baking pan.

5 In the meantime, take about 1 heaping tablespoon of the shrimp paste and flatten between the palms of your hands. Place 1 teaspoon of the filling in the center. Wrap the flattened shrimp paste up around the filling to form a closed ball. Continue with the rest of the paste and filling. Gently place the shrimp balls in the baking pan with the sauce. Cover and bake for 40 minutes. Serve immediately with Saudi-Style White Rice (page 28).

wbole fisb witb garlic and fresb coriander

Hamour Mahshi

In Dubai, I, with a group of friends, enjoyed this dish in one of the people's restaurants. Forget the fork and knife, it was finger-licking good! While I enjoyed my grouper, I thought of the long association of fish with Arab culinary tradition. From the storehouse of stories relating to fish, there is one of a host who wanted to impress his dinner guest, the Caliph Harun al-Rashid. When the Caliph was served what seemed to be a whole fish, he asked his host why the fish had been cut into such small slices and then re-shaped into the form of a fish. The answer? This fabulous treat was composed of over 150 fish tongues which had cost the host over 1,000 *dirhams*. The Caliph, however, did not appreciate this needless expense and stopped eating. Instead, he ordered his host to distribute over 1,000 dirhams to the poor to make up for the host's wastefulness. A large *hamour* will often be the main dish at a feast-meal when served over a bed of rice and garnished with limes. If grouper is not available, snapper or halibut are good substitutes or, for a less authentic but still delicious taste, try salmon. Diced Vegetable Salad with Tahini Dressing (page 52) goes well with this dish, and any type of fish or fish dish, for that matter.

Serves 4 to 6
Prep time: 1 hour
Cooking time: 45 minutes

1 whole 3-lb (1.5-kg) grouper (hamour),
    fins and tail clipped, and thoroughly
    washed (substitute red snapper or bass)
6 cloves garlic, crushed to a paste
    (see page 30)
1/2 cup (125 ml) freshly squeezed lemon
    juice
2 teaspoons salt
1 teaspoon ground black pepper
2 onions, thinly sliced
1 cup (50 g) finely chopped fresh coriander
    leaves (cilantro)
3 tomatoes, finely chopped
2 red bell peppers, deseeded and finely
    chopped
2 teaspoons Arabian Gulf Spice Mix
    (Baharat) (page 28)
Generous pinch of ground cardamom
1 cup (250 ml) extra-virgin olive oil

1 Rub the fish inside and out with half of the garlic, 2 tablespoons of the lemon juice, 1 teaspoon of the salt and 1/2 teaspoon of the black pepper. Set aside.

2 Combine the onion, coriander leaves, tomato, pepper, Arabian Gulf Spice Mix, cardamom, the remaining garlic, salt and black pepper in a bowl. Set aside.

3 Blend the remaining 6 tablespoons of lemon juice with the oil in a blender until fluffy. Pour half of this lemon mixture into the bowl with the tomato and onion mixture. Stir to mix well.

4 Preheat the oven to 350°F (175°C).

5 Spread one-third of the tomato and onion mixture, a little bit wider than the width of the fish, onto the bottom of a greased baking pan large enough to hold the fish. Stuff the fish with another one-third of the tomato and onion mixture. Place the fish over the mixture in the baking pan. Spoon the remaining one-third of the mixture over the top of the stuffed fish. Pour the remaining lemon-oil mixture over it.

6 Cover with foil then bake for 40 minutes. Uncover and scrape any vegetables still on top of the fish into the baking pan and set aside. Transfer the fish to a sheet pan or broiler pan and place under the broiler for 5 minutes, or until the fish begins to brown. Serve with the sauce and the bits of vegetables.

ELEGANT SAUTÉED FISH FILLETS WITH NUTTY RICE

Sayadia

The Arab East's coastline has given Arab cuisine Sayadia, a dish of delicately spiced fish pieces fried with onions and spices that are baked over rice. Similar to a fish pilaf, Sayadia is also referred to as "fisherman's food." This version of Sayadia is found in Saudi Arabia. Although I have eaten it in a number of restaurants throughout the Arab Gulf, the Saudi type is my favorite because of the use of garlic and the touch of hot cayenne. Also, in this version the fish fillets are fried in butter and not in the standard olive oil, which gives the dish a unique taste. What makes this dish very Gulf-like is the use of *hamour*, the favored fish in the region. However, other white fish will work just as well.

Serves 4 to 6
Prep time: 20 minutes
Soaking time: 5 minutes
Cooking time: 1 hour

1 lb (500 g) grouper (hamour) fillet, cut into 3 to 4-in (7.5 to 10-cm) pieces
    (substitute tilapia, haddock, flounder, Kingfish or other white firm-fleshed fish)
1/2 teaspoon ground black pepper
1/2 teaspoon ground cumin
6 tablespoons (3/4 stick/85 g) butter
1 large onion, minced
2 cloves garlic, crushed to a paste (see page 30)
1/2 cup (50 g) pine nuts
1 cup (200 g) uncooked Basmati or other white long-grain rice, soaked for
    5 minutes, thoroughly rinsed and drained (see page 24)
1 teaspoon salt
Generous pinch of ground red pepper (cayenne)
2 cups (500 ml) water

1 Sprinkle the fish with the black pepper and cumin and set aside.
2 Melt the butter in a medium skillet over medium heat. Sauté the fish for 6 minutes, turning over once. Remove the fish with a slotted spoon and set aside. (Do not discard the butter.)
3 Preheat the oven to 350°F (175°C).
4 In the same skillet, adding a little more butter if needed, sauté the onion, garlic and pine nut over medium-low heat for 10 minutes. Add the rice, and stir continuously for 1 minute. Stir in the salt, ground red pepper and water and bring to a boil. Transfer into a greased 2-quart (2-liter) casserole dish and arrange the fish evenly over the top. Cover and bake for 40 minutes, or until the rice is cooked. Remove the cover during the last 10 minutes of baking. Serve hot from the casserole.

SAUDI-STYLE SHRIMP 'N RICE
Ruz bil Jambury

Just as meat with rice is popular in the Arab Gulf, the nationals have also incorporated the treasures of the sea with this important staple, as exemplified in this recipe. Shrimp dishes have become part of the national pride of the region. Traditionally, as a guest, one would be offered fish and rice dishes by those living on the long coastline of the Arabian Peninsula, rather than the standard lamb and rice meals. After all, this was their main type of meat from the days of old. And the advantage of dining along the coastline? Guaranteed fresh fish and shellfish on a daily basis whether from the fish markets or straight from the sea. This Saudi Arabian dish has a tangy tomato-y, garlicky flavor with the fresh coriander leaves giving it the just-right accent. And even though my personal favorite way of enjoying shrimp is frying them with garlic, I love this dish—a testament to the pleasures of juicy shrimp cooked with rice. Shrimp should always be cooked quickly in order to preserve their sweet, delicate flavor. Cooking them takes from three to eight minutes—when pink, they are done.

Serves 6
Prep time: 20 minutes
Cooking time: 30 minutes
Standing time: 30 minutes

1 lb (500 g) medium-size (16 to 20 count) fresh shrimp, peeled and de-veined
1 1/2 teaspoons salt
6 tablespoons (2/3 stick/85 g) butter
1 large onion, minced
4 cloves garlic, crushed to a paste (see page 30)
1/2 teaspoon ground black pepper
1 teaspoon Arabian Gulf Spice Mix (Baharat) (page 28)
2 cups (400 g) uncooked Basmati or other white long-grain rice, soaked for 5 minutes, thoroughly rinsed and drained (see page 24)
3 cups (750 ml) water
1 cup (250 ml) tomato juice
2 tablespoons finely chopped fresh coriander leaves (cilantro), for garnish

1 Mix gently the shrimp with 1/2 teaspoon of the salt in a bowl and set aside.
2 Melt the butter in a medium skillet with a lid over medium-low heat. Add the onion and garlic and fry, uncovered, for 5 minutes.
3 Stir in the shrimp, pepper, Arabian Gulf Spice Mix, the remaining salt and more butter if necessary and cook for 6 minutes, still over medium-low heat, stirring frequently. Stir in the rest of the ingredients, except the coriander leaves, and bring to a boil. Cover and cook over medium-low heat for 12 minutes. Stir and remove from the heat.
4 Cover and allow to cook in its own steam for 30 minutes. Garnish with the chopped coriander leaves and serve warm with Refreshing Green Salad (page 51) or Fresh Cucumber and Tomato Salad with Sumac (page 49).

Saudi-Style Shrimp 'n Rice

CHAPTER 7
VEGETARIAN dishes

All over the world many people are heading down the vegetarian path and some inhabitants of the Arab Gulf countries are gradually getting on the same bandwagon. However, in these nations, a strict vegetarian diet does not have a mass following—that is—as of yet. In the past, fresh produce was a rare item on the daily menu. It has only been since the advent of oil age wealth (allowing for the transportation of vegetables and fruits and then irrigation) that fruit and vegetables have become abundant in the markets.

Initially, fruits and vegetables (and the recipes for them) were imported from the Greater Syria area, Iraq, Iran, the Indian sub-continent and beyond but now they have become home grown commodities. Today, in what were almost wholly meat-eating lands, one can revel in a sumptuous vegetarian feast at any time of the year.

During my many trips to the Arab Gulf countries, I often enjoyed great vegetable dishes in the elegant hotels and in the homes of the affluent. The days when one served or ate the best cut of meat to prove their status in society are now in the past. All levels of society, including the affluent, now cherish their vegetable dishes. No longer is meat the only main staff of life.

And even though most of the vegetarian dishes to be found today in the Arab Gulf countries had their origins somewhere else, Arab cooks have enhanced them with the addition of different herbs and spices, making their own unique versions. Due to the flourishing trade in the past with the Indian sub-continent and the influx of a vast number of workers after the oil boom from around the world, there can be found today in the markets of all the Gulf countries aromatics (garlic and ginger), herbs and spices galore to enhance these new non-meat dishes. Fresh or dried herbs such as chervil, basil, coriander leaves (cilantro), mint, parsley, tarragon, oregano, and thyme along with spices such as aniseed, cardamom, cinnamon, cloves, cumin, nutmeg, black pepper, saffron, and turmeric are all readily available and used to produce mouthwatering recipes. Fresh or dried chili peppers are added for a fiery kick. These flavorings, in addition to dried lemons and limes, make the vegetarian dishes of the Arab Gulf countries irresistible and satisfying.

spicy falafel patties

Falafel is very common today in the Arab Gulf countries, especially in the United Arab Emirates. From first class restaurants to the small "fast food" shops, Abu Dhabi and Dubai boast they make the best. In the past Falafel could only be found in the Greater Syria area and in Egypt, where it is said they were first set upon the tables of the Pharaohs. Today, the Arabs think of them as the universal Arab food. What was once only a hidden vegetarian pleasure among the Egyptians and Palestinians, it has now gained popularity throughout, not only the Arab Gulf, but the entire eastern Arab World. Also, menus of many restaurants throughout various countries in Europe, North America and South America give evidence that Falafel has traveled in popularity from the east to the west. There are various types of Falafel but all have broad beans or chickpeas or a combination of both as basic ingredients. Yet, either way, these crunchy, spicy vegetarian patties are great eaten on their own, in a pita bread pocket or on a bed of salad. Falafel mix can be purchased already prepared in a powder form in most large urban centers in North America. However, they in no way match those prepared from scratch. Try this recipe and see for yourself. There are three tricks to remember when making Falafel: First, do not be tempted to use canned chickpeas—the patties will become soggy and break apart, and the flavor will be disappointing; second, be sure the chickpeas are well ground or the patties will break up when frying; and third, Falafel will become dry if they darken too much in the deep-frying process, so watch them carefully when deep-frying.

Spicy Falafel Patties

Makes about 5 dozen or 10 dozen
Prep time: 1 hour
Soaking time: 24 hours
Standing time: 2 hours
Cooking time: 1 hour 30 minutes

1 small bunch fresh parsley (about 1/4 lb/ 125 g), thoroughly washed and drained
2 cups (400 g) dried chickpeas, soaked for 24 hours in 8 cups (2 liters) water in which 1/2 teaspoon baking soda has been dissolved, and drained
2 onions, minced
1 cup (50 g) finely chopped fresh coriander leaves (cilantro)
1/2 head garlic, cloves separated, peeled and crushed
1 small jalapeño pepper or other fresh finger-length green chili pepper of your choice, chopped
1 1/2 teaspoons salt
1 teaspoon ground black pepper
1 teaspoon ground cumin
1 teaspoon ground coriander
1/2 teaspoon ground cinnamon
2 teaspoons baking soda
1 large egg, beaten
Oil, for deep-frying

1 Finely chop the parsley. You should have about 2 cups (100 g). Place the chopped parsley and the rest of the ingredients, except the oil,

in a food processor. Process into a paste. Allow to stand for 2 hours.

2 Form the chickpea paste into patties by hand or by using a falafel mold or form into small balls if they are to be served as appetizers. See "Falafel Tips" (on facing page) for guidance on forming falafel.

3 Pour 2 to 4 inches (5 to 10 cm) of oil into a medium saucepan and set over medium-high heat. Heat the oil to a minimum temperature of 345°F (175°C) and no higher than 375°F (190°C), checking with a deep-frying or candy thermometer. If you do not have a thermometer, drop a small piece of bread in the oil. If the bread browns quickly (1 minute or less), the oil is the right temperature. Alternatively you can throw a drop of water in the oil. If the water sizzles upon contact, the oil is ready.

4 Deep-fry the patties in batches until they turn light brown, about 8 minutes, turning them over once if needed. Remove with a slotted spoon and set on paper towels to drain. While deep-frying, between batches, re-check the temperature to make sure it's still between 345° and 375°F (175° and 190°C). (You may need to let the oil re-heat between batches.) Remove with a slotted spoon and drain on paper towels.

5 Serve as a side dish or main course or on a bed of Diced Vegetable Salad with Tahini Dressing (page 52) tucked inside a Pita Bread (page 122) pocket with 1 or 2 tablespoons of Creamy Garlic Sauce (page 27), if desired.

hearty Bulghur simmered in Tangy Yogurt

Jareesh bil Laban

This is another of the Saudi Arabian dishes made from coarsely ground grain known as *jareesh*, which most likely originated with the Bedouin of the region. Eventually, the dish made its way to the tables of the cities of the Arab East. Evidence of the centuries-old migration of jareesh can be found in the medieval Arabic culinary texts written in both Baghdad and Aleppo. Although, the original recipe calls for jareesh, in my view, the wheat product bulghur enhances the dish. The dish has a smooth taste and is thick and similar in texture to cooked oatmeal or porridge.

Serves from 6 to 8
Prep time: 20 minutes
Soaking time: 15 minutes
Cooking time: 1 hour 10 minutes

2 cups (500 g) store-bought or Homemade Plain Yogurt (page 31)
2 cups (500 ml) water
1 teaspoon salt
4 tablespoons extra-virgin olive oil
1 cup (250 g) coarse bulghur, soaked for 15 minutes in warm water and drained
1 small jalapeño or other fresh finger-length green chili pepper of your choice, finely chopped
1¹/2 teaspoons ground cumin
¹/2 teaspoon ground black pepper
¹/2 teaspoon Arabian Gulf Spice Mix (Baharat) (page 28)
3 tablespoons melted butter, for drizzling over the top

1 Bring the yogurt, water and salt to a boil in a medium saucepan with a lid over medium heat, stirring continuously in one direction. As soon as the yogurt begins to boil, stir in the rest of the ingredients, except the butter. Cover and simmer over low heat for 1 hour, or until the bulghur is well-cooked, stirring a number of times. Add more water if the bulghur becomes too thick and begins to stick to the bottom of the saucepan.
2 Transfer to a food processor and process for 2 minutes or until the texture is smooth. Return the bulghur mixture to the saucepan and re-heat. Pour into individual serving bowls and drizzle the butter over the top and serve.

FALAFEL TIPS: The trick to successfully forming falafel by hand is to keep the dough from sticking to your hands. To do this, dampen your hands with a bit of cold water before shaping the falafel dough (and re-wet them before forming another falafel). Another simple way to avoid getting sticky dough on your hands while working with the dough is to use two tablespoons: use one to pick up some of the batter, press it down firmly in the spoon, and then push it off the spoon with another spoon into the hot oil If you are using a falafel mold, dip the mold in cold water then shake off any excess water before placing the falafel batter in the mold. This will make it easy for the falafel batter to slide off the mold into the hot oil.

PURÉED LENTILS WITH FRIED GARLIC AND PITA CROUTONS Fattat 'Adas

Lentils are perhaps one of the healthiest foods in the world, being low in fat but high in protein—higher even than meat in equal portions. This dish beautifully showcases the best of lentils' qualities. It is the perfect example of a hearty and nourishing yet tasty vegetarian meal. Found in Saudi Arabia, but is also known to a somewhat lesser extent in all parts of the eastern Arab World, this tasty dish can be described as a pottage or a thick soup. It is an interesting combination of ingredients with a mixture of lentils, tomatoes and toasted pieces of bread. The dish is a near full meal in itself. Although Fattat 'Adas uses beef broth as its base, rendering it a "quasi-vegetarian" dish, vegetable broth can be substituted to make it a 100-percent pure veggie stew.

Serves about 6
Prep time: 35 minutes
Standing time: 5 minutes
Cooking time: 1 hour 10 minutes

5 cups (1.25 liters) beef broth
1 cup (200 g) dried brown or green lentils, rinsed
2 teaspoons ground cumin
1 teaspoon salt
1 teaspoon ground black pepper
Generous pinch of ground red pepper (cayenne)
1 large onion, minced
2 tomatoes, finely chopped
1 head garlic, cloves separated, peeled and crushed
6 tablespoons extra-virgin olive oil
1 to 2 store-bought or homemade Pita Bread (page 122), cut into small pieces and lightly toasted (2 pitas will give the fattat a thicker texture)

1 Place the broth, lentils, cumin, salt, black pepper, ground red pepper, onion, tomato, half of the garlic and 2 tablespoons of the oil in a medium saucepan with a lid. Bring to a boil, cover, and cook over medium-low heat for 1 hour, or until the lentils are well-cooked (you should be able to mash them easily with a fork), adding extra water if necessary.
2 Remove from the heat and allow to cool. Place the lentil mixture in a food processor and process for a few minutes, or until smooth. Return to the saucepan and reheat.
3 Heat the remaining oil in a skillet over medium heat. Add the remaining garlic and cook, stirring frequently, until it just begins to brown. Set aside.
4 Spread the toasted bread on the bottom of a large serving bowl then spread the processed lentils over the top. Spread the fried garlic with its oil evenly over the top and serve.

NOTE: This dish is usually served family style in one dish so that those who do not like bread can scoop from the top and those who do can dip to the bottom.

spinach and chickpeas with garlic and lemon

This dish is a reflection of Saudi Arabia's history and contacts with other peoples outside of the Peninsula. With the influx of pilgrims from around the world, Saudi cuisine evolved from a meat-based Bedouin diet to one with spices and new ingredients, especially vegetables. Such is the case with Spinach and Chickpeas with Garlic and Lemon, probably more nutritious and high in fiber than most any other dish. One of my grandsons, who as a child never favored spinach or chickpeas, came to visit me one day. When he walked into the kitchen, he asked me, "*Jiddy* (grandfather), what smells so good?" I told him that it was a Saudi dish made with spinach and chickpeas. There was a split-second hesitation and then he asked, "Can I try some?" Now, I don't know if this was because he loved his grandfather or loved the aroma as he hovered around the stove, but he handed me an empty bowl and asked me to fill it up. The next thing I knew, he was asking for seconds! The dash of lemon and the fried garlic give this dish a zesty, yet elegant taste.

Serves 4
Prep time: 25 minutes
Cooking time: 20 minutes

4 tablespoons extra-virgin olive oil
1 large onion, thinly sliced
4 cloves garlic, crushed to a paste
  (see page 30)
1/2 teaspoon ground cumin
10 oz (285 g) fresh spinach, preferably
  baby leaf, thoroughly washed, drained
  and chopped (remove stems if using
  large spinach leaves)
2 cups (400 g) drained cooked or canned
  chickpeas (see page 17 for canned/
  dried equivalents)
1 tablespoon butter
1 tablespoon finely chopped fresh basil
  leaves or 1 teaspoon dried basil leaves
3/4 teaspoon salt
1/2 teaspoon ground black pepper
Generous pinch of freshly grated nutmeg
2 tablespoons freshly squeezed lemon
  juice

1 Heat the oil in a large skillet over medium-low heat. Add the onion and fry for 8 minutes. Add the garlic and cumin and cook for 3 minutes, stirring frequently.
2 Add the rest of the ingredients, except the lemon juice, and increase the heat to medium. Cook for 4 minutes, stirring frequently. Stir in the lemon juice and serve hot or cold with Saudi-Style White Rice (page 28).

fresh herb omelet Ujja

This Arab Gulf dish is a thick, filled omelet that resembles a Spanish Tortilla or an Italian Frittata. In Iran it is called Kookoo and in the Arab countries, Ujja. It includes an interesting combination of herbs, spices and walnuts. A multi-purpose dish, it is excellent for breakfast or it can be served as a main course for lunch or dinner and excels, as well, as a snack. For those who love fresh herbs, this omelet is a dish extraordinaire. It can be served hot or at room temperature.

Serves about 6
Prep time: 40 minutes
Cooking time: 50 minutes

2 cups (200 g) finely chopped green onions
   (scallions)
1/2 cup (28 g) finely chopped spinach
   leaves
4 tablespoons finely chopped fresh parsley
4 tablespoons finely chopped fresh dill
4 tablespoons finely chopped fresh
   coriander leaves (cilantro)
1 zucchini, 6 to 8-in (15 to 20-cm) long,
   finely chopped
4 tablespoons finely ground walnuts
6 eggs, beaten
1/2 teaspoon salt
1/2 teaspoon ground black pepper
1/2 teaspoon ground turmeric
2 tablespoons butter, melted
6 cups (1.5 kg) store-bought or Homemade
   Plain Yogurt (page 31)

1 Preheat the oven to 350°F (175°C).
2 Mix together the green onion, spinach, parsley, dill, coriander, zucchini and walnut in a mixing bowl. Set aside.
3 Combine the egg, salt, black pepper, turmeric and butter in another mixing bowl. Add to the zucchini and herb mixture and stir to combine.
4 Transfer into a greased casserole dish and bake uncovered for 50 minutes, or until the top of the omelet begins to brown. Serve warm with the yogurt as a side-dish.

spicy chickpea stew
Al-Nikhi

Simple to prepare, delicious and nutritious, this traditional Arab Gulf dish has a centuries-old place in the cuisine of the Arabian Gulf. At times, broad beans are substituted for the chickpeas, and the dish is called Bajelah; at other times, black-eyed peas are substituted, and the dish is called Luba. Unlike fresh vegetables, dried pulses have been available in the souks of the Arabian Peninsula for centuries. For many they were more important than fish or meat—the mainstays of the people of the Arabian Gulf. I love the unique flavor combination of cumin and dried lime with chickpeas. For this recipe I prefer to use dried chickpeas because the longer cooking time allows the flavor of the dried lime to be drawn out, along with the spices. But if you're in a rush, or you don't have dried lime on hand, I've also provided a short-cut version that uses already cooked (canned) chickpeas and lemon juice.

Serves about 8
Prep time: 10 minutes
Soaking time: 24 hours
Cooking time: 1 hour 10 minutes

2 cups (400 g) dried chickpeas, soaked for 24 hours in 6 cups (1.5 liters) water in which 1/2 teaspoon baking soda has been dissolved, and drained
4 tablespoons extra-virgin olive oil
1 1/2 teaspoons salt
1 teaspoon ground black pepper
1 teaspoon ground coriander
1 teaspoon ground cumin
1/4 teaspoon dried red pepper flakes
1 dried lime

1   Place the drained chickpeas in a large saucepan with a lid. Cover with water—to about 2 inches (5 cm) over the chickpeas—and stir in the remaining ingredients. Bring to a boil, cover, and cook over medium-low heat for 1 hour, or until the chickpeas become tender, adding more water if necessary.
2   Remove the lime and discard. Serve the Al-Nikhi in individual shallow soup bowls with its stock.

Variation
quick method for al-nikhi

Place all the ingredients for Al-Nikhi into a pot, but replace the dried chickpeas with two 19-oz (583-g) cans of chickpeas, drained, and omit the baking soda and dried lime. Bring to a boil and then reduce the heat to medium-low and cook, covered, for 20 minutes. Stir in 4 tablespoons of freshly squeezed lemon juice and serve in shallow bowls with the liquid.

sweetened vermicelli omelet
Balaleet

I was sitting in the lobby of the Marriott Hotel in Dubai waiting for a friend when I struck up a conversation about Arab food with an English expatriate. During our chat, he said that one of his choice Arab foods was Balaleet, an Emirati local favorite. The next day, when I was visiting a Canadian-Arab colleague in Dubai, I asked him about this dish. A few days later, I received an invitation to have breakfast at his home where his wife surprised me with Balaleet. The dish was excellent! An unusual but welcome change to the standard omelet, the taste lay somewhere between something slightly sweet and something slightly salty with a touch of cardamom while its appearance reminded me of an upside-down crepe. Ever since then it has been one of my cherished breakfast foods. This United Arab Emirates dish can be also found in other Arab Gulf countries. During Eid festivities boiled chickpeas and black-eyed peas may be served alongside it. Partially sweet, it is usually eaten for breakfast but can also be served with a side dish of dates and Sweet Holiday Biscuits (page 121) along with tea as an afternoon or evening snack.

Serves 4
Prep time: 10 minutes
Cooking time: 25 minutes

1/2 lb (250 g) dried vermicelli or very thin spaghetti
1/4 cup (1/2 stick/60 g) butter
4 tablespoons sugar
1/4 teaspoon ground cardamom
1/4 teaspoon ground ginger
1/4 teaspoon ground cinnamon
1/4 teaspoon salt
1 tablespoon orange or rose blossom water
Generous pinch of saffron dissolved in 4 tablespoons water
4 large eggs, beaten with a dash of salt

1   Cook the vermicelli according to the package instructions. Melt 3 tablespoons of the butter in a medium saucepan with a lid. Add the vermicelli and sprinkle on the sugar, cardamom, ginger, cinnamon, salt, rose or orange blossom water and dissolved saffron. Cover and cook over very low heat for 10 minutes, stirring a number of times.
2   In the meantime, melt the remaining butter in a medium skillet over medium-low heat. Pour the egg into the skillet and cook until set (do not stir them), then flip over to cook the other side, as if making an omelet. Place the vermicelli on a platter then place the omelet over the top and serve warm.

RICE AND LENTILS TOPPED WITH CARAMELIZED ONIONS 'Aysh Al-Dal

The root of the Arab Gulf cuisine is said to be the marriage between the Bedouin and pearl diving cultures, with the Indian sub-continent as the mother-in-law. This family of flavors has been the source of many tasty foods. Among these is 'Aysh Al-Dal, relished by anyone and everyone. The Indian word *dal* in its name indicates that the dish was likely brought from India in the medieval ages and then evolved into an Arab Gulf dish. Rice, and to a lesser extent lentils, were foods cooked, for centuries, by the Bedouin and pearl divers, usually simple and plain. The pearl divers who eked out a living diving for pearl-encrusted oysters in the Arabian Gulf, literally lived on rice alone. Those who came from the Indian sub-continent contributed the spices—hence, the creation of this mouth-watering dish, the result of the marriage. Grey, green, yellow and other cross-shades of lentils can be substituted for the brown lentils, but keep a close eye when cooking if you use a different type of lentil—some types take longer than others to cook. Serve with Tangy Hot Tomato Sauce (page 27) and Crunchy Pickled Garlic (page 26).

Serves 6
Prep time: 15 minutes
Soaking time: 8 hours 5 minutes
Cooking time: 30 minutes
Standing time: 30 minutes

1/4 cup (1/2 stick/60 g) butter
1 cup (200 g) uncooked Basmati or other white long-grain rice, soaked for 5 minutes, thoroughly rinsed and drained (see page 24)
1/2 cup (100g) dried brown lentils soaked overnight and drained
3 cups (750 ml) water
1 teaspoon salt
1/2 teaspoon ground black pepper
1/2 teaspoon ground cumin
1/2 teaspoon ground ginger
Generous pinch of ground cardamom
Generous pinch of ground red pepper (cayenne)
4 tablespoons extra-virgin olive oil
2 onions, thinly sliced
1/2 teaspoon ground cinnamon, for garnish

1 Melt the butter in a medium saucepan with a lid over medium heat. Add the rice and stir continuously for 1 minute. Add the lentils, water, salt, black pepper, cumin, ginger, cardamom and ground red pepper, and bring to a boil. Cover and cook over medium-low heat for 15 minutes, stirring occasionally to ensure that the rice does not stick to the bottom of the saucepan. Turn off the heat and allow to cook in its own steam for 30 minutes.

2 In the meantime, pour the oil into a medium skillet and set over medium-low heat. Add the onion slices and sauté until they turn light brown. Remove with a slotted spoon and place them on paper towels to drain.

3 Place the rice and lentil mixture on a serving platter. Arrange the onion slices evenly over the top. Sprinkle with the cinnamon and serve.

Serves 6
Prep time: 15 minutes
Soaking time: 8 hours 5 minutes
Standing time: 30 minutes
Cooking time: 40 minutes

1/4 cup (1/2 stick/60 g) butter
1 large onion, minced
1/2 cup (100 g) dried mung beans (maash),
   soaked overnight, rinsed and drained
1 cup (200 g) uncooked Basmati or other
   white long-grain rice, soaked for
   5 minutes, thoroughly rinsed and drained
   (see page 24)
Pinch of saffron
1/2 teaspoon ground cinnamon
1/2 teaspoon ground cardamom
1 teaspoon salt
3/4 teaspoon ground black pepper
3 cups (750 ml) water
3 tablespoons extra-virgin olive oil
4 tablespoons blanched almonds, for garnish
Tangy Hot Tomato Sauce (page 27)

1 Melt the butter in a medium saucepan with a lid over low heat. Add the minced onion and fry, uncovered, over medium-low heat until light brown. Add the mung beans and rice and cook for 3 minutes, stirring frequently. Add the saffron, cinnamon, cardamom, salt, black pepper and water and bring to a boil. Cover and cook over medium-low heat for 25 minutes, stirring occasionally to ensure the rice and the beans do not stick to the bottom of the saucepan. If the rice and beans begin to stick to the bottom of the pan, add a little water.
2 Remove from the heat and stir. Cover and allow to cook in its own steam for another 30 minutes.
3 In the meantime, pour the olive oil into a medium skillet and set over medium heat. Add the almond and sauté until light brown. Set aside.
4 Place the rice and the beans on a platter and top with the almonds. Serve immediately with the Tangy Hot Tomato Sauce on the side, allowing each person to use an amount to his or her liking.

MUNG BEANS AND RICE WITH ALMONDS   Al-Momawash Al-Mutabbaq

Before oil was discovered in Kuwait, the vast majority of people relied on a restricted diet of fish and other seafood, rice, dates, milk and the meat of camels, sheep and goats. However, meat was not consumed daily. In fact, the norm for meat consumption was either once a week or once a month. Instead, legumes mixed with rice, for example, were hearty enough to be a full meal. Such is the case with Al-Momawash Al-Mutabbaq, a rice and mung bean dish. During these years, this Kuwaiti dish, its flavor enhanced with Tangy Hot Tomato Sauce, which is served alongside it, was affordable to most and kept everyone well-fed and healthy. In those bygone days, most people with little means likely substituted turmeric for the saffron. Hence, it is said, with the addition of saffron meant affluence and thus this simple dish became one of regality. The mung bean (*maash*) is a small green bean used commonly in the northern Indian sub-continent. When the skin is removed the bean inside is yellow. Both the green and yellow varieties of the mung bean are sold in Indian shops and in many health food stores. As for myself, I prefer to use the green version since it tends to be more available in a variety of grocery stores. Serve with Tangy Hot Tomato Sauce (page 27) and Crunchy Pickled Garlic (page 26).

SPICY VEGETARIAN TURNOVERS

Samboosak ma' Khudra

Throughout the Arab Gulf countries, Samboosak abound—turnovers filled with meat, chicken or vegetable mixtures. The spices used to flavor the filling recall the inspiration for this turnover—the Indian *samosa*, which came to the Arab Gulf by way of Arab dhows sailing the seas between India and the Arabian Peninsula. Though the dhows are famous for carrying precious cargoes of porcelain, silks, spices and rare foods and goods, there is no doubt, that they carried, with no intention for trade, but for personal consumption, vegetarian Samboosak, which continues to be a favorite today of the inhabitants of the Arab Gulf. They are especially popular during Ramadan and the Iftar. Samboosak take the place of a lunch sandwich in our house and were and still are a great treat for my busy grandchildren running in and out looking for a quick something to eat. Little did they know that these turnovers were packed with nutritious ingredients. What they did know was that they were powerfully delicious! You can bake Samboosak in the oven, instead of frying them, but they will not be as tasty. This basic dough recipe, originating in the Fertile Crescent area, can be used for all types of Fatayar (savory turnovers hailing from Lebanon, Syria and Palestine) and Samboosak, such as cheese, leek, spinach and meat. This type of dough is today found throughout the Arab Gulf countries. A little flakier than ordinary bread, the pies make for a great tasting baked pocket. They freeze well and taste just as good re-heated.

Makes 36
Prep time: 2 hours
Standing time: 2 hours 40 minutes
Cooking time: 1 hour

Oil, for deep-frying

Dough
3 cups all-purpose flour (360 g), plus more
   if needed
3 tablespoons butter, melted
1/2 teaspoon salt
1/4 teaspoon ground ginger
1/2 cup (125 ml) warm milk, plus more if
   needed
2 1/4 teaspoons (1/4 oz/7 g) dry yeast mixed
   with 1/2 cup (125 ml) warm water and
   1 teaspoon sugar and allowed to stand
   for 10 minutes
1 teaspoon extra-virgin olive oil

Filling
4 cups (700 g) shredded potatoes
   (about 4 medium potatoes)
2 tomatoes, finely chopped
1 large onion, minced
1 small jalapeño or other fresh finger-length
   green chili pepper of your choice, very
   finely chopped
2 cloves garlic, crushed to a paste
   (see page 30)
2 tablespoons finely chopped fresh
   coriander leaves (cilantro)
2 tablespoons butter
1 large egg, beaten

1 1/2 teaspoons salt
1/2 teaspoon ground cumin
1/2 teaspoon ground coriander
1/2 teaspoon ground ginger
1/2 teaspoon ground black pepper

1 To make the Dough: Combine the flour, butter, salt and ginger in a large mixing bowl. Make a well in the flour mixture. Add the milk and yeast mixture then knead well, adding more warm milk or flour if necessary. When sufficiently kneaded, the Dough will behave like bread dough—it will be pliable, soft and smooth, and it should no longer stick to your hands.
2 Shape into a ball and then brush the entire outside of the ball with the olive oil. Place the oiled Dough ball in a medium bowl, cover with a tea towel, and set in a warm spot. Allow to rise until the Dough is double in size, about 2 hours.
3 Form the Dough into 36 balls and place on a floured tray. Cover with a damp cloth and allow to stand in a warm place for 30 minutes.
4 To make the Filling: Combine all the ingredients for the Filling in a mixing bowl.
5 To form the turnovers: Roll the balls into about 3-inch (7.5-cm) rounds. Thoroughly mix the Filling then place a heaping tablespoon of the Filling in the middle of each round. Fold the Dough over the Filling to form a half-moon shape. Firmly pinch the edges together to securely close the Samboosak—do this a few times to make sure you have a good seal. Repeat with the remaining rounds, making sure

to mix the Filling before making a new Samboosak. If after remixing the Filling it seems too watery, drain off a little of the accumulated juice. For more guidance on how to form the turnovers, see the illustrated steps in the recipe for Golden Meat Turnovers, page 78.
6 Pour about 2 inches (5 cm) of oil into a medium saucepan and set over medium-high heat. Heat the oil to a minimum temperature of 345°F (175°C) and no higher than 375°F (190°C), checking with a deep-frying or candy thermometer. If you do not have a thermometer, drop a small piece of bread in the oil. If the bread browns quickly (1 minute or less), the oil is the right temperature. Alternatively you can throw a drop of water in the oil. If the water sizzles upon contact, the oil is ready.
7 Deep-fry the Samboosak in batches so as not to overcrowd the pan. While deep-frying, between batches, re-check the temperature to make sure it's still between 345°F and 375°F (175°C and 190°C). (You may need to let the oil re-heat between batches.) Remove with a slotted spoon or tongs and drain on paper towels. Serve warm.

> **TIP:** You may freeze the individual dough balls for later use. To freeze them, tightly wrap in plastic ensuring there are no air pockets. Thaw at room temperature thoroughly before using.

CHAPTER 8

BREADS, RICE AND SIDE DISHES

Breads of all types are to be found in the Arab Gulf countries—from Iran and India, Europe and North America and especially the surrounding Arab lands. The most popular are Pita Bread (page 122), Sweet Holiday Biscuits (page 121), a crepe-like Bedouin bread, as well as the breads of the Indian sub-continent. Bread can be easily purchased but the best is the homemade bread. A few years ago when visiting Heritage Village in Dubai, a re-creation of a traditional Arab Gulf village, we stopped and watched two elderly women making Wafer-Thin Bedouin Pancakes (page 120). They offered us a piece to taste. When my daughter asked if there were stores where one could buy this bread, she replied: "Of course, but you cannot compare it to the bread that we make at home." Boasting, she went on, "You have now tasted the real bread! Here it is homemade!"

In all Arab homes bread is an essential food, served with every meal—the most common being the Arab Pita bread, a round leavened flat bread that when baked rises and forms a pocket. Pieces of bread are torn by hand and formed into tiny shovels to scoop up food such as Savory Lamb Tartare (page 90) and Red Bell Pepper Dip with Pine Nuts (page 43). Pita bread is great for sandwiches as well. A loaf is cut in half and each half pocket is stuffed with goodies like cheese, Spicy Falafel Patties (page108), and all types of meat. At other times, as in Lamb in a Savory Sauce with Pita Bread (page 78), bread is used as a main ingredient in the dish.

Like bread, rice in the Arab Gulf countries is found in many types and is prepared in various ways in innumerable dishes. In the main, rice side dishes are served alongside main dishes but a good number of hearty rice dishes can also be served as the main course for a light meal or as a whole snack—such as Date Syrup Rice (page 124), Rice with Arabian Truffles (page 124) and Aromatic Rice with Almonds (page 123). Rice is also one of the main ingredients in stuffed vegetables such as Onions Stuffed with Meat and Rice (page 123) and Delicious Stuffed Zucchini (page 128). For centuries a favored food in Iran, Iraq, the Greater Syria region and Turkey, these stuffed vegetables are today to be found in all the Arab Gulf countries. These two traditional common stuffed dishes and almost any other edible vegetable or leaf can be stuffed with meat or non-meat products. The subtle flavor produced from the fusion of the leaves and vegetables with their fillings give these dishes an irresistable and appetizing appeal. An expert cook can create, from daily-consumed vegetables, a range of delicious side dishes that will titillate the palate.

WAFER-THIN BEDOUIN PANCAKES

Chubab

This traditional Bedouin bread, found in the United Arab Emirates and other Arab Gulf countries, is today enhanced with ingredients not generally available to the Bedouin of the past. However, as it has been for centuries, it remains today a delightful sweet bread that is comparable to a crepe, though it uses a yeasted batter. Especially excellent for breakfast, the bread can be served warm for all meals, accompanied by cheese, dates, jam, syrup, honey or eggs. Creamy Yogurt Spread (page 29) and Labana Balls (page 29) go well with this bread, especially when freshly made. Chubab is even tastier when a little melted butter is spread over the warm pancake.

Makes 12 pancakes
Prep time: 15 minutes
Standing time: 2 hours 10 minutes
Cooking time: 20 minutes

1¹/2 cups (180 g) all-purpose flour
¹/2 cup (60 g) whole-wheat flour
2 large eggs, beaten
4 tablespoons date syrup (see Tip, page 121)
¹/2 cup (125 g) store-bought or Homemade Plain Yogurt (page 31)
2 tablespoons butter, melted, plus extra to drizzle on pancakes
¹/4 oz/7 g (1 envelope) active dry yeast and 1 teaspoon sugar dissolved in ¹/2 cup (125 ml) warm water and allowed to stand for 10 minutes
2 cups (500 ml) warm water
Butter, for greasing the skillet

1 Place all the ingredients, except the butter for greasing, in a food processor and process until very smooth. The batter should be thinner than pancake batter; add extra water if necessary. Cover with a tea towel and let stand in a warm place for about 2 hours.
2 Lightly grease a small skillet with the butter and set over medium heat. Cooking one pancake at a time, place 3 tablespoons of the batter into the hot skillet and quickly spread out the batter with the back of a small spoon to create a thin pancake. When bubbles form on the top, turn the pancake over and cook until the underside turns golden brown. Repeat with the rest of the batter. Drizzle a little melted butter on the warm Chubab and serve immediately.

sweet holiday biscuits

Khubz Mohala

A traditional bread recipe found in all the Arab Gulf nations, Khubz Mohala, a type of sweetbread, is often baked in a special oven called a *tannur*. It is a specialty bread baked for festive occasions such as religious holidays and weddings and is typically served with coffee and dates. Like scones, the bread is excellent when served with a hot beverage for a snack especially when guests drop by.

TIP: Date syrup can be purchased in Middle Eastern stores and markets that carry Mid-East and/or Asian products. However it can be easily made by bringing to a boil an equal amount of pitted dates and water, then cooking for 20 minutes. Add a little vanilla extract and cinnamon and then allow to cool. Place in a blender and blend until smooth. Store in a sealed jar in a refrigerator. Date syrup will keep well in a refrigerator for up to 2 weeks but usually much longer—the syrup can be kept until it begins to crystallize. I have kept some of my homemade date syrup for up to 3 months. Maple syrup, carob syrup, or grape syrup, the latter found in Middle Eastern stores, can be used as substitutes.

Makes 6
Prep time: 40 minutes
Standing time: 2 hours 40 minutes
Cooking time: 20 minutes

2¹/2 cups (300 g) all-purpose flour, plus extra if needed
¹/2 cup (60 g) whole-wheat flour
¹/4 oz/7 g (1 envelope) active dry yeast dissolved in a ¹/4 cup (65 ml) warm water and 1 tablespoon sugar and allowed to stand for 10 minutes
¹/2 cup (125 ml) date syrup (see Tip)
2 teaspoons rose or orange blossom water
¹/2 cup (125 ml) water, plus extra if needed
¹/2 teaspoon baking soda
Oil, to oil the dough
2 tablespoons toasted sesame seeds
2 teaspoons sugar dissolved in 2 tablespoons water and mixed with ¹/4 teaspoon baking soda

1 To make the dough, thoroughly combine the all-purpose and whole-wheat flours, dissolved yeast, date syrup, rose or orange blossom water, water and baking soda in a mixing bowl. Knead until a smooth and elastic bread dough texture is formed, adding extra flour or water if needed. Form the dough into a ball, rub it with a little of the oil and place it in a bowl. Cover with a tea towel and let rest in a warm place for 2 hours or until it doubles in size.

2 Place the sesame seeds in a medium skillet and toast over medium-low heat for about 2 minutes, or until they just begin to slightly brown. Immediately remove the sesame seeds from the skillet and allow them to cool.

3 Form the dough into 6 balls. Working on a lightly floured surface, roll out the balls to about ¹/4-inch (6-mm)-thick circles. Brush the tops with the sugar and baking soda mixture and indent the top of each circle with your fingertips. Sprinkle with the sesame seeds and place on greased cookie trays. Cover and allow to stand for 30 minutes.

4 While the circles are resting, preheat the oven to 350°F (175°C). Bake for 10 to 15 minutes, or until the tops turn golden brown.

Makes about 1 dozen pitas
Prep time: 40 minutes
Standing time: 3 hours 10 minutes
Cooking time: 20 minutes

4 cups (480 g) all-purpose flour, plus
   more if needed
1/2 teaspoon salt
2 tablespoons extra-virgin olive oil,
   plus extra for oiling dough
1/2 oz/14 g (2 envelopes) active dry
   yeast dissolved in 1/2 cup (125 ml)
   warm water and 2 teaspoons sugar
   and allowed to stand for 10 minutes
1 1/4 cups (300 ml) lukewarm water

1 Place the flour, salt and 2 table-spoons of the oil in a mixing bowl. Mix together and make a well in the center. Add the yeast mixture and the lukewarm water. Knead until smooth and elastic, adding some extra water or flour if necessary. Shape into a ball and brush the entire outside of the ball with the olive oil and place in a bowl. Cover with a tea towel and place in a warm spot. Allow to rise until double in size, about 1 1/2 to 2 hours.

2 Form the dough into balls the size of small oranges, rolling them gently between your hands. Place each on a dry cloth in a warm place and cover with a tea towel. Allow to stand for 30 minutes.

3 Working on a lightly floured surface, roll out the balls into circles about 1/4 inch (6 mm) thick. Allow to rest covered with a tea towel for about 30 minutes.

4 Preheat the oven to 500°F (260°C) with the oven rack in the center of the oven. Place the dough circles directly on the oven rack and bake for 5 to 7 minutes. Loaves may be placed under broiler for a few minutes for darker bread, if preferred.

ꝒITΛ BRΣΛꝎ Khubz 'Arabi

In tradition, and in daily life, bread is held to be a divine gift from God. Arabs eat bread with every meal, claiming that they cannot taste other foods without it. It is used for picking up meat, vegetables, and salads, and serves as a scoop for sauces, dips, yogurt, and other semi-liquids. It is ideal for enjoying any type of appetizer. When a pita is cut into two, the top and bottom separate easily and the halves form pockets, which can be filled with just about anything you like. Spicy Falafel Patties (page 108) and/or a salad is a classic filling option. This flat bread is found, in the main, in the Greater Syria area but is also today, one of the many types of bread to be found in all the Arab Gulf countries. While baking, the pita breads will puff up like a balloon and will collapse when cooled. Pita bread may be eaten immediately, or frozen for long-term storage. For short-term storage, the cooled breads should be sealed in plastic wrap or a plastic bag. To freeze pita bread, cool them and then place them in airtight plastic bags. Remove as needed and thaw at room temperature. The bread, when ready to eat, may be quickly warmed in the oven. Try it with Creamy Yogurt Spread (page 29) when the bread is just fresh out of the oven.

ONIONS STUFFED WITH MEAT AND RICE Basal Mahshi

When one thinks of stuffed onions, usually stuffing a whole onion comes to mind. I always stuffed onions in this way until a few years ago when a friend in the UAE invited me to a meal in which was included Basal Mahshi, a dish of stuffed onion layers. From then on, I have forgone stuffing the whole onion and, instead, have been stuffing onion layers in the same way as stuffing cabbage leaves. It simplifies the stuffing of an onion—an ancient food in the eastern Arab lands. The dish likely came to the Arab Gulf countries with the Greek, Turkish, Iraqi or the Greater Syria expatriates, possibly after the discovery of oil but more likely during the Ottoman period. Dissolved tamarind paste, although not having the same 'zing' in flavor, can be used as a replacement for the pomegranate syrup. Tamarind is a sour condiment used in the Arab Gulf countries and other Asiatic lands. For those who ponder the use of pomegranate juice in place of the pomegranate syrup, it would be much better to substitute tamarind paste than pomegranate juice since the juice is much milder than the concentrate. Once the stuffed onion layers are cooked they will be very tender. For this reason, it is important to invert the saucepan onto a serving platter. Other, less gentle ways of removing the stuffed onion layers, will likely cause the onion layers to tear or the stuffing to fall out. Also, when inverting the pan, the onion hearts cooked at the bottom end up on top, which makes a great presentation.

Serves 6   **Soaking time:** 5 minutes
Prep time: 1 hour 45 minutes
Cooking time: 1 hour

4 very large white onions (4 lbs/2 kg total)

Stuffing
1/2 lb (250 g) ground beef or lamb
1/2 cup (100 g) uncooked Basmati or other white long-grain rice, soaked for 5 minutes, thoroughly rinsed and drained (see page 24)
1 bunch green onions (scallions) (about 1/4 lb/125 g), trimmed and thinly sliced
4 cloves garlic, crushed to a paste (see page 30)
4 tablespoons extra-virgin olive oil
1 tablespoon sumac
1 teaspoon Arabian Gulf Spice Mix (Baharat) (page 28)
1 teaspoon salt
1/2 teaspoon ground black pepper
1/2 teaspoon allspice
4 tablespoons pomegranate syrup dissolved in 2 cups (500 ml) hot water along with 1/2 teaspoon salt or 2 tablespoons tamarind paste dissolved in 2 cups (500 ml) hot water along with 1/2 teaspoon salt

1 Place the 4 whole onions in a medium saucepan. Add enough water to cover the onion and bring to a boil. Cook over medium heat until just tender. Drain and set aside to cool.
2 Place the ingredients for the Stuffing in a mixing bowl. Mix thoroughly and set aside.
3 Slice the whole onions in half lengthwise. Carefully separate the layers of cooked onion and remove the center hearts. Chop the hearts and spread on the bottom of a medium saucepan with a lid.
4 Place 1 tablespoon of the Stuffing on an onion layer. Roll the layer around the Stuffing to close it and place it seam-side down in the saucepan. Repeat with the remainder of the onion layers and Stuffing, laying the stuffed onion rolls as close to each other as possible. To keep the rolled onion submerged in its cooking liquid, place an inverted plate over the top then pour the pomegranate syrup solution over the onion and enough of water to barely cover the plate. Bring to a boil, cover, and cook over medium-low heat for 40 minutes. Remove the inverted plate. Turn the contents onto a serving dish and serve warm.

AROMATIC RICE WITH ALMONDS

Ruzz ma' Lawz

The aroma of simmering Basmati rice and cardamom make this rice dish especially enticing. At restaurants both in Dubai and Abu Dhabi I relished this dish's subtle hint of cardamom combined with the sweet and savory tastes of plump raisins and toasted almonds. This dish will be even more delicious if you use freshly ground cardamom (see "How to Pulverize Cardamom Seeds," page 149) and serve it with Homemade Plain Yogurt (page 31).

Serves 4 to 6
Prep time: 15 minutes
Standing time: 35 minutes
Cooking time: 20 minutes

1/4 cup (1/2 stick/60 g) butter
1 1/2 cups (235 g) blanched almonds
1 cup (200 g) uncooked Basmati or other white long-grain rice, soaked for 5 minutes, thoroughly rinsed and drained (see page 24)
1/4 cup (40 g) raisins, rinsed
2 1/2 cups (635 ml) water
1/2 teaspoon ground cardamom
1/2 teaspoon ground cinnamon
1/2 teaspoon salt
1/4 teaspoon freshly grated nutmeg
Generous pinch of ground red pepper (cayenne)
2 tablespoons finely chopped fresh parsley, for garnish

1 Melt the butter in a medium skillet with a lid over medium-low heat. Sauté the almond, uncovered, until they begin to brown. Add the rice and stir continuously for 1 to 2 minutes.
2 Stir in the rest of the ingredients, except the parsley, and bring to a boil. Cover and cook over medium-low heat for 12 minutes. Stir and remove from the heat. Cover and allow to cook in its own steam for 30 minutes.
3 Spread the rice on a platter, garnish with the parsley, and serve immediately.

DATE SYRUP RICE Mahammarat Ruzz

The use of fruits and other sweets in main dishes was a basic way of cooking in the medieval Baghdadi and Iranian kitchens. Strangely, today the cuisine of Morocco in the western edge of the Arab World still combines sweet and savory while in the eastern Arab World it is only found in a few places. This dish of sweetened rice, a specialty of Bahrain, though popular in all of the Arab Gulf countries, is one of the few sweet main dishes that remain in the Gulf region. It goes well with all types of fried fish.

Serves 4
Prep time: 15 minutes
Standing time: 35 minutes
Cooking time: 20 minutes

1 cup (200 g) uncooked Basmati or other white long-grain rice, soaked for 5 minutes, thoroughly rinsed and drained (see page 24)
6 tablespoons date syrup (see Tip, page 121)
1/2 teaspoon ground cardamom
1/2 teaspoon ground cumin
1/2 teaspoon salt
4 cups (1 liter) water
2 tablespoons extra-virgin olive oil
1 tablespoon rosewater
2 tablespoons butter, melted
Generous pinch of saffron dissolved in 2 tablespoons water

1 Place the rice, 3 tablespoons of the date syrup, 1/4 teaspoon of the cardamom, cumin, salt and water in a medium saucepan with a lid and bring to a boil. Reduce the heat to low, cover, and cook for 10 minutes. Drain the rice and set aside.
2 Pour the olive oil into the same saucepan you used to cook the rice. Set over medium heat and, when hot, add the drained rice, rosewater, the remaining date syrup and cardamom. Stir continuously over medium heat for 2 minutes. Stir in the butter and sprinkle on the dissolved saffron. Turn off the heat, cover, and allow to cook in its own steam for 30 minutes. Serve warm.

RICE WITH ARABIAN TRUFFLES 'Aysh Al-Faqa'a

The truffle, known in Arabic as *faqa'a, kama, kamaieh, terfez*, is an edible subterranean fungus that is available in two types: the European variety, very aromatic and highly valued by connoisseurs of fine foods; and the Arabic variety (Middle Eastern and North African), which has a meaty mushroom taste but is blander than the European variety, though it is much more reasonable in price. In the Arab Gulf countries, truffles have been eaten, throughout the ages, as a cherished delicacy. This dish is a version of one of the many traditional dishes of faqa'a in the Arab Gulf countries. It is said that truffles, like precious metals, are a beloved treasure that the earth conceals within its bosom. The ancient Greeks believed that this delicacy was planted by thunderbolts striking the earth and hence is the offspring of thunder. The belief that truffles arrive with storms is shared by the inhabitants of the Arabian Peninsula and seems completely plausible. In the deserts, when storms suddenly break out, they crack the sand and expose the buried truffles below. The Arabic word faqa'a, which translates as "to burst or explode," apparently, confirms this belief. I use Syrian truffles in this recipe simply because they are the most readily available in markets. However, the less common Moroccan or Lebanese truffle can also be used in this recipe. If truffles are not available, any type of fresh mushroom can be substituted.

Serves 4
Prep time: 25 minutes
Soaking time: 5 minutes
Cooking time: 35 minutes
Standing time: 30 minutes

1/4 cup (1/2 stick/60 g) butter
1 onion, finely chopped
1 cup (200 g) canned/bottled Syrian truffles, drained, thoroughly washed and chopped, or 2 cups (about 7 oz/ 200 g) fresh mushrooms of your choice, thoroughly washed and chopped
2 cloves garlic, crushed to a paste (see page 30)
1 cup (200 g) uncooked Basmati or other white long-grain rice, soaked for 5 minutes, thoroughly rinsed and drained (see page 24)
2 cups (500 ml) water
1/2 teaspoon salt
1/4 teaspoon ground black pepper

1 Melt the butter in a medium skillet with a lid over medium-low heat. Add the onion and sauté, uncovered, for 8 minutes. Add the truffles and cook for 7 minutes, stirring frequently. Stir in the garlic and rice and cook for 2 minutes, stirring continuously.
2 Add the water, salt and black pepper and bring to a boil. Cover and cook over medium-low heat for 15 minutes, stirring once or twice to ensure the rice does not stick to the bottom of the skillet. Remove from the heat and stir. Cover and allow to cook in its own steam for 30 minutes. Serve hot.

TIP: Most jars or cans of Syrian, Moroccan or Lebanese truffles will contain about twice the amount of truffles needed for this recipe. Leftover truffles should be stored in a sealed container (remove them from the can) in the refrigerator, where they will keep for a week or more. When using truffles or mushrooms, always take the time and effort to thoroughly clean them to remove their hidden dirt.

THREE-SPICE RICE WITH PINE NUTS AND RAISINS Ruzz Bukhari

As its name suggests, this popular Saudi Arabian dish, identified as Hijazi cuisine (from the Western province of Hijaz), likely came to the country with the pilgrims from Central Asia, more specifically from the city of Bukhara. Today, this widely-eaten rice dish is as Saudi Arabian as any original food prepared in that country. The aroma that emanates from Ruzz Bukhari is enticing to all—even staunch meat-eaters. What makes it even more appealing are the crunchy toasted pine nuts and the soft raisins making this rice dish a new adventure. The dish can be served as a vegetarian main course with a salad or vegetable or as a side dish to all types of stews. It is a favorite choice with Tandoori Chicken, Omani-Style (page 70). Homemade Plain Yogurt (page 31) goes well with it as does Creamy Cucumber and Bell Pepper Salad (page 46).

Serves 4 to 6
Prep time: 20 minutes
Standing time: 35 minutes
Cooking time: 30 minutes

4 tablespoons oil
1 onion, minced
2 cloves garlic, crushed to a paste
    (see page 30)
1¹/2 cups (300 g) uncooked Basmati or
    other white long-grain rice, soaked for
    5 minutes, thoroughly rinsed and
    drained (see page 24)
4 tablespoons raisins
2 tablespoons tomato paste dissolved in
    4 tablespoons water
³/4 teaspoon salt
¹/2 teaspoon ground black pepper
¹/4 teaspoon ground cinnamon
¹/4 teaspoon ground cardamom
Generous pinch of ground cloves
3 cups (750 ml) water
4 tablespoons pine nuts, toasted, for
    garnish

1 Heat the oil in a medium saucepan with a lid over medium-low heat and sauté the onion, uncovered, for 10 minutes. Add the garlic and cook for 3 minutes, stirring frequently.
2 Add the rice and stir frequently for 2 minutes more. Stir in the rest of the ingredients, except the pine nut, and bring to a boil. Cover and cook over medium-low heat for 12 minutes. Stir the rice and re-cover the saucepan.
3 Turn off the heat and allow to cook in its own steam for 30 minutes. Place on a serving platter, sprinkle on the pine nut and serve.

CAULIFLOWER SAUTÉED WITH CHILI PEPPERS AND FRESH CORIANDER

Qarnabeet bil Kuzbara

This Saudi Arabian dish can be served as a main dish or as a spicy salad. An abundant use of fresh coriander leaves (cilantro) gives this cauliflower dish its unique taste, making it one of my absolute favorite dishes. I vividly remember my first experience with fresh coriander leaves. A family friend who had recently arrived from Beirut prepared a stew with the herb. That day my culinary experience was revolutionized. I went into raptures after the meal just thinking about the delicious taste of this savory herb. From that first taste over five decades ago, I have become a fanatical advocate of this exquisite, parsley-like plant. The lemon wedges are used to garnish the dish and also to be squeezed, if desired, over each serving according to individual taste.

Serves 4 to 6
Prep time: 30 minutes
Cooking time: 10 minutes

1 large head cauliflower, about 2 lbs (1 kg), cut into florets, washed, rinsed and drained
1 teaspoon salt
1/4 cup (65 ml) extra-virgin olive oil
4 cloves garlic, crushed
1 small jalapeño or other fresh finger-length green chili pepper of your choice, deseeded and very finely chopped
4 tablespoons finely chopped green onions (scallions)
2 cups (100 g) fresh coriander leaves (cilantro), chopped
1 teaspoon paprika
1/2 teaspoon ground black pepper
1 lemon, cut into wedges, for garnish

1 Place the cauliflower and salt in a medium saucepan with a lid. Pour in some boiling hot water—just enough to cover the cauliflower. Cover and cook over medium-high heat for 6 minutes. Drain the cauliflower and set aside.
2 Pour the oil into a large skillet and set over medium-high heat. Add the cauliflower, garlic and chili pepper and cook for 3 minutes, stirring frequently.
3 Stir in the green onion, coriander leaves, paprika and black pepper and remove from the heat. Place on a serving platter and garnish with the lemon wedges.

Serves 6 to 8
Prep time: 20 minutes
Cooking time: 30 minutes

4 large tomatoes, about 2 lbs (1 kg) total,
 cut into about 1/4-in (6-mm)-thick slices
4 tablespoons extra-virgin olive oil
4 tablespoons water
4 tablespoons finely chopped fresh
 coriander leaves (cilantro)
2 teaspoons garlic powder
1 teaspoon salt
1/2 teaspoon paprika
1/2 teaspoon ground black pepper
1/2 teaspoon ground cumin
1/2 teaspoon ground coriander
1/4 teaspoon ground red pepper (cayenne)

1 Preheat the oven to 350°F (175°C).
2 Place the tomato slices evenly along the bottom of a 13 x 9 x 2-inch (23 x 33 x 5-cm) baking pan. Set aside. Depending on the size of the tomatoes, you may need to overlap the slices.
3 Combine the remaining ingredients in a small bowl. Spread the spice mixture over the top of the tomato slices. Bake uncovered for 30 minutes. Serve hot from the baking pan.

AROMATIC BAKED TOMATO SLICES
Duqous

Duqous could have been developed in Kuwait, where I first enjoyed it, but it's likely an adoption of a similar Palestinian dish of fried tomatoes. This dish is excellent when served as a side dish to any type of meat or fish dish. My favorite way to serve it is alongside Spicy Meatballs in a Creamy Yogurt Sauce (page 87) and Stuffed Lamb or Veal (page 88). Note: This dish can also be prepared in the Palestinian style by heating the oil over medium heat in a large skillet and then placing the tomatoes evenly in the skillet, followed by the remaining ingredients. Cover and cook for 10 minutes, lightly shaking the pan from time to time.

delicious stuffed zucchini

Kusa Mahshi

Kusa Mahshi is one of the dishes that is widely found in Qatar today and remains very common in the eastern Mediterranean countries of Iraq and Iran. It is a delicacy slowly being discovered in the kitchens of the West. One of the supreme of stuffed vegetables, it is to its great number of culinary fans a very delicious, gourmet treat. Kusa Mahshi can be served by itself as the main course or as a side dish to all types of meat dishes. As with most stuffed vegetable dishes, Homemade Plain Yogurt (page 31) is usually served alongside. Coring the zucchini comes with some practice, so I've provided two methods: the traditional method, which requires a vegetable corer, and an easier method that simply entails cutting the vegetable in half and scraping out the pulp. For the traditionalist, the latter method is an unacceptable way of stuffing vegetables as for centuries Arab women have taken pride in coring their vegetables, the ultimate being a cored vegetable with a very thin shell. The downside of the easy method is that liquid will seep into the stuffing, making it somewhat soggy. If you do not mind a slightly wet stuffing this non-traditional method is just as tasty and works particularly well when stuffing large zucchini—over a foot long and baked in an oven. The little water that seeps in is easily absorbed by the large amount of stuffing.

Serves 8
Prep time: 1 hour 15 minutes
Standing time: 5 minutes
Cooking time: 1 hour

16 small zucchini or vegetable marrow, each
    about 5-in (12.75-cm) long (about
    4^1/$_2$ lbs/2 kg total), washed and dried
2 cups (500 ml) tomato juice mixed with
    1 teaspoon freshly grated nutmeg

Stuffing
1 lb (500 g) ground lamb or beef
1 cup (200 g) uncooked Basmati or other
    white long-grain rice, soaked for 5
    minutes, thoroughly rinsed and drained
    (see page 24)
^{1}/$_4$ cup (^{1}/$_2$ stick/60 g) butter, melted
1 large onion, finely chopped
4 cloves garlic, crushed to a paste (see
    page 30)
4 tablespoons finely chopped fresh parsley
2 tablespoons finely chopped fresh
    coriander leaves (cilantro)
1 teaspoon salt
1 teaspoon ground black pepper
1 teaspoon dried oregano
^{3}/$_4$ teaspoon allspice
^{1}/$_4$ teaspoon ground red pepper (cayenne)

Special equipment (optional)
Vegetable corer

1 To make the Stuffing: Combine all the ingredients for the Stuffing in a mixing bowl.
2 Cut the stem ends off the zucchini or vegetable marrow and reserve them if you're coring the traditional way. Core and stuff the zucchini or vegetable marrow following the illustrated steps on facing page. Patience is part of the coring procedure, so don't attempt it when you feel rushed! If you're not accustomed to coring vegetables, start with the easier method described in Steps 3 and 4 on opposite page.
3 Arrange the stuffed zucchini, tightly next to each other, in a large saucepan with a lid, and then place an inverted plate on top. Add the tomato juice and enough water to cover the plate then bring to a boil. Cover the saucepan then cook over medium heat for 1 hour. Serve hot.

TIP: When coring zucchini, there will be leftover pulp. The pulp can be reserved for later use, such as frying with eggs to make a type of omelet or a simple side dish of fried onions and zucchini pulp. Allow the cored pulp to sit in a strainer for about an hour to drain and then freeze in airtight plastic in amounts needed per dish.

Coring and Stuffing the Zucchini

1 To core the zucchini the traditional way, using a corer, follow this and the next Step. (If you do not have a corer, follow Steps 3 and 4 below.) Holding the zucchini in one hand, insert the corer in the center of the cut end of the zucchini and carefully wind the corer to the opposite end of the zucchini a number of times until it is completed cored. As you wind the corer, carefully pull out the pulp. Do not push the corer through the other end of the zucchini. Continue to core until the zucchini is hollow with a somewhat thin shell. The trick to making good stuffed zucchini is to remove as much of the pulp a possible leaving a clean and neat hollow for the stuffing. Repeat with the other zucchini.

2 With a small spoon (a long slender ice-tea spoon works well), loosely fill the cored zucchini with the stuffing. Cap the ends with the reserved stem ends, placing them stem-side in, toward the stuffing.

3 If you do not own a corer, you may use this easier method. Cut the zucchini in half lengthwise and then core, using a spoon to scrape out the pulp.

4 Stuff the two halves and then tie them together with kitchen string or close them tight with tooth picks. If you're using a large zucchini, add water only to about half-way up the zucchini.

> **NOTE:** When coring, the cored material is never pushed out on the opposite end—it remains in the corer and is pulled out.

CHAPTER 9
DESSERTS

The most important natural sweet in the nations of the Arabian Peninsula is dates. In these lands, where the date palm carries an aura of mystery and romance, there is a common belief that it is the oldest cultivated fruit tree in the world. In its native homeland, the Arabian Peninsula, the inhabitants have no doubt that it was first grown in Paradise. According to Muslim belief, the Archangel Gabriel told Adam in the Garden of Eden, "Thou art created from the same substance as this palm tree which henceforth shall nourish you." Not surprisingly, dates have long been a central ingredient in the traditional sweets of the Arab Gulf countries. Centuries ago, in pre-Islamic Arabia, two of the most popular sweets were Khabees, a type of pudding made with dates with roots in Persia, and the Bedouin Hays, a mix of curds, butter and dates. Of course, the Arabs who lived in the cosmopolitan urban centers were familiar with other sweets created in the towns or brought by traders from other countries. However, for the Bedouin, sweets made with dates, and even dates on their own, were the only desserts.

Through the centuries, especially after the dawn of Islam, both Hays and Khabees were enhanced in countless ways with nuts, spices and other ingredients. At the same time, various types of puddings, such as Sweet Date Pudding (page 143) and other sweets, such as the syrup-soaked pastries Crispy Doughnuts in Sweet Syrup (page 137) and Filo Wrapped Nut Rolls (page 142), were invented or adopted from the cuisines of conquered or neighboring cultures. In the lands of their origin and adaptation, the tempting, scrumptious and gratifying taste of Arabic sweets has inspired poets and men of letters through the centuries. Poems have been composed, songs have been sung, and legends born wherever these marvelously delicate pastries have been served. An Arab poet once said, "With our exquisite and luscious sweets, can the beauty of any woman compare?" Today, all of the many and diverse Arab pastries and sweets have an irresistable appeal: some are golden-colored when fried or baked and oozing with syrup; others are filled with a rich, nutty stuffing; some come in the form of rich, thick, fragrant-scented puddings or buttery melt-in-the mouth cookies. Besides the traditional sweets served at wedding feasts, religious festivals and personal celebrations, the tables of the Arab Gulf countries display a lavish variety of sweets such as Irresistible Baklava (page 134), Cardamom Fritters with Walnuts in Orange-Blossom Syrup (page 133), Melt-in-Your-Mouth Cardamom Shortbreads (page 138) and Saudi-Style Crepes Filled with Sweetened Almonds (page 140). The world of sweets in the Arab Gulf lands is like a picture from *The Arabian Nights*.

Serves 4 to 6
Prep time: 15 minutes
Cooking time: 20 minutes

3/4 cup (100 g) cornstarch dissolved in
   3/4 cup (185 ml) water
1/2 cup (115 g) sugar
1/4 cup (1/2 stick/60 g) unsalted butter
3 or 4 threads saffron dissolved in
   1 tablespoon rosewater
1/2 teaspoon ground cardamom
1 tablespoon pine nuts, toasted, for garnish
1 tablespoon chopped pistachios, for garnish

1 Thoroughly mix together the dissolved cornstarch and sugar in a small bowl. Set aside.

2 Melt the butter in a small saucepan over medium-low heat. Add the cornstarch and sugar mixture and cook, stirring constantly, until it becomes very thick. Reduce the heat to very low and sprinkle on the saffron-infused rosewater and cardamom. Cook for 2 minutes, stirring constantly. Spread on a serving platter and garnish with the pine nut and pistachio. Serve warm.

SWEET SAFFRON CUSTARD WITH PISTACHIOS AND PINE NUTS Khabees Al-Nasha

There are a whole series of different types of Khabees, or custards, made in all of the Arab Gulf countries, but they are especially popular in Kuwait. These traditional pudding-like sweets, enriched with butter and thickened with cornstarch, are often offered during Iftar, the time in the evening when Muslims come together to break their fast during the holy month of Ramadan. Centuries ago, Khabees was considered a food of the urban centers. In fact, it became known as a luxury food, and as one of the foods of the people of Chosroes, the great Persian king. Though the earliest Khabees were made with native ingredients of dates, flour and butter, it was not designated a Bedouin dish. Those who served it were considered to be of the urban class—those who had opted for the city life and forsaken the one of the desert. A number of varieties developed over the years, and this recipe, garnished with pine nuts and pistachios, is one of the more splendid yet easy-to-prepare versions. This aromatic custard can be served as a dessert or for breakfast.

CARDAMOM FRITTERS WITH WALNUTS IN ORANGE-BLOSSOM SYRUP Balah al-Sham

I enjoyed these wonderful fritters many times during my travels in the Arabian Peninsula, and especially at daily Iftar buffets prepared in the holy month of Ramadan. Though this sweet contains no dates, its name, Balah al-Sham, translates as "Syrian dates," as they look like a variety of dates found in Syria. These deep-fried, crispy little cylinders, drenched in a fragrant sweet syrup, are the forerunner of the Spanish churro. These sweet fried fritters can be found in all of the Arab Gulf countries, and in Egypt and Lebanon, where it is also called Balah al-Sham, and in Syria, where it is oddly called Asabi' Zaynab (the fingers of Zaynab). No one can truly claim that this sweet origi-nated in their country since fried pastries have been a common method of making desserts for hundreds of years. These fritters are at their best when eaten the day they are made.

Makes from 15 to 20 pieces
Prep time: 40 minutes
Standing time: 35 minutes
Cooking time: 35 minutes

¹/2 recipe Orange Blossom Syrup (page 27)
Neutral-flavored oil, for deep-frying
4 tablespoons finely chopped walnuts, for
   garnish

Batter
2 tablespoons unsalted butter
1¹/4 cups (300 ml) water
1¹/2 cups (180 g) all-purpose flour
1 large egg, beaten
2 teaspoons rosewater
¹/4 teaspoon ground cardamom

1 Make the Orange Blossom Syrup. It's im-portant to do this first as the syrup needs time to cool.
2 To make the Batter: Melt the butter in a medium saucepan over medium-low heat. Add the water and bring to a boil. Remove the saucepan from the heat and let stand for 3 minutes. Gradually stir in the flour and con-tinue stirring until a smooth batter is formed. Cook over low heat for 3 minutes, stirring con-stantly. Turn off the heat (but leave the pan on the heating element), cover, and allow to cook in its own steam for 20 minutes. Remove from the stovetop and allow to cool for 10 minutes.
3 Stir the egg, rosewater and cardamom into the Batter and set aside.
4 Pour about 2 inches (5 cm) of oil into a medium saucepan and set over medium heat. Heat the oil to a minimum temperature of 345°F (175°C) and no higher than 375°F (190°C), checking with a deep-frying or candy thermometer. If you do not have a thermom-eter, drop a small piece of bread in the oil. If the bread browns quickly (1 minute or less), the oil is the right temperature. Alternatively you can throw a drop of water in the oil. If the water sizzles upon contact, the oil is ready.
5 Place the Batter in a cloth pastry bag with a zigzagged nozzle edge that has a ¹/2 to ³/4-inch (1.25 to 2-cm) opening. Squeeze the Batter through the nozzle into the oil in about 3-inch (7.5-cm) lengths, cutting the Batter from the nozzle with a knife. Deep-fry the fritters in batches, squeezing just enough lengths of dough to cover the top of the oil, until golden brown, turning over once. Remove with tongs and place in the Orange Blossom Syrup for a few moments. Remove and place in a strainer and allow to drain. Place on a serving platter and sprinkle with the walnuts. Serve immediately or within the same day they are made.

IRRESISTABLE BAKLAVA

In the lands of the Fertile Crescent during the bygone ages, when the affluent held their banquets, Arab sweets reached their height of magnificence. At any of these feasts, pastries similar to Baklava, or Baklawa as it is known in Arabic, were always to be found. Made from paper-thin dough that is known in the West as filo (phyllo) or strudel dough, the family of sweets made from it can be described as delicate, crispy, crunchy, sweet and rich. This dough is the base of the many varieties of syrup-soaked sweets found on the tables of these ancient lands and, later, on the tables of Eastern Europe via the Ottoman Turks. Today Baklava and similar sweets are found in all the Arab Gulf countries. On holidays and special occasions, I vividly remember my mother and then my wife setting aside a day to prepare homemade filo dough. During those years the dough could not be purchased. If one wanted a tray of Baklava, one would literally start from scratch with flour, cornstarch and water. The process was near day-long—a small round piece of dough stretched out over and over until less than paper-thin leaves were assembled in a tray. My children recall that when coming home from school and seeing their mother's wedding ring off her finger, they knew filo dough was being made. Jewelry would easily rip the piece of see-through dough. Times have changed. Filo dough is available not only in ethnic stores but has reached the frozen section of supermarkets. It is sold frozen and should be thawed a day beforehand in the refrigerator before use. Once unrolled, the filo should be worked quickly yet carefully. If a drier type of Baklava is desired, prepare only half the Orange Blossom Syrup.

Makes about 35 pieces
Thawing time: 8 hours in refrigerator
Prep time: 45 minutes
Cooking time: 45 minutes

1 recipe Orange Blossom Syrup (page 27)
2 cups (250 g) walnuts, chopped
1 cup (225 g) sugar
2 cups (500 g) Ghee (page 135), melted or
 2 cups (4 sticks/450 g) unsalted butter, melted
1 teaspoon ground cinnamon
1 tablespoon orange blossom water
Unsalted butter or Ghee (page 135), for greasing the baking pan
One 1-lb (500-g) package filo dough, thawed

1 Make the Orange Blossom Syrup. It's important to do this first as the syrup needs time to cool.
2 Preheat the oven to 400°F (200°C).
3 To prepare the walnut filling: Combine the walnut, sugar, 4 tablespoons of the Ghee or butter, cinnamon and orange blossom water in a mixing bowl.
4 Liberally grease a 9 x 13 x 2-inch (23 x 33 x 5-cm) baking pan with Ghee or butter and set aside.
5 Remove the filo dough from the package and spread out on a dish towel. Be careful to cover the unused filo dough with a lightly damped towel or plastic wrap to prevent it from drying out as you work.
6 Assemble the baklava following the illustrated steps on facing page. While assembling the Baklava, work as quickly as you can to keep the dough from becoming dry.
7 Bake for 5 minutes, then lower the heat to 300°F (150°C). Bake for 40 minutes more, or until the sides turn light brown. If you're using a glass-baking pan, look at the sides to determine doneness: when the sides are light brown, the Baklava is ready. If you're using a metal or other opaque pan, the Baklava is done when the top edges begin to brown.
8 After the sides or top edges of the Baklava turn light brown, place the pan under the broiler, turning the pan frequently, until the top of the Baklava turns evenly golden brown. Remove from the oven then immediately spoon the Orange Blossom Syrup over each square or diamond. Allow to cool before serving.

Assembling the Baklava

1 Take one sheet of the filo dough and place it in the bottom of the prepared baking pan. Lightly brush it with some of the melted Ghee or butter, making sure the sheet of dough is completely buttered. If a sheet of filo dough hangs over the sides of the baking pan, fold it back on top of the layer. Continue adding sheets of filo dough, brushing with melted Ghee or butter between each sheet, until one-half of the filo dough is used.

2 Spread the walnut filling evenly over the top of the buttered layers.

3 Place a sheet of the filo dough over the walnut filling and brush with some of the melted Ghee or butter. Filo dough that hangs over the sides of the baking pan should be folded in on top of the layer. Continue adding sheets of filo dough, buttering each sheet before adding the next, until the remainder of the dough is used. Brush the top sheet of dough with butter.

4 Cut into approximately 2-inch (5-cm) squares or diamond shapes.

Ghee Clarified Butter

Used throughout the eastern Arab World, and especially in the Arab Gulf countries, clarified butter has a special flavor and keeps for a very long period of time if refrigerated and even at room temperature if it is kept in an airtight and moisture-free container. Also called Samn Baladi in Egypt and Samn Mufaqqas in the Greater Syria area, Ghee is widely used in the preparation of pastries, and occasionally in savory dishes or even as a liquid garnish on some dishes such as Thick and Rich Lamb Pottage (page 85). Yet, another way to enjoy Ghee is to mix a little with some honey and dip thin slices of bread into it—a delicious yet simple delicacy.

Makes 2 cups (450 g)
Cooking time: 10 minutes

2 cups (4 sticks/450 g) unsalted butter

1 Bring the butter to a boil in a medium saucepan over medium heat. Boil for 2 minutes, or until the froth begins to disappear.
2 Remove from the heat and let cool. Carefully pour the butter into a glass container with a tight-fitting lid, being careful not to pour the sediment at the bottom of the saucepan into the jar. Discard the sediment.

CARDAMOM-SCENTED FRUIT SALAD

As in North Africa, Iraq, Iran and beyond, fruit salads are becoming popular in the Arab Gulf. Today, almost every type of fruit is sold in the *souks* (marketplaces) of the Arab Gulf countries, thus providing the variety needed for fruit salads. In lands where the date once reigned supreme, other fruits are becoming equally popular. The availability of all types of fruit, from the mundane to the exotic, allows the cook to create his or her own salad medley. Feel free to use whatever fruits you like—just make sure to combine at least three different types plus raisins. The cardamom-scented lemon and honey sauce is what gives this fruit salad its Arab Gulf touch. It is a refreshing and tangy salad and can also be served as a salad accompanying an entrée.

Serves 8
Prep time: 20 minutes
Cooking time: 5 minutes
Cooling time: 10 minutes

2 seedless oranges, peeled and separated
　into segments
1 cantaloupe (about 2 lbs/1 kg), peeled and
　cut into 1/2-in (1.25-cm) cubes
2 apples, peeled, cored and cut into 1/2-in
　(1.25-cm) cubes
1/2 cup (75 g) seedless raisins, rinsed

Cardamom Honey Sauce
1/2 cup (125 g) honey
2 tablespoons water
3/4 teaspoon ground cardamom
4 tablespoons freshly squeezed lemon juice

1 To make the Cardamom Honey Sauce: Place the honey, water and cardamom in a small saucepan. Bring to a boil, stirring a few times (add a little water if a thinner syrup is desired). Stir in the lemon juice and remove from the heat. Allow to cool at room temperature.
2 Cut the orange segments in half crosswise. Place the orange segments, cantaloupe cubes, apple cubes and raisin in a large serving bowl. Gently toss the fruit with the cooled Cardamom Honey Sauce and serve immediately.

CRISPY DOUGHNUTS IN SWEET SYRUP Lugaymat Nashab

This traditional dessert is popular in every Arab Gulf country and is found, under various names, throughout North Africa and to the east as far as the Indian sub-continent and beyond. In its numerous forms, it has been around since the days of the early caliphs of Baghdad. References to bite-size pieces of fried dough, dipped in a sweet syrup, are found in medieval culinary texts where they are called Luqmat or Luqum al-Qadi, meaning "the Judge's Tidbits." There is no explanation why they were associated with a judge but no doubt, after trying them, anyone would judge them as one of the tastiest delights. It's always best to serve these fritters the same day that they are made otherwise they lose their external crispy texture.

Makes about 3 dozen
Prep time: 25 minutes
Resting time: 1 hour 10 minutes
Cooking time: 35 minutes

1 recipe Orange Blossom Syrup (page 27)
Neutral-flavored oil, for deep-frying

Batter
2 1/2 cups (300 g) all-purpose flour
1/2 teaspoon salt
1/4 teaspoon ground cardamom
Generous pinch of saffron
1/4 oz/7 g (1 envelope) active dry yeast dissolved in 1/4 cup (65 ml) water and
   1 tablespoon sugar and allowed to sit for 10 minutes until frothy
3 large eggs, beaten
2 cups (500 ml) cold water

1 Make the Orange Blossom Syrup. It's important to do this first as the syrup needs time to cool.
2 To make the Batter: Combine the flour, salt, cardamom and saffron in a mixing bowl. Make a well in the center and add the dissolved yeast, egg and water. Blend together with a wooden spoon until the mixture resembles the texture of pancake batter, adding more water if necessary and making sure there are no lumps. Cover with a tea towel and set aside for 1 hour. It should increase in size by one-half to double.
3 Pour about 2 inches (5 cm) of oil into a medium saucepan and set over medium heat. Heat the oil to a minimum temperature of 345°F (175°C) and no higher than 375°F (190°C), checking with a deep-frying or candy thermometer. If you do not have a thermometer, drop a small piece of bread in the oil. If the bread browns quickly (1 minute or less), the oil is the right temperature. Alternatively you can throw a drop of water in the oil. If the water sizzles upon contact, the oil is ready.
4 Gently drop 1 tablespoon of the Batter into the hot oil until the top of the oil is filled with the dough balls. Deep-fry until the dough turns golden brown. Remove with a slotted spoon and immediately dip the fritters into the Orange Blossom Syrup. Transfer the fritters to a serving platter with a slotted spoon. Continue until all the Batter is used. Serve immediately—the sooner the better.

CREAMY CUSTARD PERFUMED WITH ROSEWATER

Qashtaleeya

A favorite in the United Arab Emirates, this custard is ideal for those who enjoy their desserts well-spiced, especially with the taste of cardamom. It is likely that this custard came to the UAE with western expatriates and that the local people added cloves and cardamom, an Emirati favorite, and rosewater, to give it a distinct Arab Gulf flavor and aroma.

Serves 4
Prep time: 10 minutes
Cooking time: 25 minutes
Refrigeration time: 2 hours

2 cups (500 ml) whole milk
1/2 cup (115 g) sugar
1/2 teaspoon ground cardamom
Generous pinch of ground cloves
2 tablespoons cornstarch dissolved in a little water to a
   thin paste-like consistency
2 teaspoons rosewater
Pistachios, coarsely ground, for garnish

1 Bring the milk, sugar, cardamom and cloves to a boil in a medium saucepan, stirring a number of times.
2 Turn the heat to medium-low and stir in the cornstarch paste. Continue stirring until the custard becomes smooth and thick and begins to bubble, about 10 to 15 minutes. Turn the heat to very low and stir in the rosewater. Continue to stir and cook for 2 minutes. Pour into individual serving dishes and garnish with the pistachio. Chill before serving.

MELT-IN-YOUR-MOUTH CARDAMOM SHORTBREADS

Ghurayba

Ghurayba, a type of shortbread, has been around in the Greater Syria area, Iraq and other Arab countries since ancient times. Today it is also found in the Arab Gulf countries, especially Saudi Arabia, but with a twist—the addition of one of the most popular spices of the Arabian Peninsula, cardamom. Children in the eastern Arab World look forward to this delicious shortbread often made by their mothers in the family kitchen. At our farm home during my boyhood years, for any festive occasion, mother always made this simple-to-prepare, mouth-melting dessert. Of all the sweets that mother made, I think most fondly of these, perhaps because they marked nearly every memorable happy family event and gathering. This cookie recipe is a hands-on process, literally! I find it easiest to work the dough with my hands, though a wooden spoon could also be used if preferred. These cookies are particularly pretty when formed in a mold, but they are equally delicious made without one, and instructions are provided to make them either way. Many molds made for Arab sweets are designed to form just one cookie at a time, whereas most Western-style molds generally allow you to form multiple cookies at one go in the same mold. The most common mold used for Arab confections is wooden and has a long handle, and is available at Middle Eastern stores that sell kitchenware items.

Makes about 25 to 30 pieces
Prep time: 30 minutes
Cooking time: 20 minutes

1 cup (2 sticks/225 g) unsalted butter, at
    room temperature
1 cup (120 g) confectioners' sugar
1 teaspoon orange blossom water or
    rosewater
1/2 teaspoon ground cardamom
2 cups (240 g) all-purpose flour
25 to 30 blanched almonds, to garnish
    cookies made without molds (optional)
1/2 cup (60 g) confectioners' sugar, to dust
    cookies (optional)

Special equipment (optional)
Shortbread or confection molds

NOTE: Don't be fooled when the timer goes off noting that the Ghurayba is done. They may appear to be under-baked, but do not judge a cookie by its cover! They should be slightly browned only on the bottom.

1 Preheat the oven to 300°F (150°C).
2 Using your hands, work the butter until soft and smooth. Gradually add the 1 cup (120 g) of confectioner's sugar, orange blossom water or rosewater and cardamom while mixing the dough by hand until soft and smooth with a creamy consistency. Again, using your hands, mix in the flour until it is well combined and forms a soft dough.
3 Form the dough into round balls, a little smaller than a walnut, and place on an un-greased cookie sheet. Using your fingers, flatten slightly to about 1/2-inch (1.25-cm) thickness, and, place an almond, if using, in the middle of each cookie, pressing lightly. If using a mold, place a ball of dough in the mold, press gently, and then flip it over onto the cookie sheet. Repeat with the remaining dough balls. Bake for 20 minutes, or until the bottoms turn very slightly light brown. Do not allow the Ghurayba to brown. Remove from the oven and allow to completely cool on the cookie sheets. If desired, sprinkle with the 1/2 cup (60 g) of confectioners' sugar.
4 Serve or store in an airtight container at room temperature or in the refrigerator. (They will keep up to 3 to 4 weeks stored in an air-tight container at room temperature and for approximately 2 months in the refrigerator.)

SAUDI-STYLE CREPES FILLED WITH SWEETENED ALMONDS Lahooh bil Lawz

The delicate texture of these almond-filled roll-ups is reminiscent of crepes, though these crepes are yeasted, whereas traditional crepes are unleavened. For those with a sweet tooth, they can be served with date or other syrups or with honey. They are excellent with tea or coffee as an afternoon or evening snack. My preference is to have them for breakfast, dipped in honey. Back home in Canada I invited a few friends over for brunch to introduce them to these Saudi-style crepes. My guests had the option of dipping them in honey or in maple syrup, a favorite Canadian sweetener. As it turned out those who dipped them in honey and those who dipped them in the maple syrup decided that each wanted to try the other. So it was back to the kitchen to make a second batch—an effort well spent and appreciated.

Serves 6
Prep time: 25 minutes
Standing time: 2 hours 10 minutes
Cooking time: 15 minutes

1 cup (120 g) all-purpose flour
1 teaspoon baking powder
1/2 teaspoon salt
1/4 oz/7 g (1 envelope) active dry yeast
    dissolved in 1/2 cup (125 ml) warm water
    and 1/2 teaspoon of sugar and allowed to
    stand for 10 minutes
1 cup (250 ml) milk
1 large egg, beaten
2 tablespoons unsalted butter, melted
Neutral-flavored oil, for greasing skillet
1/3 cup (75 g) sugar
1/2 teaspoon ground cardamom
1/2 cup (75 g) almonds, toasted and ground

1 Thoroughly mix together the flour, baking powder, salt, yeast mixture, milk, egg and butter in a mixing bowl to make a thin pancake-like batter. Refrigerate covered for 1 to 2 hours, allowing the batter to rise.
2 Grease a medium skillet with a little oil and set over medium heat. Cooking one crepe at a time, pour 1/4 cup (65ml) of the batter into the hot skillet and quickly spread out the batter with the back of a small spoon to create a thin crepe. When bubbles form on the top turn the crepe over and cook until the underside browns. Repeat with the rest of the batter.
3 Combine the sugar, cardamom and 6 tablespoons of the toasted and ground almond in a small bowl. Place about 1 1/2 tablespoons of this mixture on one side of each crepe and roll into cigar shapes. Place on a serving dish, sprinkle with the remaining almond, and serve.

Serves 8
Prep time: 40 minutes
Cooking time: 20 minutes
Refrigeration time: 12 hours

1 recipe Orange Blossom Syrup (page 27)
16 slices white bread, plus 1 or 2 if needed
2 cups (500 ml) half-and-half cream
2 tablespoons sugar
2 tablespoons orange blossom water
4 tablespoons finely ground pistachio nuts,
   for garnish

1 Make the Orange Blossom Syrup. It's important to do this first as the syrup needs time to cool.
2 Remove the crusts from the bread slices and discard. Toast 8 of the bread slices. Cut the remaining 8 slices into tiny pieces.
3 Place the toasted bread slices side by side in a 9 x 13 x 2-inch (23 x 33 x 5-cm) baking pan. If there are any gaps, toast 1 or 2 additional slices of bread (with crusts removed) and cut to fit the gaps.
4 Bring the half-and-half cream, bread pieces, sugar and orange blossom water to a boil in a medium saucepan, stirring constantly. Reduce the heat to medium and continue cooking, stirring constantly, until the mixture thickens. Reduce the heat to the lowest possible setting to keep warm.
5 Pour the Orange Blossom Syrup over the toast in the baking pan. Spread the cream mixture evenly over the top and sprinkle on the pistachio. Cover with plastic wrap and refrigerate for at least 12 hours before serving.

SWEET BREAD PUDDING
'Aysh as-Saraaya

With a long culinary history stretching back thousands of years, the desserts of the Middle East are among the most delicious in the world. One of these is 'Aysh as-Saraaya, originating either in Egypt, Syria or Lebanon. The Arabic word for "bread" in Egypt being *'aysh*, and for "palace," *saraaya*, the name of this dessert can be translated to mean "Bread of the Palace" or "Palace Bread." Yet, 'aysh also refers to living and to life, and, after tasting it, its name could well mean "life of mansions," meaning something of luxury. This dessert, once prepared in the homes of the wealthy Emirs and Sultans, is now very popular in the homes and restaurants of all the Arab Gulf countries, particularly in the United Arab Emirates and Qatar. What better way to describe this luxuriously creamy yet light dessert than to say it is a sensational combination of toasted bread soaked in scented syrup, topped with orange blossom flavored thick cream and garnished with pistachios. This simplified "Bread of the Palace" recipe came from a group of Arab-American women living in a small Syrian community in Pennsylvania, and who were honored to provide their version for this cookbook. Here, un-crusted toast replaces the original *ka'k* (dried biscuit) or in some cases, the use of breadcrumbs for the base. It is an ideal dessert for a dinner party as it is made a day ahead to allow it to set and chill.

FILO WRAPPED NUT ROLLS

Nashab

Nashab, so named because of its cylindrical shape, like that of a rolling pin, claims a lineage that goes back to ninth-century Baghdad, when that city was at the center of the world. Today this traditional sweet, especially prepared during the time of the Eid, the Muslim holiday that marks the end of Ramadan, is well-known in the United Arab Emirates as well as in other Arab Gulf countries. These sweet and crunch nut-filled filo dough pastries are a great ending to a meal or a good snack when served with a hot cup of Arab coffee or tea.

> **NOTE:** The process of rolling up and deep-frying seventy-five or more Nashab is time-consuming, but when properly stored they will keep up to three weeks. This recipe calls for using 1 lb of filo dough because it most typically comes in 1-lb (500-g) packages, and unused dough cannot be re-refrigerated or refrozen—thereby making it impossible to halve this recipe. However, the Athens brand of filo dough does make a twin package of two 8-ounce (250-g) portions. If you can find the twin package of filo dough, you may halve the recipe to make a more manageable amount of between thirty-six and forty-four pieces.

Assembling the Nut Rolls

1 Take one piece of filo dough at a time and set it on your work surface. Place 1 level tablespoon of the filling along the middle of the bottom (short) edge, leaving about 1 inch (2.5 cm) at the bottom and 2 inches (5 cm) on the sides.

2 Fold both long sides over the filling.

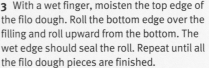

3 With a wet finger, moisten the top edge of the filo dough. Roll the bottom edge over the filling and roll upward from the bottom. The wet edge should seal the roll. Repeat until all the filo dough pieces are finished.

Makes 72 to 88 rolls, depending on number of filo sheets in the package
Prep time: 1 hour 15 minutes
Cooking time: 45 minutes to 1 hour

1 recipe Orange Blossom Syrup (page 27)
1 1/4 cups (190 g) raw cashew nuts
1 cup (100 g) walnuts
1/2 cup (75 g) blanched whole almonds
1 teaspoon ground cardamom
1 cup (225 g) sugar
One 1-lb (500-g) package filo dough, thawed
Neutral-flavored oil, for frying

1 Make the Orange Blossom Syrup. It's important to do this first as the syrup needs time to cool.
2 To make the filling, place the cashew, walnut, almond, cardamom and sugar in a food processor and process for 1 minute, or until the mixture is a thick paste. Set aside.
3 Cut the filo dough into quarters and cover with a very lightly dampened tea cloth.
4 Assemble the nut rolls, following the illustrated steps on left of page.
5 Pour 2 to 3 inches (5 to 7.5 cm) of oil into a medium saucepan and set over medium heat. Heat the oil to a minimum temperature of 345°F (175°C) and no higher than 375°F (190°C), checking with a deep-frying or candy thermometer. If you do not have a thermometer, drop a small piece of bread in the oil. If the bread browns quickly (1 minute or less), the oil is the right temperature. Alternatively you can throw a drop of water in the oil. If the water sizzles upon contact, the oil is ready.
6 Deep-fry the rolls in batches (do not overcrowd the pan), turning them over until they are evenly and lightly browned. Remove with a slotted spoon and place in the Orange Blossom Syrup for a few moments. Transfer the rolls to a serving dish with a slotted spoon and allow to cool. They are at their best when eaten freshly made. However, they can be stored in an airtight, moisture-free container in the refrigerator, where they will last in good condition for up to 3 weeks.

Filo Wrapped Nut Rolls

SWEET DATE PUDDING
Halwa

In Oman, Halwa, literally meaning "sweet," is similar in texture to the jellylike confection Turkish Delight, but softer, and is usually purchased in confectioneries in large urban centers. The making and selling of Halwa is one of the important cottage industries of Oman, a trade handed down from father to son, and is a source of national pride. Halwa is famous as a quintessential symbol of Omani hospitality and is served on special occasions and religious holidays. Today this renowned Omani sweet has become popular throughout the Arabian Peninsula. Halwa is so popular in Oman that it is sold in individual ready-to-eat portions not only in confectioneries but also in specialized fast-food stalls in the souks. In Muscat, for example, as I walked in the food section of the capital's main traditional souk, I saw a long line of people patiently waiting for their turn to receive their orders of Halwa from a Halwa stall owned and operated by a family who had been in the business for decades. According to the son, advertizing was never needed because as far as he knew, his family's Halwa had been and continued to be the best in town! In my own version of this famous sweet, which successfully recreates the flavor of the traditional Omani Halwa, I have added an egg to give a fuller body to the pudding.

Serves 6
Prep time: 20 minutes
Cooking time: 20 minutes
Refrigeration time: 4 hours

1 lb (500 g) dates, pitted and chopped
3 cups (750 ml) water
1/2 cup (115 g) sugar
3 tablespoons cornstarch dissolved in 1/4 cup (65 ml) water
1/2 cup (75 g) slivered almonds, toasted
3 tablespoons unsalted butter
2 teaspoons rosewater
1/4 teaspoon ground cardamom
1/4 teaspoon freshly grated nutmeg
Pinch of saffron
1 large egg, beaten

1 Bring the dates and water to a boil in a medium saucepan, stirring a number of times. Then cook over medium-low heat for about 3 minutes, stirring continually until the dates become very soft and lose their form.
2 Stir in the sugar and cook for a few minutes or until the sugar is dissolved. Stir in the dissolved cornstarch and cook over low heat until the mixture thickens, stirring frequently. Stir in the rest of the ingredients.
3 Cook for 2 minutes, continually stirring. Pour the mixture into 6 individual pudding bowls or into a shallow casserole dish. Allow to cool for a few hours in the refrigerator before serving.

CHAPTER 10
DRINKS

For centuries coffee and Arabia have been inseparable. The word for coffee in most languages around the world is derived from the Arabic *qahwah*. The first mention of coffee as a beverage was made around 900 A.D. in the writings of the Arab medieval physician Al-Razi, known in the West as Rhazes. Al-Razi extolled the beverage's medicinal purposes, stating that it was "hot and dry and very good for the stomach."

In the sixteenth century, Constantinople, the capital of the Ottoman Empire of which most of the Arab lands were part, became the headquarters of the coffee-drinking world. And by the end of the sixteenth century, the coffee drinking habit had spread from Turkey to the remainder of Europe.

Although the joys of coffee have spread to the four corners of the world, it is in its original homeland, the Arabian Peninsula, that it retains its mystical hold and central importance in the lives of the people. As it was in the past, even today it is almost impossible to imagine the Arabian Peninsula without the enticing aroma of roasting coffee or the soothing ring of the pestle pulverizing the freshly roasted beans. There it is a symbol of welcome and friendship—an Arab tradition since the beginning of time. For a guest to refuse a cup of coffee is to greatly insult the host. It is a social beverage offered to guests in homes and to customers by shopkeepers. Travelers will often find coffee and dates in the lobbies of hotels as a token of hospitality.

Arabs always take pride in preparing their coffee. It is the drink par excellence among the people in all the countries of the Arabian Peninsula. As an Arab proverb goes: "The best cup of coffee must be as bitter as death and as hot as love."

Though Arabs drink a lot of coffee—probably more than any other people on earth—they also consume a great deal of tea, which was introduced by Arab merchants traveling to and from China. Today, in the Arab Gulf countries, tea, including many made from herbs and spices, is the second most popular beverage after coffee, followed by soft drinks, yogurt drinks, fruit juices and non-alcoholic beer.

Iced coffee in the Arab Gulf countries is still a novelty, patronized by expatriates, tourists and other western travelers. Western firms like Dunkin Donuts and Starbucks have introduced it into this part of the world but its consumption is still limited. In the future it could spread among the Western-oriented youth, but to compete with traditional coffee, in my view, "not in this century!" Even in the boiling heat of summer, it is not likely that it will replace this traditional Arab gift to the world.

ICED YOGURT DRINK WITH FRESH MINT

Laban

Laban has been described as being somewhat like "salty butter-milk." It is a refreshing beverage and it is a great drink to serve with any type of meat dish. In the Middle East the attributes of yogurt have been appreciated since the dawn of history. The ancient Assyrians were enamored with yogurt so much that they called it *lebeny*, meaning "life." The venerable yogis of India mixed yogurt with honey and called it "the food of the gods." Cleopatra bathed in yogurt to give herself a clear complexion and soft skin, and Genghis Khan fed it to his soldiers to give them courage. One of humankind's earliest prepared foods, yogurt can claim few equals in the folklore of the culinary arts. Very popular in the United Arab Emirates and Saudi Arabia, yogurt drinks are especially important during Ramadan when they are drunk to break the fast at sundown. Many believe that after fasting all day yogurt helps in the digestion of the food that is to be eaten in the upcoming meal. Served with dates, it is a Ramadan drink par-excellence. Laban is also cooling and soothing on a hot summer day. The mint gives the drink a little more tang.

Makes Six 8-oz (250-ml) servings
Prep time: 10 minutes
Refrigeration time: 1 hour

4 cups (1 kg) store-bought or Homemade Plain Yogurt (page 31)
2 cups (500 ml) water
3/4 teaspoon salt
1 teaspoon crushed dried mint leaves
Handful of fresh mint leaves, for garnish

1 Place all the ingredients, except the fresh mint leaves, in a blender and blend for 1 minute.
2 Refrigerate until ready to serve. Serve in six 8-ounce (250-ml) glasses. If you wish, Laban may be served over ice. Garnish each glass with the fresh mint leaves.

Iced Yogurt Drink with Fresh Mint

Cardamom-Spiced Hot Milk

CARDAMOM-SPICED HOT MILK

Haleeb ma' Haal

Cardamom is what gives a unique twist to the classic cup of warm milk—a favorite night-time beverage around the world. It is also believed that Haleeb ma' Haal, enjoyed throughout the United Arab Emirates, calms and relaxes the body, making it ideal for a restful night of sleep.

Makes about three 8-ounce (250-ml) or 8 demitasse servings
Prep time: 10 minutes
Cooking time: 10 minutes

2³/4 cups (650 ml) milk
2 teaspoons sugar
¹/2 teaspoon ground cardamom

1 Bring all the ingredients to a boil in a medium saucepan, stirring constantly.
2 Simmer over medium-low heat for 5 minutes, stirring a few times. Remove from the heat and serve immediately.

Makes 6 to 8 demitasse servings
Prep time: 10 minutes
Cooking time: 10 minutes
Standing time: 10 minutes

2 cups (500 ml) water
4 tablespoons fresh finely ground coffee or
     espresso grind
2 tablespoons ground cardamom
2 whole cloves

1 Bring the water, coffee and cardamom to
a boil, in an *ibrik* or a small saucepan with a
lid, uncovered.
2 Reduce the heat to medium-low and boil for
4 minutes, stirring occasionally. Do not let the
coffee overflow.
3 Remove from the heat, cover, and set
aside for 1 minute. Place the whole cloves
in a coffee thermos and strain the coffee into
the thermos. Allow to sit for 10 minutes
before serving.

OMANI-STYLE COFFEE Khawa

The sign of a great cup of coffee, such as this Omani-style coffee, is that it tastes as good as it smells—like a rich, spiced
coffee. Hospitality in Oman begins with Khawa and a platter of dates. This strong brew, made with freshly ground coffee
beans and aromatic cardamom, has a pleasantly bitter taste. For those who take sugar with their coffee, beware—Khawa
is made without sugar and served without cream. Restaurants, of course, cater to their customers and some may serve
it with sugar on the side. In general, the preparation of Arab coffee involves bringing the water and coffee to a boil three
times. This ensures a rich and strong brew of coffee somewhat similar to espresso (see Real Arab Coffee Made Just Right,
page 149). Khawa, on the other hand, involves one long boil allowing for a stronger tasting coffee with the prominent
taste of cardamom. This, in combination with the infusion of cloves in the coffee, is what gives Khawa its unique flavor.
Omani coffee is traditionally served in small (handle-less) Arab coffee cups poured from a *midlah* or coffee thermos.
There is no standard size for the demitasse in which the coffee is served. In the past the tiny cups were somewhat standard—about 4 tablespoons—but today some are usually a little larger. However, the majority still are about a quarter-
size of a standard coffee cup. You may use any type of demitasse cup.

REAL ARAB COFFEE MADE JUST RIGHT

Qahwa Mazbut

In the Eastern Arab World, coffee, or *qahwa*, a gift that the Arabs gave the world, is made thick and black in three styles: *murra* (bitter), which is drunk by the real coffee connoisseurs and is made without sugar; *sukkar qalil* (little sugar), made with 1 teaspoon of sugar; and *mazbut* (just right), made with 1½ to 2 teaspoons of sugar. All three styles of coffee can be brewed using this recipe: simply lessen the amount of sugar for sukkar qalil or omit it altogether for murra. The brew is allowed to come to a boil three times to form foam. In the Arab World, this foam is called "the face of the coffee," and one loses face if the coffee is served without it. For Qahwa Mazbut one can use pre-ground cardamom and easy-to-find roasted coffee—either pre-ground or whole beans to freshly grind at home. However, freshly ground coffee and cardamom will give the best flavor. To Arabs any coffee served has a meaning. According to our host at the Coffee Room in the Cham Palace Hotel, located amid the magnificent ruins of Palmyra in Syria, coffee embodies three things: its rich aroma signifies the joy of meeting; its bitterness represents the sadness of departing; and its blackness reveals the dark eyes of the beloved. With metaphors such as these, it is no wonder that this gift that the Arabs gave the world remains their most cherished brew.

Makes 6 to 8 demitasse servings
Prep time: 15 minutes
Cooking time: 10 minutes
Standing time: 2 minutes

2 cups (500 ml) cold water
¼ teaspoon pre-ground cardamom or freshly pulverized cardamom seeds (see below)
1½ to 2 teaspoons sugar, to taste
5 teaspoons fresh finely ground coffee or espresso grind

1 Bring the water, cardamom and sugar to a boil in an *ibrik* or small saucepan. Remove from the heat and add the coffee. Stir and, as the foam begins to form, spoon a little of the foam into each of the tiny Arab coffee cups.

2 Return the coffee to the heat and bring to a boil again. Remove from the heat, stir, and allow to settle for about 1 minute. Repeat the same process once more, and then remove from the heat and allow to settle before serving over the foam in the cups.

3 Carefully pour the coffee into the cups to make sure that most of the grounds remain in the bottom of an ibrik or saucepan. Similar to Turkish coffee, a small amount of the fine coffee grounds will settle at the bottom of the cups—so a "bottoms-up" drinking style is not recommended!

HOW TO PULVERIZE CARDAMOM SEEDS

To pulverize cardamom seeds, you will first need to extract the seeds from the whole pods. To lessen your work, use the largest pods you can find. To extract the seeds from cardamom pods, lay a pod on a cutting board. Place the side of a chef's knife or other large knife on top of the pod. Press firmly on the side of the knife to smash the shell. Pick out the seeds with your fingers. To make a ¼ teaspoon of freshly pulverized cardamom, you will need 3 large pods containing approximately 20 seeds each. The pods I use are about ¼ x ¾ inch (6 mm x 2 cm). If you cannot find pods that large, count on needing additional pods.

Arab Coffee Demystified

Traditionally, coffee is brewed in an *ibrik*—a small, spouted metal pot with a long handle. At times, after the coffee is brewed, it is transferred into a brass serving pot called a *dallah*—the most significant serving utensil in the Arab World. However, in many parts of the eastern Arab countries an ibrik is used for the whole coffee-making procedure, including pouring the coffee into small handle-less China cups (demitasse). However, there is no difference in brewing the coffee in the traditional ibrik or in a small saucepan—the results will be the same.

Because coffee is so important in the life of the Arabs, the ceremony of making and serving coffee is replete with its own utensils. Tradition dictates that Arab coffee be served without sugar. Yet, today, on occasion, the coffee tray will include a sugar holder with a little spoon for those who are not accustomed to bitter and strong coffee. The guest has the option of adding a little or a lot depending on personal preference. The host usually goes around serving the coffee. If the guest has had enough, the guest will shake the coffee cup to indicate no more is wanted. Usually a guest will drink three of these tiny cups before shaking the cup. This whole procedure reflects the history and importance of coffee and hospitality. Whether under the coolness of a Bedouin tent, at home or in one of the Peninsula's luxurious hotels, guests are presented with traditional Arab coffee as a welcoming gesture.

sauɒı style "chaı"

Shai bil-Haal wa Qirfa

Many of the inhabitants of the Arabian Peninsula, where cardamom is used extensively, believe that this spice makes a marvelous mouth freshener. For neutralizing the smell of garlic and to freshen the breath, a few cardamom pods are slowly chewed, allowing the flavor to linger in the mouth. At times, a pod is combined with a few fennel seeds and a whole clove to create a more effective breath freshener. Sipping on this spicy Arab Gulf tea, although not quite as effective, has a similar effect. I have made this tea quite often since first being introduced to it on a visit to Dubai. It now has become an almost regular hot "*digestif*" at our table after a full meal and a lavish spread of sweets.

Makes six 6-oz (175-ml) servings
Prep time: 10 minutes
Cooking time: 15 minutes

3 cups (750 ml) water
2 teaspoons loose black tea
1 small cinnamon stick
6 cardamom pods, whole but cracked
1/2 teaspoon fennel seeds
1 cup (250 ml) milk
2 tablespoons sugar

1 Bring the water, tea, cinnamon stick, cardamom and fennel seed to a boil in a medium saucepan with a lid.
2 Cover and simmer over medium-low heat for 10 minutes. Stir in the milk and the sugar then bring to a boil again. Pour into heat-proof glasses or cups through a small strainer and serve hot.

CLOCKWISE FROM TOP RIGHT: Lemon Tea, Cinnamon Tea and Saudi Style "Chai".

LEMON TEA Shai bil-Laymoon

This is a typical lemon-flavored hot tea that I first had in Kuwait, quite by accident. After a tiring day of traveling, and the weather being somewhat unexpectedly cool, I felt like a hot cup of tea was in order. Suggesting this to my Kuwaiti host, I was surprised with his response that he never drank tea—that is, tea made from tea leaves. Not wanting to disappoint him, I awaited the cup of coffee that I was sure he was going to offer me in its place. Instead, out came his wife with a steaming cup of Shai bil-Laymoon. She then explained that the only surprise she discovered when she got married was that her husband simply did not like tea. To compensate, she introduced him to this lemon tea and after that, their shared evenings over the usual cup of coffee transitioned to the more relaxing lemon tea. Shai bil-Laymoon, I discovered, was delicious. Perhaps it was the fresh lemon, perhaps it was knowing that one lemon provides nearly 80 percent of a person's daily need of vitamin C, or perhaps the orange blossom water, but knowing that this hot version of lemonade tasted this good, spurred me on to have another cup and ask them for the recipe.

Makes four 6-oz (185-ml) servings
Prep time: 10 minutes
Cooking time: 25 minutes

3 cups (750 ml) water
1 lemon, washed and quartered
1¹/2 tablespoons sugar
1¹/2 teaspoons orange blossom water

1 Bring the water and lemon to a boil in a medium saucepan with a lid.
2 Cover and simmer over medium-low heat for 20 minutes. Strain the hot water and lemon mixture into another saucepan or teapot and stir in the sugar and orange blossom water. Bring to a boil and serve.

CINNAMON TEA Shai Qirfah

While brewing in its pot, this tea's wonderful and unexpected aroma is enticing. A favored spice among Middle Eastern Arabs and used, mostly, in making desserts, cinnamon is used to make this delicious tea in Kuwait and in most of the other countries along the Arabian Gulf.

Makes four 8-oz (250-ml) servings
Prep time: 5 minutes
Cooking time: 25 minutes

4 cups (1 liter) water
4 cinnamon sticks, each about 3-in (7.5-cm) long
1 tablespoon sugar

1 Bring the water and cinnamon to a boil in a medium saucepan with a lid .
2 Cover and brew over medium heat for 20 minutes. Remove the cinnamon sticks. Stir in the sugar and boil for 1 minute before serving.

POMEGRANATE JUICE SPRITZER

Sharab Rumman

Pomegranates originated in Persia and are among the oldest fruits in the world. Some scholars even suggest that it was a pomegranate instead of an apple in the Garden of Eden with which Eve tempted Adam. Sharab Rumman appears in almost every medieval Arabic culinary text attesting to its popularity for more than 1,000 years. A very popular drink in Saudi Arabia, it can be found in restaurants as well as in homes. In the Arab Gulf Countries this drink is usually made from pomegranate syrup, which in North America is only available in Middle Eastern or Arab markets. To make this drink more accessible I call for using fresh pomegranate juice, which is now widely available in the refrigerated sections in supermarkets. When buying fresh pomegranate juice, make sure it's pure and isn't flavored with any other type of fruit.

Makes six 8-oz (250-ml) or eight 6-oz (175-ml) servings
Prep time: 10 minutes
Refrigeration time: 3 hours

3 cups (750 ml) fresh pomegranate juice
3 cups (750 ml) club soda
2 tablespoons freshly squeezed lemon juice
1 tablespoon orange blossom water
4 tablespoons sugar
1/4 teaspoon ground cloves

1 Process all the ingredients in a blender for 1 minute.
2 Refrigerate for a few hours to chill or serve immediately over ice in glasses.

Pomegranate Juice Spritzer

hot ginger milk flavored with cloves

Shai Zanjabeel ma' Haleeb

In the Arabian Gulf countries this tea is often served as a remedy for colds and sore throats. My first experience with this slightly spicy hot milk was in Oman, in Muscat, where a sprinkling of dried thyme was added as garnish by my host who claimed this to be the best way to drink it. Other versions of this tea are made with evaporated milk and use cardamom instead of cloves; others use tea and only a small amount of ginger. Yet, no matter how this tea is made, it is a unique soothing beverage that is also a great accompaniment to food.

Makes four 8-oz (250-ml) or six 5-oz (150-ml) servings
Prep time: 5 minutes
Cooking time: 15 minutes

4 cups (1 liter) milk
1 tablespoon ground ginger
Generous pinch of ground cloves
2 tablespoons honey

1 Bring the milk, ginger and clove to a boil, in a medium saucepan, stirring constantly.
2 Reduce the heat to medium-low and gently boil for 8 to 10 minutes, stirring occasionally. Stir in the honey and serve piping hot.

aniseed tea

Shai Yansoon

Aniseed Tea is one of the more popular hot beverages served throughout the Arab Gulf countries. This slightly sweet tea with a subtle hint of licorice is a beverage of choice after enjoying a heavy meal. In fact, for centuries, a hot drink of aniseed and water has been used to relieve stomach discomfort and indigestion. As a child, my mother always had Aniseed Tea ready, whether we complained about abdominal discomforts or not, as she considered this tea to be healthy and beneficial. But as an adult I discovered that this tea is also enjoyed purely for its taste, regardless of its medicinal qualities. While at Abu Dhabi's waterfront *sheesha* (water pipe) cafes, my colleagues enjoyed puffing on their tobacco while sipping on Shai Yansoon. I, on the other hand, indulged in this delicious hot drink without the need to smoke.

Makes four 8-oz (250-ml) servings
Prep time: 5 minutes
Cooking time: 5 minutes
Standing time: 5 minutes

4 cups (1 liter) water
3 teaspoons loose green tea
2 teaspoons ground aniseed
2 tablespoons sugar or to taste

1 Bring the water to a boil. In the meantime, while the water is coming to a boil, place the rest of the ingredients in a teapot.
2 Pour the boiling water into the teapot and stir. Allow to steep for 5 minutes. Strain into tea cups or heat-proof glasses and serve immediately.

RESOURCE GUIDE

In addition to the food stores indicated below there are literally hundreds if not thousands of other stores that carry ingredients used in Arab cooking. Many are to be found in the large urban centers in the Eastern and Midwest states in the United Sates and the provinces of Ontario and Quebec in Canada. In the entries for each store I've listed specific, hard-to-find ingredients and tools (including Arab coffee service); however, these lists only reflect a smattering of the total inventory carried at each store. If you're looking for other ingredients, just ask. They probably carry what you're looking for.

Northeast U.S.

SYRIAN GROCERY IMPORTING CO
270 Shawmut Ave
Boston, MA 02118
Tel: (617) 426-1458; Fax: (617) 426-1458
Email: jwm3856@hotmail.com
Open Tuesday to Saturday 12 noon to 7 p.m.,
Closed on Sunday and Monday

The store is stocked to the ceiling with olive and nut oils; rose and orange flower waters; Middle Eastern date, fig and pomegranate syrups; dried fruit, grains and nuts of every kind; olives galore and preserved lemons in brine; as well as bulk dried spices. Basically speaking, everything a person cooking Arab food needs is here. They can ship anywhere in the continental U.S. and they even stock Syrian truffles and dried limes—not found in many U.S. ethnic food markets. The business has been in operation since the 1940s. Among other items, they carry: pomegranate concentrate/molasses, Syrian truffles, dried limes, Arab coffee, Arab coffee cups, Baharat, *dallahs*, *falafel* molds, *ibriks*, sumac, trays for serving Arab coffee, *za'tar*, zucchini corers, preserved grape leaves.

LEBANESE FOOD MARKET
1564 Hancock Street
Quincy, MA 02169
Tel: (617) 376- 4770 or (617) 699-5887
Fax: (617) 376-4776
www.lebanesefoodmarket.com
Open Monday to Friday 9.30 a.m. to 7.30 p.m.,
Saturday 9.30 a.m. to 7 p.m.

A brick-and-mortar grocery store and nationwide online grocery that offers everything one could need to prepare Arab Gulf foods. They also sell prepared Middle Eastern foods. Ships to Canada and to the U.S. Among other items, they carry: Arab coffee cups (assorted sizes and varieties), Arab coffee hand grinder, Arab coffee (ground), *falafel* molds, *ibrik* (assorted sizes), coffee pots, pastry/date confection molds (for making shortbread) pomegranate concentrate/molasses, preserved grape leaves in the jar, sumac, *za'tar*, zucchini corer.

Mid-Atlantic U.S.

BALADY FOODS
7128 5th Ave, (between 72nd St & Ovington Ave), Brooklyn, NY 11209
Tel: (718) 567-2252
Fax: (718) 228-8114
www.sultansdelight.com
Open 7 days a week from 9 a.m. to 10 p.m.

It stocks everything needed to prepare Arab Gulf recipes. Ships to U.S. and Canada. Orders can be taken by phone (800-852-5046). Among other items, they carry: Arab coffee (ground), coffee thermoses, *falafel* molds, *ibrik* (assorted sizes), coffee pots, pomegranate concentrate/molasses, concentrated pomegranate juice, preserved grape leaves in the jar, sumac, *za'tar*, zucchini corer.

BAROODY IMPORTS, INC.
1500 B Main Ave
Clifton, NJ 07011
Tel: (973) 340-4832
Fax: (973) 340-5193
Email: baroodyy@cs.com
Open Monday to Friday 7 a.m. to 6 p.m.

Wholesale Middle Eastern groceries and related products. They carry a large amount and assortment of ingredients and kitchen utensils, and will sell to individuals but items must be purchased by the case. Ships U.S. (UPS C.O.D.). Orders taken by telephone, email or fax. Major credit cards are accepted. Among other items, they carry: Arab coffee cups (assorted varieties), Arab coffee trays, Arab coffee (beans and ground), Baharat, chickpea flour, *dallahs*, dried lime powder, *falafel* molds, fresh grape leaves, *ibriks*, pomegranate concentrate/molasses/syrup, preserved grape leaves, sumac, truffles (Lebanon), *za'tar*, zucchini corers.

SAHADI'S
187 Atlantic Ave
Brooklyn, NY 11201
Tel: (718) 624-4550
Fax: (718) 643-4415
Email: mail@sahadis.com
www.sahadis.com
Open Monday to Saturday, 9 a.m. to 7 p.m.,
Closed on Sunday

Almost any product or ingredient needed to prepare Arab Gulf foods is available at the store. The website, however, carries a more limited and specialized number of items. Ships to U.S. only—orders taken on website. No telephone orders. Sahadi's is a long-standing business that has been in operation since the 1940s. Among other items, they carry: Arab coffee (beans and ground), Baharat, pomegranate concentrate/molasses, preserved grape leaves, sumac, *za'tar*.

Southeast U.S.

BARAKA INTERNATIONAL FOODS
5596 Nolensville Pike
NashvilleTN 37211
Tel: (615) 333-9285
Fax: (615) 837-8541
Open 7 days a week from 8 a.m. to 7 p.m.

It stocks a wide variety of spices and other ingredients used in Arab cooking. Baraka also has a store in Memphis but the one in Nashville is much larger. They can ship to any part of the U.S. and beyond. Among other items, they carry: Arab coffee (beans and ground), Baharat, *falafel* molds, pomegranate concentrate/molasses, preserved grape leaves, sumac, *za'tar*.

DAMASCUS MID-EAST FOOD MARKET

5721 Hollywood Boulevard
Hollywood, FL 33021
Tels: (954) 962-4552; (954) 962-4545
Email: alavi.reza@gmail.com
Open Monday to Saturday 10 a.m. to 7 p.m.,
Closed on Sunday

The store carries a wide variety of Persian and Middle Eastern groceries. It offers spices and most other ingredients used in the cooking of the Arab Gulf Countries. Telephone orders taken and will ship UPS C.O.D. Credit card payments accepted. Among other items, they carry: Arab coffee cups, Arab coffee (beans and ground), Baharat, *falafel* molds, *ibriks*, pomegranate concentrate/molasses, preserved grape leaves, sumac, *za'tar*, zucchini corers.

SEASON'S FRESH MARKET

1757 N. University Drive
Plantation, FL 33322
Tel: (954) 577-8626
Fax: (954) 577-9343
Email: seasonsfresh@bellsouth.net
www.seasonsfreshmarket.com/
Open Monday to Saturday 9.30 a.m. to 8 p.m.,
Sunday 12 noon to 7 p.m.

It stocks most ingredients needed in Arab cooking—also, will ship COD. Among other items, they carry: Arab coffee (ground), Arab coffee cups, trays to serve coffee, *falafel* molds, Baharat, preserved and fresh grape leaves, sumac, chickpea flour, truffles (special order), *za'tar*, zucchini corers, *ibriks*, pomegranate concentrate/molasses.

Midwest U.S.

ARABIAN VILLAGE MARKET

10040 Dix
Dearborn, MI 48120
Tel: (313) 841-4650
Fax: (313) 841-3900
Email: hdsaad@yahoo.com
Open 7 days a week Monday to Saturday 9 a.m.
to 9 p.m., Sunday 9 a.m. to 6 p.m.

One of the oldest Arab grocery supermarkets in Dearborn, the Village offers a vast selection of fresh foods and spices from all over the Middle East. Telephone orders accepted only. Minimum amount required on orders for shipping. UPS, COD or major credit cards accepted. Among

other items, they carry: Arab coffee, Baharat, *falafel* molds, *ibriks*, pomegranate concentrate/molasses, preserved grape leaves, sumac, *za'tar*, zucchini corers.

HILAL GROCERIES

1163 25th St.
Des Moines, IO
Tel: (515) 274-8943
Fax: (515) 274-3519
Open 7 days a week from 10 a.m. to 7 p.m.

The store stocks items such as rosewater, orange blossom water, spices, hummus, tahini and other Arab groceries. Does not ship.

THE SPICE HOUSE

1512 North Wells Street
Chicago, IL 60610
Tel: (312) 274-0378
Fax: (312) 274-0143
Email: spices@thespicehouse.com
Website: http://www.thespicehouse.com/
The Spice House has branches in Evanston, IL; Geneva, IL; and Milwaukee, WI.
Open Monday to Saturday 10 a.m. to 7 p.m.,
Sunday 10 a.m. to 5 p.m.

It offers a fabulous selection of all types of spices and spice blends from everywhere on earth, including Baharat and *za'tar*. Labels tell the purchaser from where the particular spice came and gives ideas about how it can be used. Products are made in small batches to keep them fresh. They concentrate on spices but they have some other products used in Arab cooking such as rosewater, pomegranate concentrate/molasses, sumac and tahini. Ships to anywhere on the continent including Hawaii and Alaska. Orders taken online or by telephone.

MIDDLE EAST BAKERY AND GROCERY

1512 West Foster Avenue
Chicago, IL 60640
Tel: (773) 561-2224
Fax : (773) 561-2234
Email: admin@middleeastbakeryandgrocery.com
& **middleeastbakeryandgrocery@yahoo.com**
There is also a Contact Page on the website
www.middleeastbakeryandgrocery.com
Open Monday to Saturday 9 a.m. to 8 p.m.,
Sunday 10:30 a.m. to 5 p.m. Closed on major
holidays.

It stocks most ingredients needed in Arab Gulf cooking such as dried fruits, pulses, grains and all types of nuts and spices. Ships throughout the U.S. Ships via UPS or C.O.D., or payments can be made by credit card. Orders can be emailed or made by telephone. There is a minimum amount required for placing orders. Among other items, they carry: Arab coffee (beans and ground), Arab coffee cups, Baharat, *dallahs*, *falafel* molds, *ibriks*, *midlahs*, pomegranate concentrate/molasses, sumac, *za'tar*, zucchini corers.

PHOENICIA SPECIALTY FOODS

12141 Westheimer Rd
Houston, TX 77077
Tel: (281) 558-8225
Fax: (281) 584-9912
Email: info@phoeniciafoods.com
www.phoeniciafoods.com/
Open Monday to Saturday 8 a.m. to 9 p.m.,
Sunday 8 a.m. to 7 p.m.

They carry a full line of Middle Eastern foods and they ship whatever is ordered to whoever sends in orders via UPS throughout the U.S. Orders are taken by telephone. During the summer perishable items are not shipped. Among other items, they carry: Arab coffee cups, assorted sizes and varieties, Arab coffee (beans and ground), chickpea flour, rice flour, date syrup, *falafel* molds, *ibriks*, *midlahs* (by special order), pomegranate concentrate/molasses, preserved grape leaves, serving trays (assorted), sumac, Syrian truffles, *za'tar*, zucchini corers.

SUPER GREENLAND

12715 Warren Ave
Dearborn, MI 48126
Tel: (313) 584-5445
Fax: (313) 584-5512
Email: supergreenland@ameritech.net
Open 7 days a week from 8 a.m. to 10 p.m.

This store is so authentic that customers feel they are in the Middle East. Here virtually everything relating to Arab food can be found. Does not ship. Among other items, they carry: Arab coffee cups, Arab coffee (ground), Baharat, *falafel* molds, pomegranate concentrate/molasses, sumac, *za'tar*, zucchini corers.

Southwest U.S.

SAMIRAMIS IMPORTS
2990 Mission Street
(between 25th St & 26th St)
San Francisco, CA 94110
Tel: (415) 824-6555
Fax: (415) 824-6556
Open Monday to Saturday 10 a.m. to 6 p.m.,
Closed on Sunday

It has a great selection of Middle Eastern Food, especially when it comes to spices. Among other items, they carry: Arab coffee (beans and fresh roasted on the spot), Arab coffee cups, Baharat, *dallahs*, *falafel* molds, *ibriks*, pomegranate concentrate/molasses, sumac, *za'tar*, zucchini corers. It's been open since 1965.

ALTAYEBAT MARKET
1217 S. Brookhurst St.
Anaheim, CA 92804
Tel: (714) 520-4723
Fax: (714) 535-8540
Email:mail@altayebat.com
Website: http://www.altayebat.com/
Open Monday to Saturday 9 a.m. to 7 p.m.,
Open on holidays until 6 p.m.
Closed on Sunday.

They will ship non-perishable items. Orders are taken via fax or email. Among other items, they carry: Arab coffee cups, Arab coffee (beans and ground), Baharat, *ibriks*, pomegranate concentrate/molasses, preserved grape leaves, sumac, *za'tar*, zucchini corers.

Northwest U.S.

INTERNATIONAL FOOD SUPPLY
8015 SE Stark St., At the corner of SE Stark and 8oth Portland, Oregon 97215
Tel: (503) 256 - 9576
www.internationalfoodsupply.com/
Open Monday–Saturday 10 a.m. to 8 p.m.,
Closed on Sundays.

The owner also owns Barbur World Foods and Ya Hala Restaurant. Stocks many of the dried fruits, spices and other ingredients used in Arab cooking. Will ship UPS C.O.D. Among other items, they carry: Arab coffee (ground), *falafel* molds, *ibriks*, pomegranate concentrate/molasses, preserved grape leaves, sumac, *za'tar*, zucchini corers.

THE SOUK
1916 Pike Pl # 11
Seattle, WA 98101
Tel: (206) 441-1666
Fax: (206) 956-9387
Email: info@soukseattle.com
www.soukseattle.com
Open Monday to Saturday 10 a.m. to 6 p.m.,
Sunday 11 a.m. to 5 p.m.

This small speciality store stocks a wide variety of spices, Indian products and Arab food ingredients. Will ship products. It is better to place orders over the telephone as ingredients are available in various amounts at the store itself. Shipments are made UPS, C.O.D., or UPS customer pre-pays. Among other items, they carry: Arab coffee cups (various sizes), Arab coffee (beans and ground), Baharat, cardamom (black and green), *dallahs*, *falafel* molds, *ibriks* (various sizes), *midlahs*, pomegranate concentrate/molasses, preserved grape leaves, sumac, za'tar, zucchini corers. (limited items on website)

Rocky Mountain Region U.S.

MIDDLE EAST MARKET
2254 S Colorado Blvd
Denver, CO 80222
Tel: (303) 756-4580
Fax: (303) 756-1226
Open 7 days a week 9 a.m. to 10 p.m.

It carries Middle Eastern products. Does not ship. Among other items, they carry: *falafel* molds, pomegranate concentrate/molasses, preserved grape leaves, sumac, *za'tar*

Toronto

AL-QUDS TOWN & COUNTRY MARKET
3355, Hurontario Stree,
Mississauga, Toronto, ON,
Canada L5A 4E7
Tel: (905) 275-2781
Fax: (905) 275-7588
Email: inamkuds@hotmail.com
Open 7 days a week from 8 a.m. to 10 p.m.,
Closed on Christmas day.

The store carries an excellent selection and large variety of Arab foods and ingredients used in Arab cooking. Clientele includes customers from not only Canada, but the U.S.as well. Among other items, they carry: Arab coffee (beans and

ground), Baharat (ground and whole spice), *dallahs*, *falafel* molds (copper and stainless steel), *ibriks*, *midlahs*, pomegranate concentrate/molasses, preserved grape leaves, sumac, *za'tar*, zucchini corers

ARZ BAKERY FINE FOODS LTD
1909 Lawrence Avenue East,
Scarborough
Toronto, ON
Canada M1R 2Y6
Tel: (416) 755-5084
www.arzbakery.com
Open Monday to Saturday 9 a.m. to 9 p.m.,
Sunday 9 a.m. to 8 p.m.

Exquisite house-made *labnah* and countless other cheeses as well as anything else a cook preparing Arab Gulf dishes may need. Ships only to Canada and a minimum order is required. Orders taken by telephone. Among other items, they carry: Arab coffee cups and sets (assorted varieties and sizes), Arab coffee (beans and ground), Baharat, *dallahs*, *falafel* molds, *ibriks*, *midlahs*, pomegranate concentrate/molasses, preserved grapes leaves, sumac, trays, *za'tar*, zucchini corers.

Vancouver

MEDITERRANEAN SPECIALTY FOODS
1800 Commercial Dr,
Vancouver, BC
Canada V5N 4A5
Tel: (604) 438-4033
Open 7 days a week 10:00 a.m. to 7:00 p.m.

It offers all types of Mediterranean and Middle Eastern food. Does not ship. Among other items, they carry: Arab coffee (ground), *falafel* molds, pomegranate concentrate/molasses, preserved grape leaves, *za'tar*.

Montreal

ADONIS MARKET - SAUVÉ
2001 Sauvé street O
Montreal, Quebec, H4N 1L8
Tel: (514) 382-8606
Fax : (514) 382-4386
www.adonisproducts.com/
Open Monday to Wednesday 9 a.m. to 8 p.m.,
Thursday and Friday, 9 a.m. to 9 p.m., Saturday
9 a.m. to 7 p.m., Sunday 9 a.m to 6 p.m.

Besides the Sauvé store, Adonis has two other branches, one on Boulevard des Sources and one in Laval. Stocks all types of Middle Eastern foods such as dried fruits and pulses as well as canned pulses and Middle Eastern food ingredients. The stores also stock a wide range of nuts and spices—almost all the ingredients needed in Arab Gulf food recipes. Does not ship.

NDG Store: Akhavan Supermarket
6170 Sherbrooke W.
Montreal, QC H4B 1LB
Tel: (514) 485-4887
Fax: (514) 485-7009
Email: info@akhavanfood.com
www.akhavanfood.com
Open Monday to Friday 8 a.m. to 8 p.m., Saturday 8 a.m. to 7 p.m., Sunday 8 a.m. to 6 p.m.

West-Island Store: Akhavan Supermarket
15760 Boul. Pierrefonds,
Pierrefonds, Qc, Canada H9H 3P6
Tel: (514) 620-5551
Fax: (514) 620-5371
Email: info@akhavanfood.com
www.akhavanfood.com
Open Monday to Friday 8 a.m. to 8 p.m., Saturday 8 a.m. to 7 p.m., Sunday 8 a.m. to 6 p.m.

Retail and wholesale Middle Eastern groceries and related products. Orders accepted over the phone, fax or email provided the order is paid in full by means of money transfer to the store's bank or by check cashed to the store's account before sending the order. Accepts major credit cards at store locations only. Does not sell online. Among other items, they carry: Arab coffee cups (assorted varieties), Arab coffee trays, Arab coffee (beans and ground), Baharat, chickpea flour, *dallahs*, dried lime powder, *falafel* molds, fresh grape leaves, *ibriks*, *midlahs*, pomegranate concentrate/molasses/syrup, preserved grape leaves, sumac, truffles (Lebanese), *za'tar*, zucchini corers.

London

DAMAS GATE
81 Uxbridge Rd
Shepherd's Bush
London, W12 8NR
United Kingdom
Tel: +44 (0)20 8743-5116
Open Monday to Sunday 9 a.m. to 7 p.m.

This store focuses on Middle Eastern fare and stocks all sorts of nuts and spices. Does not ship.

Online Stores

ZAMOURI SPICES, (Elbertai Company, LLC.)
P.O.Box 65
Olathe, KS 66051
Tel: (913) 829-5988
Email: info@zamourispices.com
www.zamourispices.com/

Zamouri Spices stocks almost every spice employed in Arab cooking, in addition to *ibriks*, Arab coffee (beans and ground), and Arab coffee cups and trays to serve Arab coffee. Items can be purchased online.

DAYNA'S MARKET
26300 Ford Road, Suite 239
Dearborn Heights, MI 48127
Tel: (313) 623-6231
Email: info@daynasmarket.com
www.daynasmarket.com/

A nationwide online Middle Eastern grocery, Dayna offers specialty Mediterranean products and much more. Items can be ordered online. Among other items, they carry: Arab coffee cups (assorted sizes and styles), Arab coffee (ground), Baharat, *dallahs*, *falafel* molds, *ibriks*, *midlahs*, pastry molds (to make shortbread) pomegranate concentrate/ molasses, preserved grape leaves, trays, *za'tar*, zucchini corers.

acknowledgments

First, I wish to especially thank my daughters Leila Salloum Elias and Muna Salloum who encouraged me to write this modest work. Also, I want to thank them for their valuable advice about the recipes, for providing the historical background to some of the foods and for helping to test and taste a number of the dishes.

   Also, I wish to thank the men and women who I talked to in the Arab Gulf countries and other parts of the Arab world who gave me valuable information about their ways of life and cuisine. Further, I want to thank family, friends and colleagues who gave me constructive feedback about the food dishes that I had created. After tasting my recipes, their good opinions have confirmed my belief that I had indeed re-created the authentic tastes and aromas of the Arab Gulf at my own table.

   In addition, I wish to thank those authors whose books widened my horizon on the Arab Gulf nations and provided interesting quotable material, which I've sprinkled throughout the book.

   Guiding me through the maze of fine-tuning the text of my book for publication was my editor, Holly Jennings. She was always pleasant and helpful during our discussions on the various matters relating to this book, and her dedication and enjoyment of the topic is exemplary, making it a joy to have had the opportunity to work with her.

INDEX